D1917228

Law and Economics of International Telecommunications

Under the Auspices of the
Max Planck Institute for Foreign and International Private Law
edited by Prof. Ernst-Joachim Mestmäcker

Volume 5

Prof. K. D. Gaur

Law of International Telecommunications in India

Nomos Verlagsgesellschaft
Baden-Baden

CIP-Titelaufnahme der Deutschen Bibliothek

Gaur, K. D.:
Law of International Telecommunications in India / K. D. Gaur. – 1. Aufl. – Baden-Baden: Nomos Verl.-Ges., 1988
(Law and Economics of International Telecommunications; Vol. 5)
ISBN 3-7890-1310-2
NE: GT

1. Auflage 1988
© Nomos Verlagsgesellschaft, Baden-Baden 1988. Printed in Germany. Alle Rechte, auch die des Nachdrucks von Auszügen, der photomechanischen Wiedergabe und der Übersetzung vorbehalten.

Editor's Preface

This book on the »Law of International Telecommunications in India« is part of an ongoing research project on the international communications system undertaken at the Max Planck Institute for Foreign and International Private Law in Hamburg. Like similar reports on other countries, this report is based upon questionnaires prepared at the Institute and reproduced at the end of the volume. The questionnaires are identical for all countries in order to facilitate comparative evaluations of the national reports. They serve as guidelines without, however, interfering with the authors' individual judgment in adapting their presentation to the special national situation. The project will include comparative analyses of key problem areas and the examination of the role of international organizations, the task of which is the facilitation of international communications.

Professor K. D. Gaur is head of the Department of Post-Graduate Studies and Research in Law at Utkal University in Bhubaneswar. He received an LL. M. (Gold Medal list) from Allahabad University and a Ph.D. from the Institute of Advanced Legal Studies at the University of London. Professor Gaur has worked at the Indian Law Institute. In addition, he has contributed over fifty papers to noteworthy journals and has authored chapters and monographs in a number of books.

We gratefully acknowledge a grant from the Volkswagen Foundation, which made this Report possible. We also extend thanks to Paul Aliferis, J.D., for his editorial assistance.

Preface

This study forms an attempt to survey the Law of International Telecommunications in India. It has been divided into three parts: Part I, in Chapters 1 to 5, deals with telecommunications in the technical sense, including telephone, telegraph, telex and satellite communications services; Part II, in Chapter 6, discusses computers and data processing, which are still in their infancy in India; Part III, in Chapters 7 to 14, is devoted to radio and TV broadcasting, cinema and the press.

Indian telecommunications is a (central) government-owned public utility. In operation since 1851, it is perhaps one of the oldest telecommunications systems in the world. Until recently, telecommunications services were operated by the Department of Posts and Telegraph. But to keep pace with the fast-developing technology, telecommunications direction was made the province of the independent Department of Telecommunications.

The Indian Telegraph Act of 1885 is the essential piece of legislation that controls the operation of telecommunications services both inside and outside the country. This is supplemented by the Wireless Telegraphy Act of 1933 and the Telegraph Wires (Unlawful Possession) Act of 1950.

Telegraph services in India are well-developed, efficient and heavily used. Telephone services have made rapid strides in India since Independence, but conditions are still unsatisfactory and much remains to be done; a potential customer may have to wait years for a telephone connection. Telex services, though fairly new, are being increasingly relied on, particularly for international communications.

Transborder telecommunications is handled by the Overseas Communications Services, a wing of the Department of Telecommunications. The OCS operators a variety of systems, including the Indian Ocean Commonwealth Submarine Cable link with Malaysia.

India is one of the few countries in the world to have its own operational satellite. India's INSAT-IB provides a variety of services, including telephone; telegraph; meteorological, hydrological and oceanographic data collection; disaster warnings; and radio and television broadcasting. The fact that all this has been made possible in only the last four years is a remarkable achievement in itself.

Computer technology is rapidly developing in India with the new, liberal policies of the central government. Revolutionary changes are expected in this field when super computers are installed in each of the four metropolitan towns of Delhi, Calcutta, Bombay and Madras. Data processing has progressed more slowly, and there is as yet no legislation regarding data protection.

The cinema industry in India has occupied a unique place in the life of the people, both as the single largest disseminator of popular culture and as a great unifying force toward national integration. India, the world's largest producer of films, has a variety of laws regulating film content. The court decisions involving censorship and constitutional guarantees of speech and expression have played a central role in the development of individual liberty in India.

Radio and television broadcasting are state monopolies in India. Radio broadcasting has been particularly effective in informing, educating and entertaining Indians, 85% of whom live in over 500,000 villages and have little access to the print media, illiteracy notwithstanding. The radio network has been greatly expanded since 1947. All-India Radio, the biggest broadcasting agency in the world, supervises broadcasting within India and seeks to project a true and objective image of the country and its viewpoints to listeners abroad.

Television had grown quite slowly since its introduction in the late 1960s. But since the IXth Asian Games, held in Delhi in November 1982, television has expanded rapidly and now reaches nearly 70% of the population. Such an unparalleled growth is the result of the impact of satellite telecommunications capabilities. Problems expressed about television include over-commercialism, lack of appropriate software and excessive government control. Despite a serious proposal in 1978 by the opposition Janta Party to make radio and television services more autonomous, broadcasting remains today an arm of the government.

As long as there has been a press in India, there has been press legislation to curb its independence. Despite these restraints, the press played a major role in India's struggle for independence, and it continues today to help mold public opinion and maintain a watchful eye.

As in the United States, the United Kingdom and many other Western countries, the right of freedom of speech and expression in India has been most heavily scrutinised in court cases involving the press. The Indian Constitution authorises restraints on the freedom of the press in specified areas, resulting in a number of cases testing the limits and reasonableness of such restraints.

The press is subject to other restraints in the form of laws. Laws on defamation, incitement to an offence and contempt of court have had a significant impact on the development of the press in India. In particular, the Supreme Court of India has consistently defined contempt broadly and tolerated no direct attacks on the judicial system, as they are anathema to the proper and orderly administration of justice.

The Copyright Act of 1957 was enacted to safeguard an author's interest in his work against piracy. It establishes both civil and criminal liability. International copyright has been incorporated into the provisions of the Act of 1957.

I wish to take the opportunity to acknowledge my gratitude to Professor Dr. E.J. Mestmäcker, director of the Max Planck Institute for Foreign and International Private Law, for inviting me to contribute a report on the Law of International Telecommunications in India as part of the Institute's project on worldwide telecommunications.

I convey my thanks to Mr. Paul Aliferis, J. D., of the Max Planck Institute for Foreign and Private International Law, for reviewing the report and rendering valuable suggestions.

I also express my gratitude to my wife Madhu Gaur, LL. B., who has not only provided the necessary congenial and proper working conditions for writing the report but also has helped me considerably by revising the text and providing sharp insight.

K.D. Gaur

TABLE OF CONTENTS

BIBLIOGRAPHY

A. Books

Ambedkar, B.R.	VII Constituent Assembly Debates ( )
Baruah, B.L.	This is All-India Radio (1983)
Basu, D.D.	Shorter Constitution of India (1981)
Basu, D.D.	Laws of the Press in India (1980)
Desai, M.V.	Communication Policies in India (UNESCO 1977)
Gajendragadkar, P.B.	Law, Liberty and Social Justice (1965)
Gaur, K.D.	Criminal Law: Cases and Materials (1985)
Hunnings, N.	Film Censors and the Law (1967)
Jain, M.P.	Indian Constitutional Law (1978)
Jain, S.N.	Official Secrecy and the Press (1982)
Jain Kagzi, M.C.	The Constitution of India (1983)
Khurana, B.K.	Doordarshan, INSAT-IB: Basic Information (1985)
Law Commission of India	42nd Report on the Indian Penal Code (1971)
Seervai, H.M.	Constitutional Law of India (1983)
Shali	The Indian Films (1950)
Venkataramiah, E.S.	Freedom of the Press: Some Recent Trends (Endowment Lecture 1984)
Winfield	Law of Torts (1971)

B. Essays

Benn	Privacy, Freedom and Respect for Persons, 13 Privacy 15 (J. Pennock & J. Chapman ed.)
Bhagat	Communication in India: Prospects and Policy, 18 Communicator 53 (1983)
Bhattacharya	Piracy of Films, Broadcasts and Books, 19 Communicator 17 (1984)
Boyd	Film Censorship in India: A Reasonable Restriction on Freedom of Speech and Expression, 14 J. India L. Inst. 501 (1972)
Comment	The Wages of Crying Wolf: A Comment on Roe v. Wade, 82 Yale L.J. 920 (1972)
Desai	A New Doordarshan, The Statesman, Jan. 18, 1985
Dhar	Computer, Software and Copyright: Indian Dilemma, 1985 A.I.R. Journal 50
Dhavan Rajeev	On the Law of the Press in India, 26 J. India L. Inst. 288 (1984)
Emerson	The Doctrine of Prior Restriction, 20 Law & Contem. Probs. 648 (1955)
Harley	U.S. Perspectives in Worldwide Communications, Span, July 1982, at 48
Konvitz	Privacy and the Law: A Philosophical Prelude, 31 Law & Contem. Probs. 272 (1966)
Martin	Music Video Copyright Protection: Implications for the Music Industry, 32 UCLA L.R. 396 (1984)

Mathur	Indira Gandhi on Communication, 19 Communicator 1 (1984)
Ojo	Freedom of the Press in Nigeria Since 1960: A Comparative Analysis, 18 J. India L. Inst. 529 (1976)
Ramchandran	Test of Reasonable Restriction in Article 19 of the Indian Constitution, 40 A.I.R. Journal 79 (1953)
Warren and Brandeis	The Right to Privacy, 4 Harv. L. Rev. 193 (1890–91)
Williams	The Control of Obscenity, 1965 Crim. L. Rev. 53

C. Government of India Publications

Enquiry Committee on Film Censorship	Report (1969)
Ministry of Communications	Annual Report (1984–1985)
Ministry of Information and Broadcasting	Annual Report (1983–1984)
Ministry of Information and Broadcasting	INDIA 1984; INDIA 1981
Ministry of Information and Broadcasting	Report of the Working Group on National Film Policy (1980
Second Press Commission	Report (1982)
Working Group on Autonomy for Akashvani and Doordarshan	Report (vols. I and II) (1978)

TABLE OF CASES

A. Susiah v. Muniswamy, 1966 A.I.R. 175 (Madras H.C.)
A.K. Gopalan v. State of Madras, 1950 A.I.R. 385 (S.C.)
Additional District Magistrate of Jabalpur v. S. Shulka, 1976 A.I.R. 1207 (S.C.)
Adi Pherozshah Gandhi v. H.M. Seervai, 1971 A.I.R. 385 (S.C.)
Amar Nath Bali v. State of Punjab, 1951 A.I.R. 18 (Punjab H.C.)
Arunachala Nadar v. State of Madras, 1959 A.I.R. 300 (S.C.)
Aswani Kumar v. Arabinda Bose, 1952 A.I.R. 369 (S.C.)
Associated Publishers (Madras) Ltd. v. Bashyam alias »Arya«, 1961 A.I.R. 114 (Madras H.C.)
Attorney General of Alberta v. Attorney General of Canada, 1939 A.I.R. 53 (P.C.)
Balzae v. Puerto Rico, 258 U.S. 298 (1921)
Bennett Coleman and Co. Ltd. v. Union of India, 1973 A.I.R. 106 (S.C.)
Bharat Plywood and Timber Products Ltd. v. Kerala State Electricity Board, Trivendrum, 1972 A.I.R. 47 (Kerala H.C.)
Brahma Prakash Sharma v. State of Uttar Pradesh, 1954 A.I.R. 10 (S.C.)
Brij Bhushan v. State of Delhi, 1950 A.I.R. 129 (S.C.)
C.K. Daphtary v. O.P. Gupta, 1971 A.I.R. 1132 (S.C.)
Channing Arnold v. Emperor, 1914 A.I.R 116 (P.C.)
Chintaman Rao v. State of Madhya Pradesh, 1951 A.I.R. 119 (S.C.)
Connally v. General Construction Company, 269 U.S. 385 (1926)
Cunniah and Co. v. Balraj and Co., 1961 A.I.R. 111 (Madras H.C.)
Daily Calendar Supplying Bureau v. United Concern, 1967 A.I.R. 381 (Madras H.C.)
Debi Prasad Sharma v. King Emperor, 1943 A.I.R. 202 (P.C.)
Dennis v. United States, 344 U.S. 494 (1952)
Dharma Dutt v. Ram Lal, 1957 A.I.R. 161 (Punjab H.C.)
Dineshkumar Hanumanprasad Tiwari v. State of Maharastra, 1984 A.I.R. 34 (Bombay H.C.)
Durgah Committee Ajmer v. Hussain Ali, 1961 A.I.R. 1402 (S.C.)
E.M.S. Namboodiripad v. T.N. Nambiar, 1970 A.I.R. 2015 (S.C.)
E.R.J. Swami v. State of Tamil Nadu, 1972 A.I.R. 1586 (S.C.)
Emperor v. Jagiri Lal, 1938 A.I.R. 251 (Lahore H.C.)
Emperor v. Sadashiv Narain, 1947 A.I.R. 82 (P.C.)
Entertaining Enterprises v. State of Tamil Nadu, 1984 A.I.R. 278 (Madras H.C.)
Express Newspapers (Private) Ltd. v. Union of India, 1958 A.I.R. 578 (S.C.)
Gitlow v. New York, 268 U.S. 652 (1921)
Gopal Das v. Jagannath Prasad, 1938 A.I.R. 266 (Allahabad H.C.)
Govinda v. State of Madhya Pradesh, 1975 A.I.R. 1378 (S.C.)
Griswold v. Connecticut, 381 U.S. 479 ( )
Harbhajan Singh v. State of Punjab, 1966 A.I.R. 97 (S.C.)
Hukum Chand v. Union of India, 1976 A.I.R. 789 (S.C.)
Hussainh Baksh v. Secretary of State, 1935 Indian L.R. 391 (Lahore H.C.)
Indian Performing Right Society Ltd. v. Eastern India Motion Picture Association, 1977 A.I.R. 1443 (S.C.)
Indira Neheru Gandhi v. Raj Narain, 1975 A.I.R. 2299 (S.C.)
Indira Neheru Gandhi v. Raj Narain, 1975 A.I.R. 1590 (S.C.)
Indukumar v. State of Saurashtra, 1971 A.I.R. 9 (Saurashtra H.C.)
Indulak K. Yagrik v. State of Maharastra, 1960 A.I.R. 399 (Bombay H.C.)
In re All-India Film Producers' Council of Bombay, _ A.I.R. _
In re Bharati Press, 1951 A.I.R. 12 (Patna H.C., Special Bench)
In re Editor, Printer and Publisher of Times of India, 1953 A.I.R. 75 (S.C.)
In re S. Mulgaokar, 1978 A.I.R. 727 (S.C.)

J.N. Bogga v. All-India Reporter Ltd., 1969 A.I.R. 302 (Bombay H.C.)
Jagadish Prasad Saxema v. State of Madhya Bharat, 1961 A.I.R. 1070 (S.C.)
Jagan Nath v. Union of India, 1960 A.I.R. 625 (S.C.)
K. Vishwanathswami Temple v. Assistant Engineer, [1940] 2 Madras L.J. (Reports) 254
K.A. Abbas v. Union of India, 1971 A.I.R. 481 (S.C.)
K.R. Venugopala Sarma v. Sangu Ganesan, 1972 Crim. L.J. 1098 (Madras H.C.)
K.V.V. Sharma v. Union of India, 1953 A.I.R. 269 (Madras H.C.)
Kerala State Electricity Board v. Varghese Thomas, 1961 A.I.R. 237 (Kerala H.C.)
Kharak Singh v. State of Uttar Pradesh, 1963 A.I.R. 1295 (S.C.)
Macmillan and Co. Ltd. v. K. and J. Cooper, 1924 A.I.R. 25 (P.C.)
Madan Lal Kapur v. State of Rajasthan, 1953 A.I.R. 162 (Rajasthan H.C.)
Matheu v. Vijaya Movies, 1978 Indian L.R. 275 (Kerala H.C.)
Messrs. Black Wood and Sons Ltd. v. A.N. Parasuraman, 1959 A.I.R. 410 (Madras H.C.)
Messrs. Dwarka Prasad v. State of Uttar Pradesh, 1954 A.I.R. 224 (S.C.)
Messrs. S.G. Steels Ltd. v. Union of India, 1984 A.I.R. 272 (Delhi H.C.)
Mohendra Chundra Nath Ghosh v. Emperor, 1928 A.I.R. 359 (Calcutta H.C.)
Mohini Mohan Singh v. Sita Nath, 1931 A.I.R. 233 (Calcutta H.C.)
N.B. Khare v. State of Delhi, 1950 A.I.R. 211 (S.C.)
N.T. Raghunathan v. All-India Reporter Ltd., 1971 A.I.R. 48 (Bombay H.C.)
Nandalal More v. State, 1 Crim. L.J. (Punjab) 392 (1965)
National Textile Workers' Union v. P.R. Ramakrishnan, 1983 A.I.R. 759 (S.C.)
Niharendu Dutt v. Emperor, 1942 A.I.R. 22 (P.C.)
P.N. Films Ltd. v. Union of India, 1955 A.I.R. 381 (Bombay H.C.)
Pathman v. State of Kerala, 1978 A.I.R. 771 (S.C.)
Peris Adult Theatres v. Slaton, 413 U.S. 49 (1972)
Perspective Publications v. State of Maharastra, 1971 A.I.R. 221 (S.C.)
Province of Bombay v. Khushaldas Advani, 1950 A.I.R. 222 (S.C.)
Provincial Government, Central Provinces and Berar v. Willayat Hussain, 1942 Indian L.R. 283 (Nagpur H.C.)
Provincial Government of Central Provinces and Berar v. Chakkilal, 1942 Indian L.R. 344 (Nagpur H.C.)
Queen Empress v. Bal Gongadhor Tilak, 1898 Indian L.R. 112 (Bombay H.C.)
R. v. Gray, [1900] 2 Q.B. 36
R.C. Cooper v. Union of India, 1970 A.I.R. 1318 (S.C.)
R.G. Anand v. Messrs. Delux Films, 1978 A.I.R. 1613 (S.C.)
Radha Films Ltd. v. West Bengal Board of Censors, 1952 A.I.R. 653 (Calcutta H.C.)
Raghubar Dayal Kanodia v. Union of India, 1970 A.I.R. 143 (Allahabad H.C.)
Raj Kapoor v. Laxman, 1980 A.I.R. 605 (S.C.)
Raj Kapoor v. State (Delhi Administration), 1980 A.I.R. 258 (S.C.)
Rama Sankar v. State of Uttar Pradesh, 1954 A.I.R. 562 (Allahabad H.C.)
Ramchandra Rao v. State of Madras, 1962 A.I.R. 58 (Andhra Pradesh H.C.)
Ramji Lal Modi v. State of Uttar Pradesh, 1957 A.I.R. 620 (S.C.)
Ranjit D. Udeshi v. State of Maharastra, 1965 A.I.R. 881 (S.C.)
Regina v. Hicklin, [1868] 3 Q.B. 360
Restaurant Lee v. State of Madhya Pradesh, 1983 A.I.R. 146 (Madhya Pradesh H.C.)
Romesh Choudhary v. Ali Mohamad Noshari, 1955 A.I.R. 101 (Jammu and Kashmir H.C.)
Romesh Thappar v. State of Madras, 1950 A.I.R. 124 (S.C.)
S.K. Dutt v. Law Book Co., 1954 A.I.R. 570 (Allahabad H.C.)
S.P. Gupta v. President of India, 1982 A.I.R. 149 (S.C.)
S.T. Syndicate Ltd. v. Union of India, 1975 A.I.R. 460 (S.C.)
Sabib Singh Mehra v. State of Uttar Pradesh, 1965 A.I.R. 1451 (S.C.)
Sakal Newspapers (Private) Ltd. v. Union of India, 1962 A.I.R. 305 (S.C.)
Seethrama Sastry v. N. Kalawar and Sons, 1968 A.I.R. 315 (Madhya Pradesh H.C.)
Senior Electric Inspector v. Lakshmi Narain Chopra, 1962 A.I.R. 159 (S.C.)
State (Delhi Administration) v. V.C. Shukla, et al., 1980 A.I.R. 1382 (S.C.)

State of Bihar v. Mangal Sao, 1963 A.I.R. 415 (S.C.)
State of Bihar v. Shailabala Devi, 1952 A.I.R. 329 (S.C.)
State of Bombay v. R.M.D. Chamarbaughwala, 1957 A.I.R. 699 (S.C.)
State of Kerala v. K. Balkrishna, 1961 A.I.R. 25 (Kerala H.C.)
State of Madras v. V.G. Row, 1952 A.I.R. 196 (S.C.)
State of Punjab v. Sodhi Sukhdeo Singh, 1961 A.I.R. 493 (S.C.)
State of Uttar Pradesh v. Bagoo Lal, 1956 A.I.R. 571 (Allahabad H.C.)
State of Uttar Pradesh v. Raj Narain, 1975 A.I.R. 865 (S.C.)
T.K. Abraham v. State of Travancore Cochin, 1958 A.I.R. 129 (Kerala H.C.)
Union of India v. Narayana Iyer, [1970] 1 Madras L.J. (Reports) 19
V.V. Srinivasamurthy v. State of Mysore, 1959 A.I.R. 894 (S.C.)
Vincent Panjkulangara v. Justice Krishna Iyer, 1983 Kerala Law Times 823
Virendra v. State of Punjab, 1957 A.I.R. 896 (S.C.)
Western India Theatres v. Cantonment Board of Poona, 1959 A.I.R. 582 (S.C.)
Wolf v. Colorado, 338 U.S. 25 (1948)

TABLE OF ABBREVIATIONS

AIR	All-India Radio
A.I.R.	All-India Reporter
APT	Asia-Pacific Telecommunity
AM	Amplitude Modulation
Art.	Article
BBC	British Broadcasting Corporation
CODE CRIM. PROC.	Code of Criminal Procedure
Crim.	Criminal
DCP	Date Collection Platform
DRS	Direct Reception Set
FB	Full Bench
FM	Frequency Modulation
GDP	Gross Development Programme
GHz	Gigahertz
H.C.	High Court
HTL	Hindustan Teleprinters, Ltd.
IBC	Indian Broadcasting Company
ICMC	IOCOM Cable Management Committee
IFRB	International Frequency Registration Board
INCOTEL	International Telephone Conference
Indian L.R.	Indian Law Reporter
INMARSAT	International Maritime Satellite Organisation
INSAT	Indian National Satellite System
INTELSAT	International Telecommunications Satellite Organisation
IOCOM	Indian Ocean Commonwealth Submarine Telephone Cable System
IPC	Indian Penal Code
ISBS	Indian State Broadcasting System
ISRO	Indian Space Research Organisation
ITA	Indian Telegraph Act
ITI	Indian Telephone Industries, Ltd.
ITU	International Telecommunication Union
J. INDIA L. INST.	Journal of India Law Institute
kbps	Kilobits per second
kHz	Kilohertz
kW	Kilowatt
L.J.	Law Journal
L.R.	Law Reports
L. Rev.	Law Review
MHz	Megahertz
MLOD	Multi-link Operator Dialing
M.P.E.A.A.	Motion Picture Export Association of America
mw	Medium Wave
NASA	National Aeronautics and Space Administration
NEFA	North-East Frontier Area
NIC	National Informatics Centre
OCS	Overseas Communications Service
P.C.	Privy Council
PCM	Pulse-Code Modulated
Q.B.	Queen's Bench

Rs.	Rupees
SAC	Space Application Centre
SACFA	Standing Advisory Committee on Radio Frequency Allocation
S.C.	Supreme Court
SFT	Store-and-Forward Telegraphy, Telex
SITE	Satellite Instructional Television Experiment
SLOD	Single-Link Operator Dialing
STD	Subscriber Trunk Dialing
STEP	Satellite Telecommunications Experiment Project
sw	Short Wave
TCIL	Telecommunications Consultants of India, Ltd.
TRC	Telecommunications Research Centre
TV	Television
UNDP	United Nations Development Programme
VCR	Videocassette Recorder
VFT	Voice-Frequency Telegraph
VHF	Very-High Frequency
WPC	Wireless Planning and Coordination Wing

Part I: Telecommunications Services

Chapter I: General Provisions

A. *Introduction*

Telecommunications[1] is the science of transmitting information; media employed for transmission include telegraph, telephone, radio, television, computer, telex and national and international satellites. Telecommunications technology is today in a period of revolutionary change that will have an impact on the entire fabric of society, both in developed and in developing nations. It is a basic need for the proper functioning of human society. In fact, without effective communication, a democracy cannot function and socio-economic development cannot be sustained.[2]

This new world of information and communication is becoming a fact of life. The international community is attaching increasing importance to the establishment of a more equitable and just information and communication order. Communication is central to the entire developmental process of a country in more than just the economic sense; multidimensional ramifications are felt in the social, cultural, educational, scientific, technological and political spheres. The progress of the order is doubtlessly evolving, although too slowly. Being among the world's top-ten industrialised countries and with significant satellite communications capability, India is not untouched by the latest communications developments.

There is worldwide acceptance of the important role of information and communication in bringing about a better understanding among nations, or among people or groups within a nation, of the serious imbalances and disparities in the flow of information. The necessity to pursue, and then reinforce, courses of action that encourage a freer and more reciprocal exchange of information among nations is also unquestioned.[3] Communication is the web that holds together a society, whether it is a collection of

1 The word telecommunications is made up of two words: »tele« is derived from the Greek word meaning »far,« and »communication,« from the Latin root »communico,« meaning »to share.« Thus, telecommunications is a process in which participants from a distance share information with one another. *See New Structure of International Communication: The Role of Research* 126 (1982)

2 I. Gandhi, *Report on Telecommunications (Ministry of Telecommunication, VI Five-Year Plan, 1980–85)* 1.

3 *See* Mathur, *Indira Gandhi on Communication*, 19 COMMUNICATOR 1, 3–6 (1984).

small and relatively isolated agricultural groups or a closely knit complex of interdependent groups in an industrialised country. Culture and civilisation have been, over the ages, dependent on communication. The modes of communication, initially oral or hand-written, have multiplied since the industrial revolution as a result of a succession of such inventions as telegraph, telephone, photography, film, radio, televison, teleprinters and computers.

B. *Organisational Structure of Telecommunications in India*

Indian telecommunications, operated exclusively by the Government, is one of the world's oldest government-owned public utilities. India's first telegraph line was established in 1851 between Calcutta and Diamond Harbor; the first long-distance overhead telegraph was opened in 1853 between Calcutta and Agra. India's postal system began even earlier than the telegraph, when services were made available to the public in 1837. The first postage stamp was issued in 1852 in Karachi, although it was valid only in Sind. The Postal Department was established in 1854 to meet the demands of some 700 post offices already functioning throughout the country. A money order system was introduced in 1880; the Post Office Savings Bank, in 1882; the Post Life Insurance Company, in 1884; railway mail service, in 1907; and airmail service, in 1911.

As of March 31, 1984, nearly 40,000 telegraph offices, including licensed telegraph offices working under the Railways Department and the Canal Administration, were operating in India. As of December 31, 1984, post offices numbered 144,904 (15,289 in urban areas and 129,615 in rural areas), with each post office serving an average 4728 persons and covering about 22.68 square km. In addition, 69,611 villages were being serviced by mobile counter facilities. There were 500,894 letter boxes, including 426,117 in rural areas, meaning that more than 99% of the villages were being provided daily mail delivery services by this time.[4]

Until recently, telecommunications services had been operated by the Department of Posts and Telegraph of the Ministry of Communications. But

4 MINISTRY OF INFORMATION AND BROADCASTING, INDIA 1984 423.

to make telecommunications services more effective and efficient, the Department was bifurcated on January 1, 1985 into the Department of Posts and the Department of Telecommunications, as is the case in Great Britain. The Department of Telecommunications maintains five wings to further telecommunications services both in India and abroad: (1) Wireless Planning and Coordination, (2) Overseas Communications Services, (3) Telecommunications Consultants of India, Ltd., (4) Indian Telephone Industries, Ltd., and (5) Hindustan Teleprinters, Ltd. (the Overseas Communications Service is responsible for India's external telecommunication services and will be treated in depth in Chapter IV). In addition, the Department of Telecommunications maintains a variety of support organisations: (1) Telecommunications Research Centre, (2) Telecommunications Training Centre, (3) Technical and Developmental Circle, (4) Telegraph Stores and (5) Telephone and Telecommunications Factories.

The Wireless Planning and Coordination Wing (WPC) was established in 1952 as a branch of the Ministry of Communications. The WPC assigns frequencies for telecommunications purposes to all users: the Department of Telecommunications, the Overseas Communication Service, All-India Radio, the Defence and Police Departments, private users, radio amateurs, etc. The Wireless Advisor to the Government of India is the head of the Wing. The main functions of the WPC are:

(a) regulation, planning, coordination, assignment and administration of the use of radio frequencies in India;
(b) spectrum management of radio frequencies and coordination of orbit frequencies in respect of satellite systems (geostationary and non-geostationary);
(c) coordination of all matters connected with the International Telecommunication Union (ITU) and the Asia-Pacific Telecommunity (APT), including coordination and harmonisation of national policies in preparation for ITU and APT meetings;
(d) licensing of wireless stations (except broadcasting receivers), which include amateur radio stations and the wireless stations of the police and the railways;
(e) conducting of examinations for the awarding of Certificates of Proficiency for wireless operators on board ships and aircraft and for the awarding of Operator Certificates for amateur stations;
(f) site clearance of wireless installations and related matters concerning the Standing Advisory Committee on Radio Frequency Allocation (SACFA); and

(g) direction and control of the Monitoring Organisation.[5]

The Telecommunications Research Centre, established in 1956, initiates design and development work for the indigenous manufacture of all kinds of telecommunications equipment, systems and accessories and functions as a principal advisor to the Department of Telecommunications in all technical matters. During its thirty years of existence, the work of the TRC has embraced a wide spectrum of design and development activities. This has resulted in the better utilisation of existing resources, the introduction of a number of new and modern services and facilities and the production in India of a variety of transmission and switching equipment evolved without foreign collaboration. Financial outlays of the TRC are prepared pursuant to a science and technology plan, which, after approval by the Planning Commission, is included in the overall Telecommunications Plan for obtaining the necessary budgetary allocations.

The Telecommunications Training Centre exists to give thorough basic training to new employes in the telecommunications field. Working and operative staff, e.g., linemen, mechanics and telephone operators, are trained in Circle or District Training Centres spread throughout the country. There are fifteen Circle Training Centres and eleven District Training Centres. The centres also conduct refresher courses for in-service personnel, so as to keep them abreast of the latest developments in telecommunications technology. Junior supervisory staff, e.g., engineering supervisors, are trained in one of twelve Regional Training Centres. Engineers, e.g., assistant divisional engineers, are trained in the Telecommunications Training Centre at Jabalpur in Madhya Pradesh and in the Advanced Level Telecommunications Training Centre in Ghaziabad in Uttar Pradesh. The latter centre, set up with the assistance of the United Nations Development Project, is primarily meant for imparting training in highly sophisticated technologies to medium- and upper-level management cadres.

The Technical and Development Circle has its headquarters at Jabalpur (Madhya Pradesh) and is the testing organisation for telecommunications activities. The Circle is responsible for the acceptance-testing of telephone and trunk installations of all types (electronic, crossbar, manual, etc.); transmission systems of all types (coaxial, microwave, ultrahigh frequency, pulse-code modulated, open-wire carrier, voice-frequency telegraphy, etc.);

5 MINISTRY OF COMMUNICATIONS, ANNUAL REPORT 9 (1984–1985).

and telecommunications materials purchased and supplied by various concerns. Five regional centres were established in 1973 for the acceptance-testing of switching and transmission equipment. These centres are located in Bombay, Calcutta, Delhi, Jabalpur and Madras (a sixth centre at Hyderabad handles transmission equipment only). To cope with the increased production of transmission equipment and telephone instruments and accessories, test rooms have been organised at Bangalore and Naini; as there are two separate Indian Telephone Industries factories at Naini – one for transmission equipment and the other for telephone instruments and accessories – two test rooms are functioning there. In addition to testing, the Circle also prepares engineering instructions, test schedules and specifications for the Power Telecommunication Coordination functions, and it renders technical advice to the Department of Telecommunications on all important telecommunications problems.

Indian Telephone Industries, Ltd. (ITI), located in Bangalore, is a public-sector undertaking with factories at Bangalore, Naini, Rai Bareli, Palghat, Srinagar and Manikapur. Engaged since 1948 in the manufacture of a wide range of telecommunications equipment, including telephone exchange equipment, telephone instruments and long-distance transmission equipment, ITI caters to the needs of the Department of Telecommunications, the Railways Department, Defence Services and others. ITI has entered into collaboration with CIT Alcatel of France for the manufacture of electronic switching systems and with FACE Standard of Italy for the transfer of technology for the manufacture of new telephones.

Hindustan Teleprinters, Ltd. (HTL) of Madras is a public-sector company under the administration of the Department of Telecommunications. HTL manufactures teleprinters, ancillary equipment, data modems and electronic typewriters. HTL has entered into collaboration with Sagen of France for the yearly manufacture of 8000 electronic typewriters. HTL's regional offices are in Bombay, Delhi and Calcutta.

Telecommunications Consultants of India, Ltd. (TCIL) of Delhi is a public-sector undertaking set up in March 1978 under the administrative control of the Department of Telecommunications. It offers consulting services in all aspects of telecommunications. During 1979–80, TCIL secured orders worth Rs. 96 million (US $9.6 million), mostly from foreign countries.

Four departmental telecommunications factories, under the administrative control of the Telecommunications Board, have been organised at Calcutta, Bombay, Jabalpur and Bhilai. They manufacture vital telecommunications equipment, such as microwave towers, coin-collecting boxes, pole lines, open-wire system hardware and switching equipment. The average yearly production of these factories is of the order of Rs. 200 to 220 million (US $20 to 22 million). The production increased to Rs. 350 million (US $35 million) by the end of 1985. The factory at Calcutta is nearly 100 years old and is being modernised. Modern galvanising plants are being installed at Jabalpur, Calcutta and Bhilai, and a modern foundry unit is being set up at Kharagpur.

Six wholesale store depots and a number of retail depots are entrusted with the jobs of procuring, storing and supplying materials to the Telecommunications Circles and Districts.

Chapter II: Legal Framework of Domestic Telecommunications

A. *Indian Telegraph Act of 1885*

Telecommunication services in India are maintained and operated pursuant to the provisions of the Indian Telegraph Act of 1885 (ITA). The Act is divided into five parts. Part I is preliminary.[6] Part II deals with the privileges and powers of the government.[7] Part III empowers the government to place telegraph lines and posts.[8] Part IV prescribes penalties for various categories of violations and offences under the Act.[9] Part V includes supplementary provisions concerning the power to employ additional police in places where mischief to a telegraph is repeatedly committed and also extends the scope of the Act to the presidency metropolitan towns of Calcutta, Bombay and Madras.[10]

B. *Part I of the ITA: The Act Defined*

Section 1 defines the scope, extent and operation of the Act. Section 3 gives a technical and legal definition to key words. The word »telegraph«[11] has a comprehensive meaning under the Act, and it includes all modern means of receiving or transmitting communication by electricity, including wireless,

6 Indian Telegraph Act of 1885, 1885 India Cen. Act 13 §§ 1–3.
7 *Id.* at §§ 4–9
8 *Id.* at §§ 10–19.
9 *Id.* at §§ 20–32.
10 *Id.* at §§ 33–34.
11 *Id.* at §3 (1): »›telegraph‹ means an electric, galvanic or magnetic telegraph and includes appliances and apparatuses for making, transmitting or receiving telegraphic, telephonic or other communications by means of electricity, galvanism or magnetism.«

telegraph, telephone,[12] teleprinter, telex and radio.[13] Section 3 as well defines »telegraph officer,«[14] »message,«[15] »telegraph line,«[16] »post«[17] and »telegraph authority«[18] (the Indian Wireless Telegraphy Act of 1933 also defines »wireless telegraphy,«[19] »wireless telegraphy apparatus«[20] and »wireless transmitter«[21]).

12 Seethrama Sastry v. N. Kalwar and Sons, 1968 A.I.R. 315 (Madhya Pradesh H.C.).

13 Provincial Government of Central Provinces and Berar v. Chakkilal, 1942 Indian L.R. 344 (Nagpur H.C.): telegraph as defined in the Telegraph (Amendment) Act of 1914, 1914 India Cen. Act 7, includes a radio, which is an apparatus for receiving communication by means of electricity. State of Bihar v. Mangal Sao, 1963 A.I.R. 445 (S.C.): wireless transmitter transmits sounds as electromagnetic waves, and the sound waves are detected and received by the receiving apparatus; hence a receiving set (radio) is a telegraph within the meaning of the Act. 1964 M.P.L.J. 831: telegraph includes telephone.

14 Indian Telegraph Act of 1885, § 3(2): »›telegraph officer‹ means any person employed either permanently or temporarily in connection with a telegraph established, maintained or worked by the Central Government or by a person licensed under this Act.«

15 *Id.* at § 3(3): »›message‹ means any communication sent by telegraph or given to a telegraph officer to be sent by telegraph or to be delivered.

16 *Id.* at § 3(4): »›telegraph line‹ means a wire or wires used for the purposes of a telegraph with any casing, coating, tube or pipe enclosing the same, an any appliances and apparatuses connected therewith for the purpose of fixing or insulating the same.« *See* Senior Electric Inspector v. Lakshmi Narain Chopra, 1962 A.I.R. 159 (S.C.): electric lines used for the purpose of wireless telegraph are telegraph lines.

17 Indian Telegraph Act of 1885, § 3(5): »›post‹ means a post, pole, standard, stay, strut or other above-ground contrivance for carrying, suspending or supporting a telegraph line.«

18 *Id.* at § 3(6): »›telegraph authority‹ means the Director-General of Posts and Telegraphs, and includes any officer empowered by him to perform all or any of the functions of the telegraph authority under this Act.«

19 Indian Wireless Telegraphy Act of 1933, 1933 India Cen. Act 17 § 2(1): »›wireless communication‹ means any transmission, remission or reception of signs, signals, writings, images and sounds, or intelligence of any nature by means of electricity, magnetism or Radio waves, Hertzian waves without the use of wires or other continuous electrical conductor between the transmitting and the receiving apparatus. *Explanation*; ›Radio Waves‹ or ›Hertzian Waves‹ means electro-magnetic waves of frequencies lower than 3000 gigacycles per second propagated in space without artificial guide.«

20 *Id.* at § 2(2): »›Wireless telegraphy apparatus‹ means any apparatus, appliance, instrument or material used or capable of use in wireless communication, and includes any article determined by rule made under section 10 to be wireless telegraphy apparatus, but does not include any such apparatus, appliance, instrument or material commonly used for other electrical purposes, unless it has been specially designed or adapted for wireless communication or forms part of some apparatus, appliance, instrument or material specially so designed or adapted, nor any article determined by the rule made under section 10 not to be wireless telegraphy apparatus.«

21 *Id.* at § 2(2A): »›wireless transmitter‹ means any apparatus, appliance, instrument or material used or capable of use for transmission or remission of wireless communication.«

C. *Part II of the ITA: Privileges and Powers of the Government*

Section 4 of the ITA gives the federal government the exclusive privilege of establishing, operating and maintaining telegraphs. In delegation of this privilege, the government may grant a license to any person, under any such conditions and in consideration of such payments as it thinks fit, to establish, operate or maintain a telegraph within any part of India. Section 8 empowers the government to revoke any license upon the breach of any enumerated conditions due thereunder.

In the event of an emergency or in the interest of public safety, section 5(1) of the ITA allows the federal government or a state government to take possession of any licensed telegraph and to order the interception or detention of messages brought for transmission to, transmitted by or received by any telegraph, if it is necessary or expedient to do so in the interests of the sovereignty and integrity of India, the security of the state, friendly relations with foreign states or public order or the prevention of the incitement to the commission of an offence.[22]

The federal government can establish and maintain a telegraph upon any part of the land of railways (which is a government undertaking), and the railways must provide reasonable access for operating the same.[23] Section 6-A of the ITA authorises the government to promulgate rates, conditions and restrictions for the transmission of messages to locations outside of India. Section 7 of the ITA empowers the government to frame rules for the conduct of any or all telegraphs established or maintained by the government or of those operated by persons licensed under the Act.

Section 9 of the ITA exempts the government from any responsibility for loss or damage that might occur as a consequence of the negligent performance by any telegraph officer of his duty with respect to the receipt, transmission or delivery of any message, and it exempts telegraph officers from responsibility for any loss or damage, unless such loss or damage is malicious or fraudulent.

22 Indian Telegraph Act of 1885, § 5(2). *See also* Hukum Chand Shyam Lal v. Union of India, 1976 A.I.R. 789 (S.C.) Held, power under § 5(1) of the Act of 1885 does not confer misguided and unbridled power to the central or state government to take possession of any telegraph; the occurrence of a public emergency is the *sine qua non* for the exercise of power under this section.

23 Indian Telegraph Act of 1885, § 6.

D. *Part III of the ITA: Power to Place Telegraph Lines and Posts*

The ITA, in sections 10 through 19, empowers the Telegraph Authority to place and maintain telegraph lines and posts and to do such things as are necessary for discharging this function. Section 10 legalises civil trespass over the land of others for the purpose of establishing or maintaining a telegraph installation and provides for payment of full compensation for any damage done during the course of such operation.

In assessing compensation under section 10(d)[24] for damage caused to fruit-bearing or -yielding trees by the laying of electrical wires and poles, it is permissible and often simplest to base compensation on the *usu fruct* of which the owner of the land has been deprived, without embarking upon an inquiry into the market value of the land before and after the damage was caused.[25]

But this does not preclude a court from applying a market-value test in appropriate cases. The market-value test is not the only test for assessing damages, and, in the case of damage by destruction of fruit-bearing or –yielding trees (such as coconut, jack and rubber trees) or of peeper vines, the compensation payable may be deemed to be the present worth. For example, in *Ramchandra Rao v. State of Madras* (now Andrha Pradesh),[26] a claim for compensation under section 10(d) of the ITA was brought before the Andrha Pradesh High Court for damages stemming from the cutting of the plaintiff's coconut trees by the Electric Department, which was laying transmission lines through the plaintiff's fields. The court held that the damages incurred by the owner of the fields ought to be assessed by reference to the deterioration of the property value by reason of the acts that resulted in the damages.

24 *Id.* at § 10(d): »›The telegraph authority may, from time to time, place and maintain a telegraph line under, over, along or across, and posts in or upon, any immoveable property. Provided that – ... in the exercise of the powers conferred by this section, the telegraph authority shall do as little damage as possible, and, when it has exercised those powers in respect of any property,... shall pay full compensation to all persons interested for any damage sustained by them by reason of the exercise of those powers.«

25 Kerala State Electricity Board v. Varghese Thomas, 1961 A.I.R. 237 (Kerala H.C.). *See also* K. Vishwanathswami Temple v. Assistant Engineer, [1940] 2 Madras L.J. (Reports) 254; Hussainh Baksh v. Secretary of State, 1935 Indian L.R. 391 (Lahore H.C.).

26 1962 A.I.R. 58 (Andhra Pradesh H.C.) *See also* Satvanaravan Laxminarayan Hegde v. Malikarajun Bhavanappa Tirumale. 1960 A.I.R. 315 (Andhra Pradesh H.C.)

E. *Part IV of the ITA: Violations of and Penalties Under the Act*

Part IV of the ITA, in sections 20 to 32, prescribes penalties for violating the provisions of the Act. The object of the ITA, in imposing conditions for, and a system of, penalties, is to provide an effective, modern facility through a utility service and to maintain public administration, order and safety.[27] Penalties vary from a fine of Rs. 50[28] to three years of imprisonment, depending upon the gravity of the offence. Some of the serious offences for which penalties have been provided under the ITA are: establishing, operating or maintaining an unauthorised telegraph;[29] breaching a condition of license;[30] using an unauthorised telegraph;[31] opposing the establishment of a telegraph on railway land;[32] trespassing in or obstructing the operation of a telegraph office;[33] unlawfully attempting to learn the contents of a message;[34] intentionally damaging or tampering with a telegraph;[35] injuring or interfering with a telegraph line or post;[36] unlawfully intercepting or disclosing a telegraph message or divulging the object of signals;[37] fraudulent sending of a message by a telegraph officer without payment;[38] misconduct;[39] retaining a message delivered by mistake;[40] bribery;[41] and attempting to commit an offence.[42]

F. *Part V of the ITA: Supplemental Provisions*

Part V of the ITA, in sections 33 and 34, deals with supplemental provi-

27 *Seethrama Sastry*, 1968 A.I.R. 315.
28 Indian Telegraph Act of 1885, § 29–A.
29 *Id.* at § 20.
30 *Id.* at § 20–A. *See Mangal Sao*, 1963 A.I.R. 445: held, use of a radio without a license is an offence under section 20 of the Act.
31 Indian Telegraph Act of 1885, § 21.
32 *Id.* at § 22.
33 *Id.* at § 23.
34 *Id.* at § 24.
35 *Id.* at § 25.
36 *Id.* at § 25–A.
37 *Id.* at § 26.
38 *Id.* at § 27. *See* Emperor v. Jagiri Lal, 1938 A.I.R. 251 (Lahore H.C.): held, as the charge is not payable in advance but is to be recovered in terms of monthly bills submitted to the telephone, the mere transmission of the message without payment by the accused does not fall within the mischief of the section.
39 Indian Telegraph Act of 1885, § 28.
40 *Id.* at § 30.
41 *Id.* at § 31.
42 *Id.* at § 32.

sions. Section 33 confers power on the state governments to employ additional police force in places where it appears both that any act causing or likely to cause wrongful damage to any telegraph is repeatedly and maliciously committed and that the employment of such force is necessary. The cost of the additional force is to be charged to and realized from the inhabitants of the locality. Section 34, as stated earlier, extends the application of the Act to the metropolitan towns of Delhi, Calcutta, Madras and Bombay.

G. *The Indian Wireless Telegraphy Act of 1933*

An important source of revenue for the Indian State Broadcasting Service is the fees for licenses, issued under the ITA, that authorise the establishment, operation or maintenance of wireless apparatuses. However, the possession of these apparatuses was not regulated by the ITA, resulting in a loss of revenue. Thus, the Indian Wireless Telegraphy Act of 1933[43] was enacted to license the actual possession of wireless telegraphy apparatuses, such as radios. Subsequent rules have obviated the necessity for two licenses – one for possession of a wireless telegraphy set and one for its establishment, operation or maintenance.[44]

Section 3 of the Act[45] prohibits the possession of a »wireless telegraphy apparatus« without a valid license, and section 4[46] gives exclusive power to the federal government to exempt any person from the provisions of the Act. It should be noted that a license to establish, operate or maintain a wireless telegraphy apparatus (which includes a wireless receiving set) issued under section 4 of the ITA is effective from the first day of the month in which the license was issued. Thus, the illegal possession of an apparatus between the first day of the month and the actual day of issue is made valid by the subsequent issue of a license; the licensee cannot then be prosecuted for the possession of a telegraph apparatus, in contravention of section 3 of the Act of 1933, between the first day of the month and the date of the issue

43 1933 India Cen. Act 17.

44 *Chakkilal*, 1942 A.I.R. 344.

45 Indian Wireless Telegraphy Act of 1933, § 3: »Save as provided by section 4, no person shall possess a wireless telegraphy apparatus except under and in accordance with a license issued under this Act.«

46 *Id.* at § 4: »The Central Government may by rules made under this Act exempt any person or any class of persons from the provisions of this Act either generally or subject to prescribed conditions, or in respect of specified wireless telegraphy apparatus.«

of the license.[47] In practice, the detection of unlicensed apparatuses and the successful prosecution of offenders is difficult, as it is first necessary to locate unlicensed apparatuses and then prove that they had actually been established, operated or maintained.

For the purposes of the Act of 1933, the Telegraph Authority, constituted under the ITA, shall be the authority competent to issue licenses to possess wireless telegraphy apparatuses.[48] Section 6 of the Act of 1933, which prescribes offences and penalties for contravention of its provisions, reads:

> (1) Whoever possesses any [wireless telegraphy apparatus other than a wireless transmitter] in contravention of the provisions of section 3 shall be punished, in the case of the first offence, with a fine which may extend to one hundred rupees, and, in the case of a second or subsequent offence, with a fine which may extend to two hundred and fifty rupees.
> (1-A) Whoever possesses any wireless transmitter in contravention of the provisions of section 3 shall be punished with imprisonment which may extend to three years, or with a fine which may extend to one thousand rupees, or with both.
> (2) For the purpose of this section, a Court may presume that a person possesses wireless telegraphy apparatus if such apparatus is under his ostensible charge or is located in any premises or place over which he has effective control.
> (3) If in the trial of an offence under this section the accused is convicted, the Court shall decide whether any apparatus in respect of which an offence has been committed should be confiscated, and if it so decides, may order confiscation accordingly.

Section 7 of the Act of 1933 authorises the central government to search any premises in which a telegraphy apparatus is suspected of being illegally kept or concealed and to take possession thereof. All confiscated wireless telegraphy apparatuses, as well as those having no ostensible owner, will belong to the central government.[49]

H. *The Telegraph Wires (Unlawful Possession) Act of 1950*

The Telegraph Wires (Unlawful Possession) Act of 1950[50] was enacted in

47 Provincial Government, Central Provinces and Berar v. Willayat Hassain, 1942 Indian L.R. 283 (Nagpur H.C.).

48 Indian Wireless Telegraphy Act of 1933, § 5: »The telegraph authority constituted under the Indian Telegraph Act of 1885 shall be the authority competent to issue licenses to possess wireless telegraphy apparatus under this Act, and may issue licenses in such manner, on such conditions and subject to such payment as may be prescribed.«

49 *Id.* at § 8.

50 1950 India Cen. Act 74.

order to regulate the possession of telegraph wires and to create an offence for the unlawful possession thereof. It is a small act, consisting of only eight sections. Section 2(b) defines »telegraph wire« as: »any copper wire, the gauge of which, as measured in terms of pounds per mile, is between 147 and 153 or between 196 and 204 or between 294 and 306.« Section 3 casts a duty on the part of those in possession of telegraph wires to make a declaration in writing stating the quantity in their possession. Section 4 directs persons in possession of telegraph wires in excess of 10 pounds to convert them into ingots, and section 4-A prohibits the sale or purchase of any quantity of telegraph wires without the permission of such authority as may be prescribed under the Act. Section 5 prescribes punishment for unlawful possession of telegraph wires to the extent of five years of imprisonment; in cases of second or subsequent offences committed under the Act of 1950, a fine of Rs. 2000 is also authorised. Section 6 makes failure to make a declaration required by section 3 or contravention of the provisions of sections 4 or 5 punishable with up to six months of imprisonment, with a fine or with both. Section 7 directs that no court take cognizance of an offence under the Act unless a complaint is made by, or under the authority of, the central government and that no court inferior to that of a Presidency Magistrate of the first class try any offence punishable under the Act. Section 8 empowers the central government to make rules to carry out the purposes of the Act.

Chapter III: Domestic Telecommunications Services

A. *Telegraph*

1. *Indian Language Telegraph Services*

The Hindi telegraph was introduced in India on June 1, 1949 and was expanded with the introduction of the phonecom system. The Hindi code, based on the English Morse code phonetic system, relies on Devangari, the script in which the national language of Hindi is written. For the numerals, the English signals have been retained. Telegrammes in any other Indian language, provided they have been written in the Devangari script, are also accepted at all stations where the Hindi telegraph service exists. Telegraph money orders and registered abbreviated telegraphic addresses in Hindi have been allowed as well.

2. *Store-and-Forward Telegraphy*

Indian telegraphy has come of age. On August 1, 1982, thirteen towns in Tamil Nadu, including Madras and Hyderabad in Andhra Pradesh, were networked by way of a computer grid, allowing telegrammes to reach their destinations more quickly. The use of computer technology, which drastically reduces delays at the transit points from several hours to mere minutes, is employed through a »store-and-forward« telegraph (SFT) system.

SFT, as the name indicates, is a nerve centre into which the telegrammes from outlying stations are fed by specially tuned teleprinters. An alert memory system, which can store up to 38,000 words, sifts through the telegrammes, rearranging destinations according to priority and then sending them out to teleprinters. The SFT outperforms the existing modes of telegraphy basically by economising on the time taken at the transits. This system is ten times faster than an ordinary, direct teleprinter link between any two places; at best, an operator can put out 40 words a minute on a normal teleprinter between Hyderabad and Madras, but the SFT can spew out 400 words a minute.

The SFT, manufactured by the Electronics Corporation of India, Ltd. as a result of joint research with telecommunications engineers in Tamil Nadu, is capable of tackling a common problem now faced when telegraph lines go out of order and a backlog of telegrammes accumulates. The present SFT model can store messages intended for 6 of the 13 outlying stations and, when the line is restored, can resume transmission to clear the backlog without confusion. When bigger SFTs, handling 64 or 128 stations, are developed, the problem of interrupted lines can be tackled on a still-larger magnitude. The SFT system can effectively cope with the needs of the massive telegraph network in the country. India has 20,000 telegraph stations, which presently clear 62 million telegrammes every year. The bulk of this gigantic task is concentrated at just 415 stations. If each of these were equipped with an SFT, a message could reach its destination faster than a person carrying it on a jet plane.

Cost-benefit calculations show that in the long run the SFTs should be profitable for the Department of Telecommunications, after breaking even on the capital costs over the first two years. An SFT system costs Rs. 1,000,000, and each outlying teleprinter terminal costs Rs. 70,000. The fear that telegraphic traffic may fall, thus reducing revenues, is unfounded; the number of telegrammes sent yearly has gone from 26 million in 1956 to a present level of 62 million, even though the number of trunk telephone calls has risen steeply from 4 million to 200 million (excluding STD calls) during the same period. SFTs have been recently introduced in Bombay, Ahmedabad, Calcutta and Lucknow; this is a big leap forward for Indian telegraphy.

3. *Voice-Frequency Telegraphy*

The installation of a voice-frequency telegraph (VFT) system has resulted in an increase in the number of telegraph circuits between important stations, which normally operate by frequency modulation. The use of VFT has yielded a marked improvement in the performance of teleprinters, as reflected by the speedier transmission of messages. VFT systems are required for the following purposes:

(a) transmission of inter-exchange telex traffic;
(b) long-distance telex connections;
(c) leased teleprinter circuits, both for private and public subscribers;
(d) teleprinter circuits for public telegraph services;
(e) operation of teleprinter concentrators;
(f) operation of Gentex; and
(g) operation of Intelex

4. *Other Telegraph Services*

Radio-telephone service and high-speed wireless telegraph services have been introduced in various parts of the country. Wireless monitoring stations are presently in operation at Bangalore, Bombay, Calcutta, Delhi and Jabalpur. Direct international wireless circuits exist between Bombay and London, Melbourne, Shanghai, Tokyo, New York, Kabul and Djakarta, and between Delhi and London and Moscow. Additionally, a submarine cable telegraph connects: (1) Bombay with London, via Aden, Port Sudan, Alexandria, etc., for European traffic; (2) Madras with Penang, Singapore, Hong Kong, etc., for Far Eastern traffic; and (3) Bombay with Zanzibar and Aden, for East and South African traffic.
The so-called Gentex system – a scheme envisaged for the modernization of the public telegraph network – is envisaged for the modernisation of the public telegraph network. A pilot project with 50 lines is working at fourteen selected telegraph offices. It is proposed to extend this service to metropolitan cities with 800 additional lines; this would cover all central telegraph offices and a majority of Department of Telegraph offices.

B. *Telephone*

1. *Telephone Service Before Independence*

The telephone came to India as early as 1881, five years after its invention by Bell, when a 50-line telephone exchange was installed at Calcutta. The Orient Telephone Company soon thereafter introduced telephone services in Bombay, Madras, Ahamedabad and a few other towns. The first telephone exchange with automatic lines was installed in 1913 at Simla. This was followed in 1930 by India's first carrier system, installed between Delhi and Agra. During the Second World War, telephone services were strengthened by the employment of high-grade lines covering some 12,800 km. Although originally, telephone services were in the hands of private companies, the Government of India took over the licensed private telephone companies in 1943; the telephone industry has since functioned as a government undertaking.

2. *Telephone Service After Independence*

In 1947, with the independence of India, the development of telephone services began making rapid progress, as shown in Annexure I. The table reveals that the number of telephone lines has grown more than 30-fold (Item 3). Telephone services, which were available in only about 650 cities and towns in 1948, have now spread to over 31,000 cities, towns and villages (Items 5 + 14). In response to the large demand for telephones[51] and other telecommunications facilities, the Department of Telecommunications has undertaken a number of steps and devised plans for the rapid expansion and modernisation of the telecommunications system.[52]

3. *Telephone Switching Techniques*

Manual telephone switching is being progressively automatised. The step-by-step (strowager) system was a forerunner of automatic switching in the country. A common-control switching system was introduced in the mid-1960s, primarily to meet the demands of a nationwide, subscriber trunk-dialing service. By eliminating the need for manual operators and by enabling subscribers to switch directly their long-distance calls, the trunk service has been completely transformed. Subscribers have greeted the new service with great enthusiasm, and tremendous increases in trunk traffic and revenue have resulted.

In the last decade, electronic switching systems have been developed on a worldwide level and are accepted as the systems of the future. Electronically switched telephone exchanges of more than 20,000 trunk lines have been installed at Bombay, Delhi, Madras and Calcutta, and the Department of Telecommunications is taking steps in the current Five-Year Plan towards the introduction of electronic switching of local, trunk and telex exchanges as well. Electronic switching equipment for local, trunk and telex exchanges is being imported on a limited basis to gain experience before any large-scale changeover to the electronic system takes place.

51 INDIA 1984, *supra* note 4, at 426. About 18 million potential subscribers are waiting for connections, about 25% of the number of working connections.

52 The World Bank, recognising the importance of telecommunications in the proper management of the socio-economic development of India, has been extending considerable support to telecommunications development in the form of loans and credits. It has also been instrumental in the extension of bilateral credits from other countries.

4. *Telephone Transmission Techniques*

There has been a continuous technological evolution of transmission techniques in India. Formerly, open-wire physical circuits were the common mode of transmission for telegraph and telephone messages. The open-wire circuits were progressively replaced by 3-channel, 8-channel and 12-channel open-wire carriers and by 12-channel and 24-channel VFT systems. The trunk network was comprised almost entirely of open-wire routes, until the introduction in the mid-1950s of a symmetrical-pair cable carrier system. By the end of the 1950s, a coaxial system was introduced and has ultimately proved to be the backbone of transmission between the four metropolitan towns of Delhi, Bombay, Calcutta and Madras. The capacity of the coaxial cable system, initially 960 channels, was increased to 2700 channels per pair of tubes by the installation of 12-MHz, coaxial line equipment. A 60-MHz, coaxial cable system, allowing 19,800 simultaneous telephone conversations, has been introduced on a experimental basis between Bombay and Thane.

Along with the development of the coaxial cable system, a variety of other telephone transmission systems exist in India. A line-of-sight, radio-relay microwave system was introduced in the early 1960s; 2-GHz and 7-GHz narrow-band and 4-GHz and 6-GHz wide-band microwave systems have also been employed. In addition, an ultrahigh-frequency system, operating at 400 MHz and capable of providing sixty voice channels, is in use in the national transmission network. Single-channel and multichannel VHF systems, employing underground cables, have been developed for meeting the needs of the rural-sector pulse-code-modulated (PCM) system in working the junctions between the various exchanges in metropolitan towns. Optical-fibre systems, introduced on an experimental basis in the local telephone network of Pune for junction working, are likely to prove attractive in both the local and long-distance networks. Due to the technical and economic advantages offered by digital techniques, the Department of Telecommunications is gradually switching to digital communication for transmission and local switching networks. Two digital exchanges were commissioned during the VIth Five-Year Plan (1981-85). This was followed by the introduction of one coaxial system and ten new digital routes; several digital microwave systems have as well begun functioning. In the future, all transmission systems will be digital. A large factory, capable of manufacturing up to 20,000 digital exchanges, has been set up at Mankapur in Uttar Pradesh.

5. *Main Transmission Network Objectives*

The objectives for the design of the main transmission network are as follows:

(a) Main centres would be connected with each other by at least two independent and direct coaxial/microwave media, besides interconnection via satellite.
(b) Primary centres would be connected to their main centres by two independent and direct media, one of coaxial cable and the other of microwave; high-usage routes between any two primary centres should preferably have two independent media.
(c) Secondary centres would be connected to their primary centres by either the coaxial cable or microwave medium.
(d) All revenue district headquarters that are not secondary centres would be connected by a reliable cable/radio medium to the nearest primary/secondary centre.
(e) Subdivision (tehsil) headquarters and important towns in a district would be connected to the nearest secondary centre by a reliable cable/radio medium.
(f) The requirements of governmental organisations and departments for vehicle channels for TV and for data transmission, facsimile and telemetry would either be included within the broadband public network already existing or planned or else assigned to dedicated separate networks or links.

6. *Telephone Dialing Systems*

India's first subscriber trunk-dialing (STD) service was introduced on November 26, 1960 between Kanpur and Lucknow. Having since grown by leaps and bounds, the service is now in operation in 305 cities. About 66% of all telephone subscribers have access to STD, and more than 80% of all trunk calls are dialed by the subscribers themselves, accounting for 50% of the trunk circuit occupancy. For the convenience of those who do not have their own telephones, many public telephones have been equipped with STD facilites.

To implement STD, the Department of Telecommunications employs a network of trunk automatic exchanges. Thus far, national trunk switching centres exist at Bombay, Madras, Calcutta and Delhi, consisting of eleven primary and three secondary trunk automatic exchanges. The general objective is to provide all district headquarters with STD facilities and then to progressively expand these facilities to other cities and towns. This is proposed to be achieved by: (i) the expansion of existing trunk automatic exchanges to the extent feasible, (ii) the opening of second units wherever necessary and (iii) the establishment of new trunk automatic stations. A number of cities and towns have now been connected to various trunk automatic exchanges, thus providing them with a national subscriber-dialing facility. To achieve full, nationwide subscriber dialing, all trunk automatic exchanges will gradually be connected to the network on a regional basis. However, due to a shortage of capacity in the trunk automatic exchanges at the main centres, a fully interconnected, national subscriber grid has not yet been established. But the introduction of more than 20,000 store programme controlled (electronic) trunk automatic exchanges at the four trunk switching centres and the planned employment of digital trunk automatic exchanges should both facilitate and modernise the nationwide dialing system.

Along with the expansion of STD services, the Department of Telecommunications is making continuous efforts to improve and modernise the manual trunk services by incorporating improved techniques and operational methods. The T-43 trunk switchboard is bound to provide the necessary facilities for reliable trunk operation and has remained to a large extent a standard feature of the manual trunk exchanges in India. Single-link operator-dialing (SLOD) and multilink operator-dialing (MLOD) systems, using 2-wire strowager transit exchanges, have been introduced. However, 2-wire switching has been restricted to two-link workings due to excessive transmission losses at each transit point. In order to extend the scope of MLOD, a new design, developed by the Telecommunications Research Centre, was field-tested at Ahmedabad and Coimbatore, and its performance was considered satisfactory. During 1980-85, a number of these 4-wire MLOD centres were set up in a phased manner. Each MLOD centre was connected to trunk automatic exchanges in its area, with access to other MLOD centres within the region, so that interregional traffic could be switched through. 8400 SLOD and 630 MLOD systems now connect various district headquarters with Delhi, Bombay, Calcutta, Madras and other state capitals. As a part of the programme for the development of rural communications, direct-dialing facilities have been established for even the smallest-capacity manual exchanges (e.g., 10 lines), providing the taluka (i.e., subdivision of a district) and district headquarters with access to the villages. A group-dialing scheme, which enables one taluka subscriber to dial another taluka subscriber within a district without the assistance of an operator, has been introduced in many districts, particularly in Andhra Pradesh, Tamil Nadu and Kerala.

International subscriber dialing was introduced for the Delhi-London and Bombay-London routes, so that subscribers in Delhi and Bombay could dial London without the help of an operator. This service has now been extended to almost all countries in the world and, within India, to many important cities, including state capitals.

7. *Related Telephone Services*

The Department of Telecommunications operates thirteen coast stations at Bombay, Calcutta, Cochin, Goa, Kandla, Madras, Mangalore, Okhla, Porbander, Port Blair, Ratnagiri, Tuticorin and Vishakhapatnam. Besides monitoring international distress frequencies and providing ship-to-shore radio telegramme service, these stations offer long-range, high-frequency ship-to-shore telephone service, under which subscribers in Bombay, Calcutta and Madras can telephonically contact ships up to 750 km at sea. Short-range, very-high-frequency ship-to-shore telephone service is also available in Bombay, Calcutta, Madras and Cochin and allows subscribers to telephonically contact ships within 50 km of the coastline.

An »Own Your Telephone« scheme, introduced in 1949, now covers all telephones in the country. But due to the short supply of telephone facilities and equipment, a new, »Advance Deposit« scheme was introduced on September 1, 1975 by the Department of Telecommunications to discourage new telephone connections. Under the latter plan, a prospective telephone consumer is required to deposit an advance sum of Rs.1000 to 5000 along with the application for a telephone connection. The deposit is then applied toward telephone connection charges.

8. *Constraints on Telephone Development*

Although the Indian telecommunications sector has made spectacular progress during recent years, with both a tremendous expansion and a technological transformation, telecommunication services have lagged in terms of quantity and quality behind the requirements of the country. The quality of service is far from satisfactory, in that there has been a substantial number of unsatisfied telephone demands throughout the country, despite a 30-fold increase since 1948 in the number of telephone connections. Similarly, there has been heavy congestion in telephone traffic in local systems, in large metropolitan towns and in the trunk network. Both of these factors, contributing in a large measure to the considerable dissatisfaction with the services provided by the Department of Telecommunications, have overshadowed the many remarkable achievements made during the last four decades.

The root of the problem stems from the allocation of inadequate resources for telecommunications development. The resources made available in successive Five-Year Plans, though considerably increased, have remained inadequate to meet the growing demands for local telephone and trunk circuits. This has resulted in the overloading of both the local and trunk networks. Without adequate financial resources, it is not possible to allocate adequate material resources, shortages of which have proved to be a big constraint on telephone development, financial allocations notwithstanding.

To meet the demand for telephones, that is, to service the existing economic growth levels, a 12% yearly expansion is required for local telephone services, with a correspondingly higher rate of growth in regard to the trunk network; the resources allocations in the past have never permitted a rate of growth of more than 10%. To improve its position, telephone communication must receive a higher percentage of the total plan outlay for the public sector than what it has been getting.

Annexure II lists the comparative figures for investment in telecommunications, in absolute terms and as a percentage both of the national Gross Development Programme (GDP) and of the total annual capital formation, in a few developed and developing countries. It is evident that investment in telecommunications in India falls considerably short, as a percentage of total plan outlay, of that of advanced and many developing countries, such as Bangladesh, Sri Lanka, Brazil and Singapore.

9. *Telephone and Consumers*

Consumers cannot demand telephone service as a matter of right. It is instead a privilege, which the government and the Telephone Authority can extend if they see fit to do so in a given case. For instance, if, in controlling or meeting the heavy demand for telephone connections, any particular category of applications is thought essential and is given preference by the authorities, it cannot be attacked as discriminatory[53] or as *ultra vires* under the Constitution.[54]

When the Telephone Authority refuses to continue to extend telephone facilities to a subscriber unless the amount payable for the use of the telephone for a previous period is paid, it cannot be said that an opportunity of a hearing must be given before disconnection.[55] Disconnection of the telephone of a particular subscriber cannot be treated as a punishment. It is instead a matter of contract to which the subscriber and the Telephone Authority are bound; breach on the part of one allows the other to take steps accordingly. However, the authorities are not allowed to disconnect a telephone on the ground that the subscriber was neither residing nor maintaining a place of business at the premises where the telephone was installed.[56]

Any dispute between a telephone consumer and the Telephone Authority concerning any telegraph line will be referred to arbitration, according to Section 7-B of the Telegraph Act of 1885.[57] This section was held to govern the question of whether a telephone installed in a subscriber's business premises could be disconnected.[58] But a dispute relating to the actual reading of a telephone meter, involving as such questions as to whether the meter had been correctly and honestly read or whether the reading had been correctly

53 Matheu v. Vijaya Movies, 1978 Indian L.R. 275 (Kerala H.C.). Held, there is no unqualified right on the part of any subscriber or of any transferee to have his application for a telephone or for a transfer of the telephone invariably allowed or granted.

54 INDIA CONST. art. 14: »The State shall not deny to any person equality before the law or the equal protection of the laws within the territory of India.«

55 Raghubar Dayal Kanodia v. Union of India, 1970 A.I.R. 143, 145 (Allahabad H.C.); Bharat Plywood and Timber Products Ltd. v. Kerala State Electricity Board, Trivendrum, 1972 A.I.R. 47 (Kerala H.C.).

56 1974 K.L.T. 43. *See also* Hukum Chand v. Union of India, 1976 A.I.R. 789 (S.C.): held, if the telephone of the subscriber were to be disconnected on the ground of misuse, then the authorities would have to give the consumer an opportunity to be heard, consonant with the principles of natural justice, before taking any action.

57 Indian Telegraph Act of 1885, § 7–B: »(1) Except as otherwise expressly provided in this Act, if any dispute concerning any telegraph line, appliance or apparatus arises between the telegraph authority and the person for whose benefit the line, appliance or apparatus is, or has been, provided, the dispute shall be determined by arbitration and shall, for the purposes of such determination, be referred to an arbitrator appointed by the Central Government either specially for the determination of that dispute or generally for determination of disputes under this section. (2) The award of the arbitrator appointed under sub-section (1) shall be conclusive between the parties to the dispute and shall not be questioned in any court.«

58 1964 Madhya Pradesh L.J. 831, 1964 Jabalpur L.J. 566.

and honestly noted, is clearly outside the purview of section 7-B of the ITA.[59]

Subletting a telephone is opposed to public policy and prohibited by section 4 of the ITA.[60] Accordingly, the Andrha Pradesh High Court held in *Seethrama Sastry v. N. Kalwar and Sons*[61] that in view of the object of the ITA and of the provisions of section 20-A,[62] a subscriber of a telephone who sublets it without the written consent of the Telephone Authority and in contravention of the specific conditions of his agreement with the government cannot recover from the sublessee the charges of the phone in pursuance of the arrangement.

In *Union of India v. Narayana Iyer*,[63] an important question arose as to whether the deficit incurred in the operation of the Posts and Telegraph Department could be properly recovered by an increase in the telephone tariff. The respondent, a telephone user, questioned the validity of the increased tariff, which was issued under the Indian Telegraph (Amendment) Rules of 1966 and levied pursuant to section 7(2)(a) of the ITA. It was contended that the charge for the use of the telephone was levied as a fee and, as such, there must be a reasonable correlation between an increase in the telephone rates and the services rendered by the Department of Posts; that is, an increase in telephone rates to make up for losses incurred by the Department was not permissible. It was further urged by the respondent that the increased rates were arbitrary, unjust, unreasonable and beyond the

59 *Raghubar Dayal Kanodia*, 1970 A.I.R. 143.

60 *See generally*, p. 35 *supra*.

61 1968 A.I.R. 315 (Andhra Pradesh H.C.).

62 Indian Telegraph Act of 1885, § 20A: »If the holder a license granted under section 4 contravenes any condition contained in his license, he shall be punished with fine which may extend to one thousand rupees, and with a further fine which may extend to five hundred rupees for every week during which the breach continues.« *See also Chakkilal,* 1943 A.I.R. 143: license for domestic purposes, station installed in shop: conviction can only be possible by evidence not merely of the situation of the radio but of its use to attract or amuse the public.

63 [1970] 1 Madras L.J. (Reports) 19. The Union of India, represented by the Secretary of the Ministry of Communications in Delhi, and the General Manager of Telephones in Madras appealed the judgment of the Single Bench striking down the enhanced tariff. Under the 1960 Tariff Rules in the Madras District, telephone installation charges were fixed at Rs.40 and rent for a telephone installed in a subscriber's premises at Rs.50 per quarter year, with 150 free calls per quarter year (10 paisa for every extra call over and above the free calls). The impugned tariff raised the installation charges to Rs.50, the rent to Rs.75 per quarter and the extra-call charges to 15 paisa.

power conferred under section 7(2)(a)[64] of the ITA, since telephone services, being a public utility, could not be run by the government with purely business ends.
The court rejected the respondent's contention and held that the impugned tariff could not be struck down as unlawful, that the charges levied could not be termed unreasonable and that a fundamental right of the subscriber could not be shown to have been adversely affected by the rise in rates. The court further held that section 7(2)(a) of the ITA and rule 443 of the Amendment Rules of the 1966, both of which fix the tariff rate, were neither *ultra vires* under the Constitution nor in excess of the rule-making powers given to the central government by the ITA. The court said that the charge made by the Department of Posts and Telegraph in respect of the provision of public utility services was not a fee, it was essentially a rate or a tariff of rates determined by a process of lawfully delegated legislation. The Department was therefore entitled to a reasonable return under its rate base and could employ all principals of modern accounting in the determination of its rate, for example, for appropriation of surplus for capital expansion. A reasonable rate of tariff, said the court, is a question of fact and depends on such factors as gross income and expenditure, application of surplus and extent of net profits. But even if the tariff were not reasonable, it would not be function of the courts to adjust the tariff; that is the province of the legislature.

C. *Telex*

1. *Telex Services*

The major development in telegraph services since Independence has been the installation of telex exchanges. Telex service on a national basis was introduced in India in 1963. This service has become extremely popular and

64 Indian Telegraph Act of 1885, § 7(2)(a) empowers the central government to make rules for the conduct of telegraph. It says: »... rules made under this section may provide for ... the rates at which, and other conditions subject to which, messages shall be transmitted within India.« Rule 451(c) of the Indian Telegraph Rules of 1951 (substituted by the Indian Telegraph Third Amendment Rules of 1984) says: »the charges for ordinary and S.T.D. trunk calls between any two exchanges or two long-distance charging centres not being situated within a radial distance of fifty kilometres shall be reduced by 50% ... (i) on all Sundays and National Holidays and (ii) between 00.00 hours and 05.00 hours and between 22.00 hours and 24.00 hours on other days.«

important in this day of industrialisation, trade and news reporting. As a result, within a short span of twenty-three years, a large number of telex exchanges with full intercommunication on an automatic basis have been established in the country. Telex connections are provided by the Department of Telecom munications practically on demand. Telex exchanges have gone from 4 in 1963 to 136 in 1980. The total equipped capacity – at the end of 1963-64, only 800 – had reached 22,015 by 1979-80; working connections increased from 601 to 17,893 over the same period. By the end of the VIth Five-Year Plan, telex communications had increased considerably.

It has been proposed that during the VIIth Five-Year Plan (1986-90) the equipped capacity of local lines be increased to cater to the needs of industries, banks and commercial houses in the far-flung areas of the country; where rural development is being planned, it is proposed that small telex exchanges of twenty-line capacity be installed, until such time as other solutions become available. It is further planned to increase the existing capacity of telex exchanges in suburban areas in order to meet demands and to increase the capacity of the four metropolitan telex centres in Bombay, Calcutta, Madras and Delhi. The expanded exchanges would be store programme-controlled, which offers a wide range of facilities and provides improved services.

2. *Security Deposit for Telex Services*

In the recent case of *Mssrs. S.G. Steels Ltd. v. Union of India,*[65] the validity of the imposition of a security deposit of Rs.10,000 on existing telex subscribers, by way of amended rule 505-B of the Indian Telegraph (Second Amendment) Rules of 1983,[66] was challenged on the following grounds:

(a) The government cannot unilaterally change the terms of the original contract between the parties, which contained no provision for a security deposit.

(b) The amendment to rule 505-B is prospective, and, therefore, no security deposit can be imposed on existing telex subscribers.

65 1984 A.I.R. 272 (Delhi H.C.).

66 Indian Telegraph (Second Amendment) rules of 1983, rule 505–B: »(1) Every subscriber who has a telex connection on the date of commencement of the Telegraph (Second) Amendment Rules of 1983 shall within a period of three months from such commencement deposit a sum of Rs.10,000 to the Telegraph Authority as security for the said telex connection. (2) If the subscriber fails to deposit the amount specified in sub-rule (1) within the period specified therein, the Telegraph Authority may withdraw the telex service and remove any telex or other apparatus belonging to the Telegraph Authority.«

(c) Imposition of a security deposit is arbitrary and violative of article 14 of the Constitution.
(d) Imposition of a security deposit is beyond the rule-making power of the central government, as the only sanction provided by the Indian Telegraph Act of 1885, in cases of breaches of terms by subscribers, is disconnection.

Rejecting the petitioner's contentions that the government cannot unilaterally change the terms of the agreement, the court observed that, under the provisions of the Indian Telegraph Act and Rules, the government has a monopoly on such forms of communication as telegraph, telephone and telex, both in matters of installation of the instrument of communication and in the nature of the service rendered. Private citizens have no rights. The government, in exercise of its prerogative powers, makes services available to citizens via license, on satisfaction of certain conditions. These licenses therefore cannot be termed an agreement between the parties similar to a commercial agreement.

The court further held that the new rule 505-B is authorised by section 7(2)(h)[67] of the Indian Telegraph Act of 1885 and is, therefore, not *ultra vires*; sanctions are not necessarily limited to disconnection. More importantly, the nature of a security deposit is not that of a sanction or penalty. It is only a precautionary or anticipatory measure that may not be imposed arbitrarily.

As regards the petitioner's argument that the imposition of a security deposit amounts to the giving of retrospective effect to the amendment, the court observed that the liability is not in the nature of an increase in past charges but is in the nature of recurring charges. This has to be paid only once. Technically speaking, under the provisions of the Act and the Rules, a license is yearly, from May 1 to April 30. In that sense, a license renewed on May 1, 1983 can be treated as a new license and a security deposit can be imposed. The only difference between a new license and an existing license would be that once the security deposit is paid, it would not be required to be repaid so long as the license is renewed. The rule does not suffer from any infirmity of retroactivity.

67 Indian Telegraph Act of 1885, § 7(2)(h): »Rules under this section may provide for all or any of the following, among other matters, that is to say ... the time at which, the manner in which, the conditions under which and the persons by whom the rates, charges and fees mentioned in this sub-section shall be paid and the furnishing of security for the payment of such rates, charges and fees.«

Chapter IV: Transborder Telecommunications Services

A. *Overseas Communications Services*

India's external telecommunications services are operated by the Overseas Communications Services (OCS), a wing of the Department of Telecommunications.[68] With its headquarters in Bombay, the OCS is responsible for the planning, establishment, maintenance and operation of India's external telecommunications services. Through its four »International Traffic Gateway Centres« in Bombay, Delhi, Calcutta and Madras, the OCS provides a variety of overseas services. For high-frequency radio communications, the Gateway Centres maintain transmitting and receiving stations at Poona/Dhond, Kalkaji/Chattarpur, Halisahar/Hathikanda and Korathur/Padianallur. A Troposcatter communications link between India and the U.S.S.R., commissioned in November 1981, is supervised by the Gateway Centres via a terminal station at Srinagar in Kahmir. The OCS also maintains two international satellite communications earth stations (the Vikram Satellite Earth Station at Arvi near Pune and the Ahmed Satellite Earth Station at Dehra Dun), which employ the Indian Ocean Satellite of the International Telecommunications Satellite Organisation (INTELSAT). These two earth stations are connected by broadband microwave links with the Bombay and Delhi Gateway Centres. A wide-band, submarine telephone cable (IOCOM) system operates across the Indian Ocean between the Madras Gateway Centre and Malaysia. Approximately 99.5% of India's external telecommunications traffic is routed through the satellite, IOCOM and Troposcatter media.[69]

The specific responsibilities of the OCS include:

(a) maintaining the highest of international communications operating standards, as determined by the Consultative Committee of the International Telecommunication Union;

68 ANNUAL REPORT, *supra* note 5, at 25. The Overseas Communications Services was constituted as a government department on January 1, 1947, consequent on the nationalisation of the Indian Cable and Communication Company.

69 A very small fraction of traffic is transmitted by high-frequency radio stations located in Delhi and Calcutta.

(b) operating and maintaining India's international telecommunications services by providing the necessary transmission media and Gateway exchanges;
(c) coordinating the operational aspects of the telegraph, telephone and telex services with the Department of Telecommunications, which provides the subscribers' terminal equipment and the national network;
(d) advising the government on tariff policies in regard to India's external telecommunications services;
(e) settling the traffic revenue accounts due from or owed to foreign governments;
(f) participating in the Commonwealth Telecommunications Partnership under the Commonwealth Telecommunications Financial Agreement of 1973;
(g) participating in INTELSAT, which provides international satellite communications, by acting as India's signatory to the INTELSAT Agreement, by contributing to the establishment of the space segment and by acting as the operating entity in the utilisation of the space segment;
(h) participating in INMARSAT, which provides satellite communications for ships at sea, by contributing to the establishment of the space segment and a low-cost earth station in India;
(i) participating in the IOCOM Cable Management Committee (ICMC), which is responsible for the operation and maintenance of the IOCOM submarine telephone cable system;
(j) developing new transmission media, such as the submarine cable system;
(k) developing indigenous capability for the manufacture of specialised communications equipment and for the training of workers in new technologies; and
(l) planning for the future requirements of India's telecommunications traffic, in keeping with the modern trends of technology.

In addition, the OCS provides:

(a) international telephone service;
(b) international telephone conference (INCOTEL) service, whereby an Indian party can have a telephonic conference with up to four foreign parties located anywhere in the world (available only from the Bombay Gateway);

(c) international telegraph service;
(d) international telex service;
(e) fully automatic telex service (via INMARSAT) for ships located anywhere in the Indian, Atlantic or Pacific Oceans;
(f) store-and-forward telex (SFT) service from Delhi to Hong Kong, Japan, the U.S. and the U.K.;
(g) international facsimile (Bureaufax) service, which can transmit to or receive from other countries drawings, letters and other documents in a matter of minutes (now operational between Bombay and Delhi and Hong Kong, Japan, Kuwait and Singapore);
(h) programme transmissions (»voice casts«) for press correspondents, news agencies and broadcasting organisations covering international events in India;
(i) live relay of international satellite television broadcasts;
(j) leased data service for international banking houses, the Meteorological Department and others;
(k) leased teleprinter service; and
(l) leased voice-grade service.

B. *OCS Development Plans*

The OCS maintains a research and development wing to assist in the implementation of OCS expansion schemes and to develop indigenous know-how and capabilities. The wing devotes itself to designing and manufacturing some of the sophisticated communications equipment unique to OCS requirements. In addition, the OCS seeks to provide continuous improvement of internal telecommunications services and to bring them on a par with facilities in the more advanced countries of the world. To that end, the OCS has adopted short- and long-term plans to modernise equipment and facilities and to introduce the latest technologies. A new submarine telephone cable system, the Gulf Cable, now operates between India and the United Arab Emirates; a high-grade, trans-India microwave link, meeting international standards, to connect Madras and Bombay with the IOCOM and Gulf cables is also planned. Establishment of a coastal satellite earth station to provide 24-hour communications facilities via satellite for ships at sea is another project at an advanced stage of completion. Another important developmental plan of the OCS is the proposed expansion of the Calcutta

Gateway Centre, to provide it with facilities similar to those at the other OCS Gateways.

C. *International Store Programme-Controlled Exchanges*

India's first electronic, or store programme-controlled, telex exchange was commissioned by the OCS at the Bombay Gateway in 1977, providing customers with an international subscriber-dialed telex facility. Installation of similar exchanges at Delhi in 1980 and at Madras in 1982 further improved the service to the public. Following the introduction of the telex exchanges, India's first store programme-controlled telephone exchange was commissioned by the OCS at the Bombay Gateway in 1981; similar exchanges followed at the Delhi, Madras and Calcutta Gateways. Featuring advanced and highly sophisticated technology and adopting modular hardware and software configurations, both the telex and the telephone exchanges have helped to improve the international communications service. The exchanges have a number of unique operational and maintenance features not possible in conventional electro-mechanical systems, and they offer such new facilities to the public as international subscriber dialing to all major countries. With these improved exchanges, the OCS can now offer direct telephone links with 42 countries on 864 channels. The international subscriber-dialed service, available at present to Australia, France, Hong Kong, Japan, Singapore and the U.K., is being progressively expanded to more countries. The international subscriber-dialed telex service is available to 175 countries,[70] and direct international telex service is available to 44 countries via satellite on 945 channels.

As with telephone and telex services, India also has a modern, automatic, store programme-controlled, international telegramme transmission and switching system. Available at all four Gateway Centres, the system offers better service to the public by the improved handling of international telegrammes. Outgoing telegrammes are fed into the system by operators with the help of video keyboards that all but eliminate errors. The system automatically transmits and routes the telegrammes to various destinations in the world, receiving likewise incoming telegrammes without delay. The system

70 *See* Annexure III.

facilitates a variety of monitoring, supervisory, storage and retrieval functions, safeguarding the accuracy and security of public telegrammes. The system enables very large volumes of international telegrammes, particularly during peak hours, to be handled with minimum delay.

D. *Indian Ocean Commonwealth Submarine Cable*

The Indian Ocean Commonwealth submarine telephone cable system, or IOCOM, provides a direct telephone link between India and Malaysia. Extending some 1350 nautical miles (2500 km) from Madras, across the Bay of Bengal, to Penang, the cable marks the culmination of the joint endeavors of the OCS and six other Commonwealth telecommunications administrations, namely: JTM (Malaysia), OTS (Sri Lanka), TELECOM (Singapore), Cable and Wireless (Hong Kong), OTC (Australia) and TELEGLOBE (Canada). Capital participation was broadly proportional to anticipated usage. The OCS was the project coordinator.

The submerged system consists of a 0.99-inch coaxial cable, 173 electronic repeater amplifiers and eleven equalisers spliced into the cable at regular intervals along its length; the terminal equipment is located at Madras (India) and at Kuala Muda (Malaysia). The cable itself has at its core a steel rope for strength. Around this rope is wrapped an inner copper conductor; this is in turn covered by a polyethylene dielectric to achieve an exact diameter. An outer aluminium conductor is then folded longitudinally around the cable. Finally, the cable is wrapped in a polyethylene outer sheathing. At the shore ends, the light-weight cable is wrapped with galvanised steel wires sandwiched between layers of polypropylene and bitumen compounds.[71]

The terminal equipment is comprised of a high-voltage repeater power feed, wide-band transmission equipment and supervisory and monitoring facilities.

Two-way transmission over the single submarine coaxial cable is achieved by using the lower portion of the cable frequency spectrum (below 2296 kHz) for transmission in one direction and the upper portion of the spectrum (above 2788 kHz) for transmission in the opposite direction. Directional filters are used at each terminal station and at each submerged repeater to

71 The total quantities of material involved in the IOCOM system were: 2760 tons of steel, 240 tons of copper, 195 tons of aluminum, 1198 tons of polyethylene and 175 tons of polypropylene.

separate the two bands. The submerged repeater amplifiers are energised by means of a DC line current fed along the centre conductor of the cable in one direction and through the sea bed in the reverse direction. The normal, full-system voltage between the two ends of the cable is 4580 volts. The equipment at one terminal has control of the line current and functions as the master. Fully automatic, »repeater supervisory monitoring equipment« enables the continuous monitoring of the repeater performance and initiates alarms in the event of any deviations. In order to minimise loss of circuits due to equipment faults, strategic items of transmission equipment have been duplicated.

The IOCOM complex in Madras, comprised of India's part of the submarine cable system, a Gateway terminal building and associated electronic telephone and telex exchanges, was completed at a cost of approximately Rs.350 million (US $32 million) with the joint financing of the government of India and the U.K., under the Indian-U.K. Mixed Project Ground; India's share was Rs.240 million, and the U.K.'s, Rs.110 million. The Madras complex is housed in a building adjoining the OCS complex (Videsh Sanchar Bhawan). The first floor of the building, where the transmission and reception equipment is located, has been specially screened to eliminate radio and electrical interference.

E. *Operative Telecommunications Circuits (as of December 31, 1984)*

1. Via Satellite

(a)	Telex circuits	862
(b)	Telephone circuits	781
(c)	Leased telegraph circuits	135
(d)	Voice-frequency bearer circuits	57
(e)	Telegraph circuits	43
(f)	Leased voice-grade circuits	17

2. Via IOCOM Cable

(a)	Telex circuits	82
(b)	Telephone circuits	80
(c)	Leased telegraph circuits	8
(d)	Voice-frequency bearer circuits	7

(e)	Telegraph circuits	1
(f)	Leased voice-grade circuits	1

3. Via Troposcatter Medium

(a)	Voice-grade circuits	2

4. Via High-Frequency Radio

(a)	Telegraph circuits	4
(b)	Leased telegraph circuits	4
(c)	Telex circuits	1
(d)	Telephone circuits	1
(e)	Leased voice-grade circuits	1

Chapter V: Satellite Telecommunications

A. *Satellite Communications*

In June 1977, India began a two-year experiment in satellite telecommunications known as the Satellite Telecommunications Experiment Project, or STEP. The project was the result of an agreement made between the Indian Space Research Organisation and the Symphonic Organisation, whereby one of the two transponders aboard the French-West German Symphonic satellite was made available for experiments in such areas as remote-area communications, digital communications, multiple access, integration of satellite circuits into a terrestrial network and multiple audio-visual transmission. The project successfully provided India with a system test for a geosynchronous communications satellite and sharpened her expertise in the design, development, fabrication and operation of a communications system involving a geostationary satellite.

On July 18, 1980, India joined the exclusive group of nations possessing their own satellite launch capabilities when its SLV-3 launch vehicle placed a 35-kg Rohini satellite (RS-I), developed at the Indian Space Application Centre (SAC), into a near-earth orbit.[72] A series of Rohini satellites, to carry selected scientific and application payloads to be launched by future SLV vehicles, are under development at SAC. A Rohini-II satellite was successfully launched on May 31, 1981, asserting India's satellite supremacy in the developing world.

India's first three-axis, geostationary satellite, Apollo, was launched on June

72 MINISTRY OF INFORMATION AND BROADCASTING, INDIA 1981, 75–79. The first Indian satellite, Aryabhata, named after the famous ancient Indian astronomer and mathematician, was designed and built at the Indian Space Research Organisation's Satellite Centre. The 360-kg satellite was launched on April 19, 1975 from a Soviet Cosmodrome using a Soviet Intercosmos rocket into a near-circular orbit of 600 km at an inclination of 51° to the equator. A second Indian satellite, Bhaskara I, was launched on June 7, 1980 from a Soviet Cosmodrome for earth observations. The 44-kg, experimental satellite, named after two ancient Indian astronomers, was also designed and built at the Indian Space Research Organisation. It contained sophisticated instruments for carrying out remote sensing experiments over India, using TV cameras and a microwave radiometer. Bhaskara experiments were useful in such studies as forestry, hydrology, snow cover and snow melt, geology, soils, land use and the ocean surface. Bhaskara II, India's second earth observation satellite, was launched on November 20, 1982 from a Soviet Cosmodrome in Volvograd.

19, 1981, using the Ariane launch vehicle of the European Space Agency. While the communications payloads of the 600-kg satellite were built at SAC, important subsystems, like the apogee boost motor and the secondary propulsion systems, were built at the Vikram Sarabhai Space Centre (named after the late Prof. Vikram A. Sarabhai, the founder of the Indian space programme). The experience provided India with the technological expertise necessary for the building and operation of future geosynchronous satellites.[73]

B. *Indian Satellite System (INSAT)*

India launched its first multipurpose domestic satellite, INSAT-IA, on April 10, 1982 into a geostationary orbit at 74° East. Due to troubles with the unfolding of the solar cell, the power supply necessary for the satellite's seven-year life was exhausted. Since the satellite could not become operational, it was abandoned in September 1982. This was a major setback for India's satellite communications programme.

However, within eighteen months of the launching of INSAT-IA, India was able to launch a second, 1193-kg, multipurpose satellite. INSAT-IB, the product of an agreement between India's Department of Space and the U.S. National Aeronautics and Space Administration (NASA), was built by the Ford Aerospace and Communication Corporation. It was launched on August 30, 1983 from the U.S. space shuttle Challenger and came into operation on October 15, 1983. INSAT-IB is controlled by the Indian space scientists from the Master Control Facility at Hassan, about 200 km from Bangalore, in southern India. With the launching of INSAT-IB, India entered a new era in space communications. It should be noted that during the short span of one decade, India acquired more expertise in direct satellite broadcasting than

73 The word »space« may mean different things to different people. It may mean the earth's near environment, interplanetary areas or the very outer fringes of the universe. Space research essentially relates to the study and exploration of the earth's environment, both near and remote. Space science is by no means a recent development. Descriptions of various planets and phenomena in the skies are found in the Vedic texts of ancient India. Modern astronomy and telescopes came to India with the establishment of the Madras observatory in 1972 and the Kodaikanal Observatory in 1978. In modern terms, Indian advances in space sciences can perhaps be traced to the establishment of both an observatory at Colaba and the Indian Meteorological department in Bombay in 1823. *See* Yash, *Space Projects for Developing Countries* (June 20, 1977) (paper presented at a meeting of the UN Committee on the Peaceful Uses of Outer Space held in Vienna in June–July 1977).

any other country in the world. In fact, India can even share this kind of information with other countries, including developed countries.[74]

The most outstanding features of this satellite communications system are the multipoint accessibility on the uplink and the broadcasting abilities on the downlink. A geostationary communications satellite is simultaneously accessible to all the earth stations within its coverage area, and, similarly, satellite broadcast transmissions can be received by all earth stations in the coverage area. These two special features of satellite communication lend it great versatility. Some of the important services provided by INSAT-IB are detailed as follows:

1. *Telephone*

The telephone component of INSAT-IB is comprised of twelve satellite transponders – capable of providing 6000 to 8000, 2-way, long-distance telephone circuits – and thirty-one earth stations: five main-area locations with 11-metre antennas (Delhi, Bombay, Calcutta, Madras and Shillong), eight primary-area locations with 8-metre antennas (Ahmedabad, Ernakulam, Jalandhar, Lucknow, Patna, Bhubaneswar, Hyderabad and Jaipur), fifteen remote-area locations with 4.5-metre antennas (Leh, Gangtok, Arumachal Pradesh, Mezoram, Agartala, Nagaland, Andaman, Nicobar, Jodhpur, Srinagar, Locadives, Minicoy, Bhuj, Imphal and Goa) and one road-transportable and two air/road-transportable stations.

INSAT-IB serves one-third of the total circuit requirement on the inter-main routes of Delhi-Bombay, Delhi-Calcutta, Madras-Bombay, Madras-Calcutta and Calcutta-Shillong, and one-half of the total circuit requirement on the Delhi-Madras and Bombay-Calcutta routes. The satellite transponders also handle three-fourths of the total circuit requirement on eight of the primary-main routes and will service as well the traffic to remote-area locations that are to be connected to the main stations at Delhi, Bombay, Calcutta and Madras.

It should be noted that the full capacity of the twelve satellite transponders has been utilised, and, as such, the balance of traffic must necessarily be met by terrestrial media. Provisions have been made in the VIIth Five-Year Plan for meeting the balance of traffic on the inter-main routes and on selected primary-main routes not serviced by the satellite. There are as well a very large number of routes that need to be developed to connect secondary and smaller centres to the national network. All traffic requirements just cannot

74 *See* Harley, *U.S. Perspectives in Worldwide Communications*, Span, July 1982, at 48.

be met by any satellite system, and terrestrial systems are required to fill the gaps.

2. *Meteorology*

INSAT-IB allows the remote collection of meteorological, hydrological and oceanographic data from unattended automatic data-collection platforms (DCPs) and the transmission of this data to a central data-processing centre. For this purpose, a total of 200 DCPs are scheduled to be installed at a variety of locations on the subcontinent. INSAT-IB also provides timely warnings of impending disasters from cyclones, floods, etc., by direct broadcast to the areas likely to be affected.

3. *Television and Radio*

The revolutionary impact of INSAT-IB on India's television and radio broadcast capabilities is dealt with extensively in Part III, Chapters XI and XII, infra.

C. *Next-Generation Satellites*

The planning for India's next generation of satellites is presently underway in the various sections of the concerned departments. The second-generation satellites will undoubtedly be much larger than INSAT-IB and likely not be multipurpose. The world trend in satellite communications is toward simpler, smaller earth installations working with larger satellites with specific purposes, such as meteorology or telecommunications. Long-distance telecommunications would continue to form the bulk of the total service requirements for an INSAT-II system, but such new services as general data communications and rural telecommunications could also be advantageously provided. For the latter example, a number of small, low-cost earth terminals, working in demand-assignment modes, would be installed in various rural pockets located in assorted secondary switching centres of the national network. This would effectively take the benefits of satellite communications technology to the doorsteps of India's villages and help connect Rural Public Cell offices, particularly in hamlets not serviceable by terrestrial media.

PART II: Remote Data Processing

Chapter VI: Computers and Data Processing

A. *Computer Technology in India*

India's Department of Electronics has made substantial efforts in developing indigenous hardware and software capability. National research and development centres include the National Centre for Software Development and Computing Techniques in Bombay and the National Informatics Centre (NIC), which provides a computer network infrastructure to enable the development of interactive, computerised data bases for the various organs of the Government of India.[75] The NIC has already developed several information systems for, and installed ten computer terminals in, governmental departments, allowing them direct access to the NIC's maxi-computer, Cyber 170/720.

To meet the computing needs of various regions, the Department of Electronics has been establishing regional computer centres. The regional computer centre at Calcutta is already in operation and serves over eighty users. A regional computer centre for the northern region has been set up at Chandigarh, and two other centres have been set up at Pune and Kanpur. To extend computer application to more-specialised areas and to maximally utilise computer facilities, infrastructure and manpower already in place, the Department of Electronics has undertaken to develop a computer-aided design programme and a computer-aided management programme with the assistance of the United Nations Development Project (UNDP).

The major Indian producer of computers is the Electronics Corporation of India, Ltd. in Hyderabad, a public-sector undertaking. It has already produced and installed 184 various computer systems, such as the TDC-12, TDC-316 and Micro-78 systems. A few private-sector companies have as well successfully developed and marketed dedicated microprocessor-based systems for financial inventory and other applications. Research work is also in progress for the use of Indian languages in computers.

75 *See* ANNUAL REPORT, *supra* note 5, at 58–60.

B. *Data Communications*

Data communications[76] in its simplest form is the transfer of information from a data-collecting source to either data-processing equipment or simple storage. With the worldwide explosion of information technology, there is a need for the fast and safe transport of data over distance; fast and accurate delivery of data are the basic parameters of an efficient data-communications system. In India, a variety of data networks are being planned and implemented by the Department of Telecommunications and other users.
Data communications means, to a telecommunications engineer, the transmission of digital signals over long distances using a telecommunications network. However, from a consumer's point of view, data communications usually takes one of the following forms:

(a) terminal-to-terminal communications, as applied to telex and telefax;
(b) terminal-to-computer communications, as applied to information retrieval, such as airline reservations, inventory control and other similar applications; and
(c) computer-to-computer communications, applicable to distributed processing, computer resource sharing and other applications.

Data-communication services in India began with imported, customer-owned modem equipment. The Department of Telecommunications then started to provide leased, dedicated telecommunications circuits between mainframe computers and their remotely located terminals. In the early years, however, commissioning and testing of high-speed circuits were difficult for the Department of Telecommunications because of a lack of the specific instruments required for the measurement of relevant parameters. Thus, computer use was generally restricted to computer centres, and teleprocessing capability was often unavailable. But due to decreased hardware costs, the availability of indigenous computers, microprocessor systems and modems has grown; this has in turn boosted the demand for data circuits in many fields, including educational research institutions, police, security, railways, airlines, industrial and commercial undertakings and establishments, travel and tourism and a number of allied industries and under-

76 *See* 34 TELECOMMUNICATIONS 273, 330 (1984).

takings. Nevertheless, a lack of facilities for data processing remains a problem, and users requiring infrequent use of data links and those with low traffic were therefore excluded from the telecommunications processing demand estimation done by the Department of Electronics for the VIth Five-Year Plan. With the increasing computerisation in various organisations, on-demand data-transmission service is targeted for the VIIth Five-Year Plan (1986-90).

The Department of Telecommunications' emphasis in data communications has generally been toward:

(a) provision of data links on a leased-circuit basis, using point-to-point link configuration;
(b) provision of a data service of up to 1200 bps on an intracity basis at Delhi, Calcutta, Bombay and Madras, utilising the data-capability feature of store programme-controlled telex exchanges;
(c) provision of a data service on an intercity basis between the above four centres, also using telex exchanges;
(d) realisation of a low-speed data service, using the public switched telephone network by way of STD calls; and
(e) implementation of research aimed at evolving an appropriate, full-fledged public data network (circuit-switched, packet-switched or a combination of both).

C. *Leased Data Services*

Leased data services are provided by dedicated circuits using modems and are rendered either locally, by long distance or by use of a premium digital-data system. The premium digital-data service is a new service based on the philosophy of a digital-data network. In this service, group-band modems, operating in a group of twelve channels, are operated at speeds of 64 kbps between major locations.

This speed of 64 kbps is subdivided into combinations of 2400, 4800 and 9600 bps through group-band multiplexers (synchronous). The group-band modems and multiplexers are located at long-distance transmission facilities. The local leads to subscriber premises are driven by voice-band or base-band modems at appropriate speeds. An alternate voice/data facility is available with all imported modems by use of a special telephone; it is not presently available with the indigenous ones. This facility is likely to be introduced very shortly.

D. *Packet Switched Network*

A market survey, recently conducted by In-House Consultancy and British Teleconsult, to assess the requirements of data users in India concluded that a switching network is required that would reduce costs, have smaller call overheads and support different types of subscribers and services. To meet this requirement, the introduction of a public packet switched network was suggested. To that end, the Department of Telecommunications is to set up a simple, experimental packet switched network that will use an indigenously available computer. The proposed network will comprise three nodes, located at Delhi, Madras and Bombay. Each switching node will support thirty-two asynchronous lines, four synchronous lines and synchronous X-25 lines for networking. Each system will possess self-diagnostic capability, and, in the event of fault, it should recover within a period of three hours.

E. *Fees for Services*

The following criteria are taken into account in the charging of consumers for data-communications services by the Department of Telecommunications:[77]

(a) Duration of the call,
(b) Volume of data transacted on both sides;
(c) Minimum charge;
(d) Rental for the access arrangement;
(e) Charge for facilities, like the provision of closed-user groups, etc.;
(f) Time of origination with respect to times of traffic peaks; and
(g) Distance.

77 The fees for data and facsimile services are prescribed by §§ 16 and 17 of rule 434, such sections being inserted into the rule by the Indian Telegraph (Seventh Amendment) Rules of 1983.

Part III: Audio-Visual Media Programmes

Introduction

India, with 700 million people, is the largest democracy in the world. The predominantly rural population has low levels of literacy and purchasing power, making the traditional modes of entertainment-cum-instruction and other forms of face-to-face communication, as with agriculture or health extension work, as important as the modern media of mass communication.[78] In this welfare society, the powers of the press, radio and television derive, as does that of religion, from organisation; their principal instrument of enforcement is belief, or social conditioning.

India's Ministry of Information and Broadcasting is responsible for informing, educating and entertaining the people, with a view to creating awareness among them of the nation's potentials for development and its problems. By widening their horizons, the Ministry seeks to solicit the participation of the people in the implementation of the government's policies, plans and programmes for bringing about economic development and social change, for achieving national security and for providing national integration.[79] In other words, the Ministry attempts to provide, through its various media units, an audio-visual link between the people and the government.[80]

However, the technology of modern telecommunications required by the Ministry to carry out its monumental task is as yet only nascent in India. As a result, many Indians turn to the press for information and to the cinema for entertainment. The press and cinema media, though outside the strict periphery of *telecommunications*, are worthy of discussion for their substantive, rather than alternative, *communications* role, which radio and TV are at present unable to fill.

Another striking difference exists between broadcasting and the press and

78 The term »mass communication« stands for dissemination of information, ideas and entertainment by use of communications media.

79 M.V. DESAI, COMMUNICATION POLICIES IN INDIA 11 (UNESCO 1977). *See also* Annexure IV for the organisational chart of the Ministry of Information and Broadcasting.

80 The various media units of the Ministry are: (1) All-India Radio, (2) Doordarshan (television), (3) Press Information Bureau, (4) Films Division, (5) Directorate of Advertising and Visual Publicity, (6) Publications Division, (7) Song and Drama Division, (8) Research and Reference Division, (9) Directorate of Field Publicity, (10) Photo Division, (11) Register of Newspapers for India, (12) Central Board of Film Censors, (13) Directorate of Film Festivals, (14) National Film Archives, (15) Indian Institute of Mass Communication, (16) Film and Television Institute of India, (17) Childrens's Film Society, (18) Film Finance Corporation, (19) National Motion Pictures Export Corporation, (20) National Film Development Corporation and (21) Directorate of Evaluation.

cinema. In India, broadcasting is a state monopoly and is directly controlled by the government, unlike most Western countries and similar to the control exercised in Eastern countries. The film and press media, however, are by and large in the hands of private management. Thus the meaning of the constitutional guarantee of speech and expression found in Article 19(2), a right virtually unavailable in the broadcasting sector, has been tested primarily with regard to the press and cinema, concurrent with various legislative efforts by the government to acquire regulatory power over them.

For these reasons, it is clear that an analysis of telecommunications in India that omitted a discussion of the press and cinema would be incomplete. Moreover, any deregulation of broadcasting would bring with it the same questions of the extent of constitutional freedoms, whose limits already have been demarcated in landmark decisions involving the press and cinema. As the distinction between telecommunications and traditional information sources begins to blur – as, say, with home video cassettes – so grows the relevance of those decisions. Beyond that, the promotion and exhibition of films have a direct impact on televison and other audio-visual media, as films contribute the most important programme material for television.

Chapter VII: Constitutional Rights and Freedom of the Media

A. *Freedom of Speech and Expression*

Freedom of speech is protected by article 19(1)(a) of the Indian Constitution. This freedom encompasses the right to express freely one's convictions or opinions by speaking, writing, printing pictures or in any other manner.
The freedom of speech and expression is the foundation of a democracy, because without free public discussion, public education, which is so essential for the proper functioning of a popular government, is impossible.[81]
Media freedom is fundamental to the life of an individual in a democratic polity; the media is held as one of the vital pillars of a free society and is an instrument of social and political change.[82]
The Constitution does not employ the term »freedom of the press« unlike the United States Constitution, which expressly mentions the »liberty of the press,« i.e., the freedom to publish what one pleases without previous permission. But the freedom of expression necessarily includes the freedom of propagation of ideas, with the latter ensured by liberty of publication and circulation, both essential elements of the freedom of the press. Moreover, the press is merely another manifestation of the individual or citizen; press editors and managers are all citizens, and when they write in newspapers, they are thereby exercising their individual right of expression.[83] It is, then, settled law in India that the right of freedom of speech and expression includes the liberty of the press as well.[84]
This right extends to communication media other than the press – cinema and theatre, for example. Thus, »media freedom« will be used to denote the general workings of the right of freedom of speech and expression on the various media sectors. Television and radio, being state-owned, are little influenced by any media freedoms, as will be shown.
The freedom of speech and expression of the individual and the media does

81 Romesh Thappar v. State of Madras, 1950 A.I.R. 124, 128 (S.C.); Queen Empress v. Bal Gongadhor Tilak, 1898 Indian L.R. 112 (Bombay H.C.); Emperor v. Sadashiv Narain, 1947 A.I.R. 82 (P.C.): Niharendu Dutt v. Emperor, 1942 A.I.R. 22 (P.C.).

82 P.B. GAJENDRAGADKAR, LAW, LIBERTY AND SOCIAL JUSTICE 89–90 (1965).

83 B.R. AMBEDKAR, VIII CONSTITUENT ASSEMBLY DEBATES 716–17 (   ).

84 Sakal Newspapers (Private) Ltd. v. Union of India, 1962 A.I.R. 305 (S.C.).

not, however, confer an absolute right to speak or to disseminate without responsibility whatever one wishes, nor does it provide unrestricted or unbridled immunity for every possible use of language and prevent the punishment of those who abuse this freedom. Unlike the United States Constitution, which says »the Congress shall make no law ... abridging the freedom of speech,«[85] the Indian Constitution in article 19(2) attempts to strike a balance between individual liberty and state control[86] and authorizes the state to impose certain reasonable restrictions:

> Nothing in subclause (a) of clause (1) shall affect the operation of any existing law, or prevent the State from making any law, insofar as such law imposes reasonable restrictions on the exercise of the right conferred by the said subclause in the interest of the sovereignty and integrity of India, the security of the State, friendly relations with foreign States, public order, decency or morality, or in relation to contempt of court, defamation or incitement to an offence.

It is worthy to note that for a limitation on the exercise of the right of freedom of speech and expression to be valid, it must be imposed by a valid law (a restriction imposed by executive action will be invalid), be reasonable and be proximately related to the purposes mentioned in article 19(2).[87]

B. *Historical Background*

In India before Independence, there was no constitutional or statutory guarantee of individual or media freedom. At most, some common-law freedom could be claimed by the press, as observed by the Privy Council in *Channing Arnold v. Emperor*[88]:

> The freedom of the journalist is an ordinary part of the freedom of the subject, and to whatever length the subject may go, so also may the journalist, but apart from Statute Law, his privilege is no other and no higher. The range of his assertions, his criticisms or his comments is as wide as, and no wider than that of, any other subject.

The leaders of the Independence movement attached great significance to

85 U.S. CONST. amend. I.
86 A.K. Gopalan v. State of Madras, 1950 A.I.R. 27, 93 (S.C.).
87 D.D. BASU, SHORTER CONSTITUTION OF INDIA 77 (1981); M.P. JAIN, INDIAN CONSTITUTIONAL LAW 444 (1978).
88 1914 A.I.R. 116, 117 (P.C.).

this freedom of speech and expression for both the individual and the media.[89] With this object in view, the Constitution of India in article 19(1)(a) guaranteed to every citizen the basic human right of freedom of speech and expression; articles 19(1)(b)-(e) and (g),[90] 20,[91] 21[92] and 22[93] guaranteed the individual certain other rights as well. In addition, article 19(1)(a) was made suspendable only while a proclamation of emergency, ordered by the president under articles 352 and 358, was in effect. Article 19(2) was initially somewhat more liberal and was confined to a limited number of subjects, as evident from the original text of the clause:

> Nothing in subclause (a) of clause (1) shall affect the operation of any existing law insofar as it relates to, or prevents the State from making, any law relating to libel, slander, defamation, contempt of court or any other matter which offends against decency or morality or which undermines the security of, or tends to overthrow, the State.

But article 19(2) was amended twice – first in 1951 and again in 1963 – in order to widen its scope and give greater powers to the state to curb the freedom of expression. The first amendment resulted from three successive decisions of the Supreme Court that had defined liberally the freedom of the

89 E.S. VENKATARAMIAH, FREEDOM OF THE PRESS: SOME RECENT TRENDS 14–25 (Endowment Lecture 1984).

90 INDIA CONST. art. 19(1) provides that: »All citizens shall have the right – ... (b) to assemble peaceably and without arms; (c) to form associations or unions; (d) to move freely throughout the territory of India; (e) to reside and settle in any part of the territory of India; (f) [deleted by Constitution (Forty-Fourth) Amendment Act of 1978]; (g) to practice any profession, or to carry on any occupation, trade or business.«

91 INDIA CONST. art. 20: »(1) No person shall be convicted of any offence except for violation of a law in force at the time of the commission of the act charged as an offence, nor be subjected to a penalty greater than that which might have been inflicted under the law in force at the time of the commission of the offence. (2) No person shall be prosecuted and punished for the same offence more than once. (3) No person accused of any offence shall be compelled to be a witness against himself.«

92 INDIA CONST. art. 21; »No person shall be deprived of his life or personal liberty except according to procedure established by law.«

93 INDIA CONST. art. 22: »(1) No person who is arrested shall be detained in custody without being informed, as soon as may be, of the grounds for such arrest nor shall be denied the right to consult, and to be defended by, a legal practioneer of his choice. (2) Every person who is arrested and detained in custody shall be produced before the nearest magistrate within a period of twenty-four hours of such arrest excluding the time necessary for the journey from the place of arrest to the court of the magistrate and no such person shall be detained in custody beyond the said period without the authority of a magistrate. (3) Nothing in clauses (1) and (2) shall apply – (a) to any person who for the time being is an enemy alien or (b) to any person who is arrested or detained under any law providing for preventive detention.«

press: the *Cross Road Newspaper*,[94] *Organiser Newspaper*[95] and *Bharati Press*[96] cases.

1. *Cross Road Newspaper Case*

In *Romesh Thappar v. State of Madras*,[97] the Supreme Court struck down section 9(1)(A) of the Madras Maintenance of Public Order Act of 1949,[98] which had sought to impose restrictions on the freedom of the press guaranteed under article 19(1)(a) of the Constitution. The Court held invalid the notification banning the entry into, or the circulation, sale or distribution in, the State of Madras or any part thereof of a weekly journal entitled *Cross Road*, published in Bombay.

The Court rejected the government's contention that public safety and the maintenance of public order, for which reasons the Act was passed, fell within the »security of the State« envisioned by article 19(2), allowing the imposition of a restriction by a state on the right of free speech. The Constitution, said the Court, had not included such as reasonable grounds for restraint; article 19(2) permits restrictions on the freedom of speech and expression only in those cases where danger to the security of the state is involved. An enactment that is capable of being applied to cases where no such danger could arise cannot be held to be constitutional and valid to any extent.

2. *Organiser Newspaper Case*

In *Brij Bhushan v. State of Delhi*,[99] the Supreme Court declared unconstitutional an order issued under section 7(1) of the East Punjab Safety Act of 1950, which directed the editor and publisher of the newspaper *Organiser* to submit for scrutiny, in duplicate and before publication, all communal matters and news and views about Pakistan, including photographs and cartoons.

The Court held that the imposition of precensorship on a journal is a restric-

94 Romesh Thapper v. State of Madras, 1950 A.I.R. 124 (S.C.).
95 Brij Bhushan v. State of Delhi, 1950 A.I.R. 129 (S.C.).
96 State of Bihar v. Shailabala Devi, 1952 A.I.R. 329 (S.C.).
97 *Romesh Thapper*, 1950 A.I.R. 124.
98 The impugned act authorised the state government to prohibit or regulate the entry into, or the circulation, sale or distribution in, the province of Madras of any document or class of documents for the purpose of securing the safety of the public or maintaining public order in the province.
99 *Brij Bhushan*, 1950 A.I.R. 129.

tion on the liberty of the press, which is an essential part of the freedom of speech and expression guaranteed under article 19(1)(a) of the Constitution, and that the imposition of restriction on the grounds of public safety and maintenance of public order is not embraced by article 19(2).

3. *Bharati Press Case*

In *State of Bihar v. Shailabala,*[100] a pamphlet entitled »Sangram« (»Revolution«) was printed at the respondent's press and allegedly circulated in a Bihar town. The leaflet, written in Bengali, contained a clear invocation to the readers to join an all-out, deadly struggle to bring about a violent revolution that was to result in the complete annihilation of those who the writer considered »oppressors,« directors of wrongs and injustices, participants in parochial national politics and persons who disgraced the Mother Land. The government of the State of Bihar determined that the pamphlet contained objectionable matters proscribed by section 4(1)(a) of the Indian Press (Emergency Powers) Act of 1931[101] and ordered the press to furnish security in the amount of Rs.2000, as authorised by section 3(3) of the Act.[102]

The respondent moved the High Court of Patna, pursuant to section 23 of the Act, to set aside the order. The high court, by a majority of 2-1, allowed the application and declared section 4(1)(a) *ultra vires*. Although article 19(2) of the Constitution could authorise legislation that restrained the publication of matters that incited or encouraged the commission of murder or any other cognisable offence[103] involving violence, section 4(1)(a) was invalid because it was worded in general terms and could therefore be applied both to aggravated offences, like political assasinations, and to ordinary murders or cognisable offences involving violence.[104]

100 *Shailabala Devi*, 1952 A.I.R. 329. *See also* Srinivas Bhatt v. State of Madras, 1951 A.I.R. 70 (Madras H.C.); Indukumar v. State of Saurashtra, 1951 A.I.R. 9 (Saurashtra H.C.).

101 § 4(a)(1) deals with word, signs or visible representations that incite or encourage, or tend to incite or encourage, the commission of any offence of murder or any cognisable offence involving violence.

102 § 3(3): »Whenever it appears to the Provincial Government that any printing press ... is used for the purpose of printing or publishing any newspaper, book or other document containing any words, signs or visible representations of the nature described in section 4, sub-section (1), the Provincial Government may, by notice in writing to the keeper of the press, ... order the keeper to deposit with the Magistrate security ...«

103 INDIA CODE CRIM. PROC. § 2(c) defines a cognisable offence as »an offence for which a police officer may, in accordance with the First Schedule or under any other law for the time being in force, arrest without warrant.«

104 The decision of the Patna High Court is reported in In re Bharati Press, 1951 A.I.R. 12 (Patna H.C., Special Bench).

On appeal, the Supreme Court reversed and upheld section 4(1)(a) as valid and permissible under article 19(2). The Court observed that inciting or encouraging the commission of a violent offence, like murder, could not but be a matter that would undermine the security of the state or lead to its overthrow. However, in the absence of any evidence linking the pamphlet with any agitation or movement at the time it was written, it could not be held that the pamphlet fell within the mischief proscribed by section 4(1)(a). Thus, although section 4(1)(a) was constitutionally valid, the order issued under it was not.

C. *Amendments to Article 19(2) of the Constitution*

The above-noted decisions acknowledging the freedom of the press did not find favor with the government. With the Constitution (First Amendment) Act of 1951, it engineered an amendment to article 19(2) to nullify the wide and harmful implications of those judgments. The amendment added to article 19(2) the word »reasonable« in respect of permissible legislative restrictions on the right of freedom of speech and expression, and it provided for three additional grounds that would permit the imposition of legislative restrictions, namely: (i) friendly relations with foreign States, (ii) public order and (iii) incitement to an offence.

Over the course of time, it was noticed that some political parties and disgruntled elements were agitating for secession from India. To stop such nefarious acts, Article 19(2) was further amended via the Constitution (Sixteenth Amendment) Act of 1963,[105] which inserted »sovereignty and integrity of India« as another basis for curbing the freedom of expression and conferred adequate power on the government to preserve and maintain the sovereignty and integrity of India.

Thus, article 19(2) now enables the legislature to impose reasonable restrictions in the public interest on the right of freedom of speech and expression on the following grounds:

(a) Security of the State;
(b) Friendly relations with foreign States;

105 The amendment was the recommendation of the 1962 Committee on National Integration and Regionalism.

(c) Public order;
(d) Decency or morality;
(e) Contempt of court;
(f) Defamation;
(g) Incitement to an offence; and
(h) Sovereignty and integrity of India.

The preservation of »public order« is one of the added grounds for imposing restrictions on the freedom of speech and expression. The term public order is of broad import and is synonymous with public peace, safety and tranquility. The state may, in the interest of public order, prohibit and punish utterances tending to incite a breach of the peace or riots or the use of threatening, abusive or insulting words or behavior in any public place or at any public meeting with the intent to cause a breach of the peace.
The expression »security of State« has two dimensions – external and internal. To protect the state from external dangers, article 19(2) sanctions laws that seek to prevent or curb the advocacy of the rendering of assistance to the state's enemies, the impeding of the successful operation of any war activities and the like. As regards the internal security, any utterance advocating by crimes of violence the overthrow of the government is subject to restriction under article 19(2). Security of the state encompasses serious and aggravated forms of public disorder and not ordinary breaches of public order and safety.
»Friendly relations with foreign States« serves as well as a basis for media restrictions. This prevents the jeopardisation of the good and friendly relations with a foreign country by unrestrained and malicious propaganda directed against that country.[106] This provision has the sanction of article 2(1) of the Covenant on Freedom of Information and the Press, prepared by the United Nations.

106 Jagan Nath v. Union of India, 1960 A.I.R. 625 (S.C.). The petitioner was detained under the Preventive Detention Act of 1950, as he was likely to act in a manner prejudical to the relations of India with Pakistan. The petitioner had sent to a foreign newspaper for publication dispatches of news and views containing false, incomplete, one-sided and misleading information about the State of Jammu and Kashmir, which were not only prejudicial to the government of India vis-a-vis Pakistan but also to the relations of India with foreign powers generally. Held, even though a Commonwealth country (Pakistan was at that time in the Commonwealth) will not be regarded as a foreign state for the purposes of Article 367(3) of the Constitution, a country would be a foreign power for other purposes.

D. *Requirement of Reasonableness*

In safeguarding the freedom of the media, the Supreme Court discharges the role of sentinal on the *qui vive*: it determines the constitutionality of impugned statutes. It is the constitutional obligation of all courts to ensure that the restrictions imposed by a law on the media are reasonable[107] and relate to the purposes specified in article 19(2);[108] the mere fact that a law confers discretion on the executive would not invalidate the law as being unreasonable, so long as the law lays down a policy as to when the discretion could be exercised.[109]

In determining the reasonableness of a restriction, the Supreme Court reviews it under the »average prudent man« standard[110] and is guided by certain other principles: the restriction must strike a balance between the freedom and social control,[111] it must bear a rational and direct relation to the object that the legislature seeks to control,[112] and it must not be arbitrary or excessive.[113] In *State of Madras v. V.G. Row*, Chief Justice Patanjal Shastri of the Supreme Court said:

> The test of reasonableness, wherever prescribed, should be applied to each individual statute impugned, and no abstract standard or general pattern of reasonableness can be laid down as applicable to all cases. The nature of the right alleged to have been infringed, the underlying purposes of the restrictions imposed, the extent and urgency of the evil sought to be remedied thereby, the disproportion of the imposition, the prevailing conditions at the time, should all enter into the judicial verdict. In evaluating such elusive factors and forming their own conception of what is reasonable in all the circumstances of a given case, it is inevitable that the social philosophy and the scale of values of the Judges participating in the decision should play an important part, and the limit to their interference with legislative judgment in such cases can only be detected by their sense of responsibility that the constitution is meant not only for people of their way of thinking but for all, and that the majority of the elected representative of the people have, in authorising the imposition of restrictions, considered them to be reasonable.[114]

107 Chintaman Rao v. State of Madhya Pradesh, 1951 A.I.R. 118, 120 (S.C.).
108 Express Newspapers (Private) Ltd. v. Union of India, 1958 A.I.R. 578, 618 (S.C.).
109 Virendra v. State of Punjab, 1957 A.I.R. 896 (S.C.).
110 N.B. Khare v. State of Delhi, 1950 A.I.R. 211 (S.C.).
111 Messrs. Dwarka Prasad v. Sate of Uttar Pradesh, 1954 A.I.R. 224, 227 (S.C.).
112 Arunachala Nadar v. State of Madras, 1959 A.I.R. 300, 303 (S.C.).
113 Romesh Thapper v. State of Madras, 1950 A.I.R. 124 (S.C.).
114 1952 A.I.R. 196, 200 (S.C.).

In *Chintaman Rao v. State of Madhya Pradesh,*[115] Justice Mahajan of the Supreme Court very aptly summed up the scope of the term »reasonableness«:

> The phrase »reasonable restriction« connotes that the limitation imposed on a person in the enjoyment of the right shall not be arbitrary or of an excessive nature, beyond what is required in the interest of the public. The word »reasonable« implies intelligent care and deliberation, that is, the choice of a course which reason dictates. Legislation which arbitrarily or excessively invades the right cannot be said to contain the quality of reasonableness and unless it strikes a proper balance between the freedom guaranteed ... and the social control permitted ... , it must be held to be wanting in that quality.

Thus a restrictive legislation will not be *ultra vires* if it satisfies the test of reasonableness, within the ambit of article 19(2) of the Constitution. Such a restriction may be held unreasonable either because it is too stringent and, therefore, unreasonable, because there is some procedural flaw in the law sanctioning it or because it does not fall within one the interests mentioned in article 19(2).[116]

E. *Censorship: A Restriction on Fundamental Rights*

The term »censorship« commonly denotes an act of an official who has the power to examine publications, movies, mail, etc. and to remove from circulation, or prohibt the dissemination of, anything considered obscene or objectionable. There may be differences in degree and scope, but some sort of either self-regulatory or statutory censorship is employed in almost every country, whether socialist or capitalist. As the modern welfare state is interested not only in the material well-being, but also in the moral well-being, of its citizens, censorship is invoked as a regulatory mechanism to safeguard the best interests of its society. Censorship is, however, a restriction of the right of freedom of speech and expression and, as such, it must be exercised with great care and circumspection; the liberty openly to express one's views must be balanced against the need to forestall the potential harm resulting from an abuse of such liberty.

115 1951 A.I.R. 118, 119 (S.C.). *See also* Pathman v. State of Kerala, 1978 A.I.R. 771 (S.C.); H.M. SEERAVAI, 1 CONSTITUTIONAL LAW OF INDIA 441–85 (1983).

116 *See* N. HUNNINGS, FILM CENSORS AND THE LAW 226–27 (1967), Boyd, *Film Censorship in India: A Reasonable Restriction on Freedom of Speech and Expression*, 14 J. INDIA L. INST. 501 (1972).

Nevertheless, all forms of speech and expression in India are subject to censorship, which takes two basic forms. Films and dramatic performances are subject to pre-exhibition censorship,[117] or precensorship, which prohibits their presentation without prior governmental approval. It is comparatively easier to implement precensorship for films than for other forms of expression, and the effect of such censorship on dramatic performances is only marginal. On the other hand, newspapers and printed matter are subject to censorship under a post-publication penal model, which imposes sanctions for the publication of any prohibited matter; precensorship is not practically feasible here because many of the objectionable materials are published by the underground press.[118] This model also regulates the areas of drawing, sculpture, dance and speech. Since radio and television are government run, they operate under the supervision of the Ministry of Information and Broadcasting.

Pre-exhibition control is the most effective form of censorship,[119] since the perceived evil is eliminated before it can be disseminated. Such a preventive measure is more effective than a subsequent punishment. But prosecuting a person for disseminating objectionable material and preventing him from disseminating it are entirely different matters. If the objectionable material is prosecutable only, the matter is then subject to judical resolution. But in the case of precensorship, which is an executive action, a court of law cannot examine the legality of the order unless the order is *mala fide*. However, the only difference under the law between pre- and post-exhibition censorship is the time at which control is exercised, and this is not a material difference, thus negating the question of discrimination.[120]

Censorship may also take the form of prohibitive orders. Under section 144 of the Criminal Procedure Code (1973),[121] the district magistrate or, in certain towns, the commissioner of police can issue directives in the interest

117 *See, e.g.*, Kerala Dramatic Performance Act of 1961.

118 Williams, *The Control of Obscenity,* 1965 CRIM. L. REV. 53.

119 Censorship may be: (1) self-regulatory (carried on by the industry itself); (2) official (censorial powers are exercised by an authority constituted for that purpose, such as the Board of Film Censors); (3) under a criminal law model (the producer of distributor of the material is punished for violations of standards set forth in the criminal law, Peris Adult Theatres v. Slaton, 413 U.S. 49, 84 (1972)); (4) under a civil law model (the power to censor is conferred on civil courts); (5) under a constitutional law model (the constitution guarantees freedom of speech and expression but expressly permits the state to impose reasonable restrictions).

120 K.A. Abbas v. Union of India, 1971 A.I.R. 481 (S.C.).

121 INDIA CODE CRIM. PROC. § 144 authorises the magistrate to issue orders in urgent cases of nuisance or apprehended danger.

of public order prohibiting the holding of meetings and processions, the delivering of public speeches or the making of public demonstrations. Protests and demonstrations in front of foreign embassies may be, and sometimes have been, banned in the interest of friendly international relations. Such orders are essentially preventive in nature, but they may also contain a penal provision, which punishes contravention of the order.

Ideally, censorship should operate within well-defined parameters. But it is nearly impossible to lay down absolute and universal standards for determining which depictions are obscene and objectionable or decent and moral, what language amounts to defamation or incitement to an offence, or which depictions affect the security of the State or friendly relations with foreign States. These are matters that simply have to be evaluated in the context of the circumstances in which they can or do occur.

Chapter VIII: Cinema

A. *Cinema in India*

The movie is a form of expression. Like such other mass media as newspapers, books, radio and television, cinema plays a creative role in the effective dissemination of ideas,[122] although to a great extent the object of cinema is commercial. Because of its capacity for social penetration, cinema is very significant in the day-to-day life of Indians. Perhaps the single most-telling influence on the lives of millions of people, next to religion, is that of the cinema. Thus what passes for entertainment on the silver screen also has an influence on social attitudes and actions that endures beyond the actual viewing. Cinema is, in a word, a kind of social touchstone.[123]

India is among the earliest countries in the world to have screened cinema films. The history of film exhibition in India dates back to July 7, 1896, when representatives of the Lumiere Brothers began public showings with their cinématographe at Watson's Hotel in Bombay. Indian audiences thus had their introduction to projected motion pictures in the same year as British, Russian and American audiences, barely six months after the first cinématographe show at the Grand Cafe in Paris. Short-film activity in India followed at the beginning of the twentieth century.

During the last sixty years, India produced several films that are counted among the world's finest. The Indian film industry, unlike other national film industries, has a polyglot home market and makes films in more than fifteen Indian languages. With the production in 1979 of 714 feature and 635 short films[124] (excluding trailers and advertisements), India emerged as the biggest producer of films in the world. Every day, a large number of people

122 K.V.V. Sharma v. Union of India, 1953 A.I.R. 269, 272 (Madras H.C.); K.A. Abbas v. Union of India, 1971 A.I.R. 481 (S.C.).

123 Raj Kapoor v. Laxman, 1980 A.I.R. 605, 606 (S.C.). Cinema is one of the major mass media, with millions of viewers and millions in investments. *See* 5 INDIA TODAY 19 (1980)

124 The Cinematograph (Certification Amendment) Rules of 1984 classify film into one of three categories based on length. »Feature films« are fictionalised story films exceeding 2000 metres in 35 mm or corresponding lengths in other gauges or on video (Rule 2 (xi)). »Long films« are those with a length exceeding 2000 metres in 35 mm or corresponding lengths in other gauges or on video (Rule 2 (xi)). »Short films« are those with a length of up to and including 2000 metres in 35 mm or corresponding lengths in other gauges or on video (Rule 2(xvi)).

in India watch films in theatres, over television or through informal, open-air shows organised by the Field Publicity units of the central and state governments and various other agencies.[125] It is no wonder that film plays a very important role in the country and has an exceptionally powerful hold on the Indian public.

The number of cinemagoers in India is perhaps the largest in the world. It is estimated that an average 25 million people daily go to films in India.[126] These figures have increased with the expansion of television in the country. At present, at least two to three movies a week are broadcast over television, which has a wide range of viewers.

Despite the obvious importance of cinema in contemporary life, there had been, prior to 1978, only two major attempts to examine the problems of Indian cinema and the Indian film industry in a national perspective. These were the Indian Cinematograph Committee of 1927-28 and the Film Enquiry Committee of 1951. But in 1979, the government appointed a working group, consisting of nineteen members with K.S. Karenth as its chairman, to study the present state of the film industry in such areas as production, distribution, exhibition and taxation and to suggest a national film policy that would foster the growth of Indian cinema.

The committee recommended that the entire film industry be brought within the purview of central policy and control. Ideally, this would imply the transfer of the subject matter of cinema from the State List to the Union List.[127] The committee further suggested that a national film policy, in the Indian context, be based upon a clear recognition of the following facts:

125 MINISTRY OF INFORMATION AND BROADCASTING, REPORT OF THE WORKING GROUP ON NATIONAL FILM POLICY 1 (1980).

126 ENQUIRY COMMITTEE ON FILM CENSORSHIP, REPORT 75 (1969) (hereinafter cited as Khosla Committee Report). There are 7522 permanent and 4754 touring cinema houses in the country. Every cinema house in India is required by law to exhibit only approved films of a length not exceeding 60,960 metres. *See* SHALI, THE INDIAN FILMS 20 (1950).

127 Schedule VII of the Constitution provides the relevant entries that authorise the federal and state governments to legislate on matters relating to films. These are:

Union List (List I)

Entry 52: Industries, the control of which by the Union is declared by Parliament by law to be expedient in the public interest.

Entry 60: Sanctioning of cinematograph films for exhibition.

State List (List II)

Entry 24: Industries subject to the provisions of (Entries 7 and 52 of) List I.

Entry 33: Theatres and dramatic performances: cinemas subject to the provisions of Entry 60 of List I; sports, entertainments and amusements.

Entry 62: Taxes on luxuries, including taxes on entertainments, amusements, betting and gambling.

(a) Cinema today is the single largest disseminator of popular culture.
(b) Despite the growth of television and the availability of other means of entertainment, cinema remains the most popular audio-visual medium of entertainment for the masses.
(c) With the tradition of film making in India spread over some seventy years and with the national and international recognition attained by outstanding Indian films, cinema in India is no longer only a medium of entertainment, but it has emerged as a major art form that gives expression to the vision of distinguished artists.
(d) The wide popularity of cinema, and its known strength as an audio-visual communication medium, invests it with pervasive power for social influence. Cinema has, therefore, the potential to play an important role as a medium of enlightenment, information and education and as a catalyst for social change.
(e) Cinema is a major industry in India, involving fairly high levels of investment and engaging a significant number of semi-skilled, highly skilled and creative people.
(f) The backing of industry is common for films of all kinds, from fiction films to specialised films, and is irrespective of their content.
(g) Cinema is technologically sophisticated and is continuously evolving.
(h) Cinema in India generates a considerable amount of revenue for the government, with very little investment of public funds.
(i) Indian cinema has a vast potential for earning foreign exchange.

The committee recommended that a national film policy have the following broad objectives:

(a) to provide facilities to undertake research and development for the »indigenisation« of film technology and to keep abreast of the latest cinematic developments;
(b) to expand training facilities in the creative and technical areas of cinema, with a view to cinema growth in India; and
(c) to ensure that taxation policies aim at a horizontal expansion of revenue resources and not at a vertical rise in taxation levels, thereby encouraging the growth of cinema and not contributing to making the market for cinema uncertain and speculative.

B. *Federal/State Powers in Regard to the Cinema Industry*

The Cinematograph Act of 1918 gave the federal government plenary power over cinematography, including the exhibition of films. Later, the power to license cinemas was delegated to the provincial governments, pursuant to the policy of devolution of powers. The scheme of legislative powers for the states and the federal government under the Constitution then gave complete authority to state governments over the production and exhibition of films within each state.

The power of the state governments to license cinema theatres arises out of sections 10 and 11 of the Cinematograph Act of 1952, read with entry 33 of the State List. The powers of the federal government were confined to the sanctioning of cinematograph films for exhibition, i.e., to certification through the Central Board of Film Censors.[128]

Pursuant to entry 62 of the State List, an entertainment tax on the exhibition of films is levied by the respective state governments[129] instead of by the federal government. However, the tax policies of the various states differ widely. Still, the common basic objective of taxation is generation of maximum revenues, and all types of direct and indirect taxes are levied on the film industry: entertainment taxes, show taxes and customs and excise duties.[130] Some states also levy an additional surcharge on the entertainment tax.

Entertainment tax is collected by the states from the basic admission rates of Rs.1, Rs.2 and Rs.3. The lowest state entertainment tax rate on the basic admission fee of Rs.1 is 37.56%, including surcharge, in the State of Maharastra; some Maharastra towns, such as Bombay, Pune, Nagpur and Sholapur, have higher rates. The highest rate is in Uttar Pradesh, whose tax,

128 The Cinematograph Act of 1952, 1952 India Cen. Act 37, § 4 prescribes the procedure for the certification of films for exhibition. *See infra* p. XX

129 *Supra* note 127. *See* T.K. Abraham v. State of Travancore Cochin, 1958 A.I.R. 129 (Kerala H.C., F.B.). In the absence of a statutory definition of »luxuries,« it would be a matter of opinion and will depend on the price and nature of the article in question; held, the levy of an annual fee for a license under section 1 of the Travancore Tobacco Act of 1951 is a luxury tax falling within the ambit of Entry 62 of List II. V.V. Srinivasamurthy v. State of Mysore, 1959 A.I.R. 894 (S.C.). Held, the words »entertainment« and »amusements« are wide enough to include theatres, dramatic performances, cinemas, sports and the like. State of Bombay v. R.M.D. Chamarbaughwala, 1957 A.I.R. 699 (S.C.). Tax on gambling and betting is demanded from the promoter, as he indemnifies himself by charging entrance fees from the gamblers. *See also* Western India Theatres v. Cantonment Board of Poona, 1959 A.I.R. 582 (S.C.); Attorney General of Alberta v. Attorney General of Canada, 1939 A.I.R. 53 (P.C.).

130 *See* REPORT *supra* note 125, at 38.

including surcharge, is 125%.[131] It is perhaps appropriate for the federal government to adopt a uniform policy in regard to entertainment tax; by doing so, it could make a serious attempt to rationalise the entertainment tax and reduce rates.[132]

C. *Film Censorship: The Cinematograph Act of 1952*

The prime objectives of film censorship, as envisaged by the government, is to ensure that the medium of film remains responsible and sensitive to the values and standards of society, that artistic expression and creative freedom are not unduly curbed and that censorship remains responsive to social change. Whether they are regarded as a pure and simple form of entertainment, as works of art designed to give aesthetic pleasure or as a medium of information, education and propaganda, films are forms of communication and expression. But as shown above, a reasonable restriction upon the right of freedom of speech and expression, in the form of censorship or otherwise, is permitted by the Constitution,[133] and the need for the censorship of such a significant medium of expression as film is well recognised and resorted to in India, in the wider interests of society. As pointed out by the Khosla Committee:

> A modern sound film, specially the version in vivid, realistic colours, is unique among all art forms and media for its evocative potential. The viewer is apt to forget the real world around him, because it is completely hidden from him by the impenetrable curtain of darkness which surrounds and envelops him. The impact made by the film is vivid, immediate and compulsive, and the effect may last for a few hours or for many months.[134]

Although the licensing of cinematograph exhibition in India began as long ago as 1912 with the emergence of cinema in the country, film censorship was of minimal significance in India prior to Independence in 1947. While

131 Entertainment tax rates for the various states are listed in Annexure V.

132 *See* REPORT, *supra* note 125, at 39.

133 Madanlal Kapoor v. State of Rajasthan, 1953 A.I.R. 162 (Rajasthan H.C.). The requirement of reasonableness under article 19(2) and (6) of the Constitution includes both substantive and procedural reasonableness. *See* Ramchandran, *Test of Reasonable Restriction in Article 19 of the Indian Constitution*, 40 A.I.R. JOURNAL 79 (1953).

134 Khosla Committee Report, *supra* note 126, at 60. The committee consisted of seventeen members, headed by Justice G.D. Khosla, chief justice of the Punjab High Court. *See also* Boyd, *supra* note 116, at 501.

film industry censorship had long existed, film censorship per se did not come into being until the passage of the Cinematograph Act of 1918. The Act provided for the exhibition of films only in places licensed for such a purpose.[135]

The first noteworthy change in post-Independence film censorship transpired in 1948, when a so-called »Production Code« was drafted, with a view to ensuring that cinema played its proper role in the building of a healthy national life.[136] Two years later, in 1951, the Film Enquiry Committee, commissioned by the Government of India in 1949, submitted its report on the state of the Indian motion picture industry and made a number of suggestions for its rationalisation. Pursuant to these recommendations, the Cinematograph Act of 1952 was passed. The Act established a central Board of Film Censors for the purpose of certifying films for public exhibition. The Board consists of twelve to twenty-five members, drawn from various sections of society, and a full-time chairman.

The Act requires that any person desiring to exhibit any film, including video films,[137] must first make an application in a prescribed form to the Board for a certificate in respect thereof. The films are examined by the regional officers, with the aid of an advisory panel consisting of non-officials. The Board then carefully examines the film. Pursuant to its powers under the Act, it can approve the film for public exhibition and assign it an appropriate category,[138] order the deletion of objectionable matters[139] or refuse to sanction the exhibition of the film.[140] Section 5-B(1) of the Act (more or less a replica of article 19(2) of the Constitution) sets forth the guiding prin-

135 Khoshla Committee Report, *supra* note 126, at 14.

136 *Id.* at 4.

137 By way of the Cinematograph (Certification) Amendment Rules of 1984, video films produced in India shall be certified separately for public exhibition. An applicant for the certification of a video film must produce a certificate of authorisation from the producer of the film or its copyright holder.

138 Under § 4 of the Cinematograph Act of 1952, the Board may grant one of the following certificates.

(i) »U«: unrestricted public exhibition;

(ii) »A«: restricted to adults only (above 18 years);

(iii) »UA«: unrestricted public exhibition subject to the film's being endorsed with a caution to parents/guardians that they satisfy themselves as to whether they would like their children or wards below the age of 12 years to see the film.

(iv) »S«: public exhibition restricted to the members of any profession or any class of persons having regard to the nature, content and theme of the film.

A certificate granted by the Board shall be valid for a period of 10 years from the date of issue of the certificate. § 5–A(3).

139 *Id.* at § 4(1)(iii).

140 *Id.* at § 4(iv).

ciples for censorship authorities in the certification of films for public exhibition:

> A film shall not be certified for public exhibition if, in the opinion of the authority competent to grant the certificate, the film or any part of it is against the interests of the sovereignty and integrity of India, the security of the State, friendly relations with foreign States, public order, decency or morality, or involves defamation or contempt of court or is likely to incite the commission of any offence.

Pursuant to the powers granted by section 5-B(2), the Ministry of Information and Broadcasting could then issue directions to guide the Board of Film Censors in achieving, as far as possible, uniform standards for determining whether a film is suitable for public exhibition.[141]

A person aggrieved of the decision of the Board may, within thirty days of the receipt of such order, either appeal to the Appellate Tribunal[142] or seek a revision from the central government.[143] Every appeal must be made by a written petition, and it must be accompanied by a brief statement of the reasons for the order appealed against and the prescribed fees. The Tribunal, after making a necessary inquiry and giving both the appellant and the Board an opportunity to be heard in the matter, may make such an order in relation to the film as it thinks fit; the Board must dispose of the matter accordingly.

D. *Suspension or Revocation of Certificate*

Under section 5-E(1) of the Cinematograph Act of 1952, the federal government is empowered to suspend or revoke a certificate and to direct the person concerned to deliver the certificate to the Board, if the film was being exhibited in a form other than that in which it was certified or in contravention of the provisions of the Act or the rules made thereunder. The aggrieved party, within sixty days from the date of the decision, may apply to the government for a review of the order.

Under section 6 of the Act, the federal government, through the Ministry of

141 *See* Annexure VI.

142 Cinematograph Act of 1952, § 5–C. The provision for appeal was added by the Cinematograph (Amendment) Act of 1983. The Tribunal consists of a chairman and not more than four other members, appointed by the government under § 5–D. The central government may appoint such persons as are qualified to appointed judge of a high court.

143 *Id.* at § 6.

Information and Broadcasting, may at any stage call for the record of any proceeding in relation to any film that is pending before, or has been decided by, the Board or the Tribunal, and it may direct that:

(a) a film that has been granted a certificate shall be thenceforth uncertified in all or any part of India;
(b) a film that had been granted a »U,« »UA« or »S« certificate shall carry thenceforth an »A« certificate; or
(c) the exhibition of any film shall be suspended for such a period as may be specified in the direction.

E. *Enforcement and Penal Sanctions*

There is no separate enforcement machinery for monitoring compliance with the provision of the Act. This is the responsibility of the police, already overburdened with the task of enforcement of law and order. Section 7 of the Act of 1952 provides for penal sanction in case of contravention of the provisions of the Act, and section 7-A empowers the police to seize such films as are exhibited without certificates or are exhibited in contravention of the orders issued by the Board of Film Censors, the central government or any other appropriate authority.[144]

Section 7-F of the cinematograph Act of 1952 bars the institution of legal proceedings against any decision taken by an appropriate authority under the Act:

> No suit or other legal proceeding shall lie against the Central Government, the Tribunal, the Board, the Advisory Panel or any officer or member of the Central Government, the Tribunal, the Board or the Advisory Panel, as the case may be, in respect of anything which is in good faith done or intended to be done under this Act.

Thus, it is not possible to challenge a decision except on the ground of *mala fide*,[145] which is quite difficult to establish.

To curb the widespread illegal trade that has resulted from the large-scale

144 INDIA CODE CRIM. PROC. §§ 193–198.

145 S.T. Syndicate Ltd. v. Union of India, 1975 A.I.R. 460 (S.C.); Province of Bombay v. Khushaldas Advani, 1950 A.I.R. 222 (S.C.); P.N. Films Ltd. v. Union of India, 1955 A.I.R. 381 (Bombay H.C.); Radha Films Ltd. v. West Bengal Board of Censors, 1952 A.I.R. 653 (Calcutta H.C.).

piracy of films, section 7 of the Act was amended by the Cinematograph (Amendment) Rules of 1984 to enhance the punishment for offences defined in the section from two years to three years, to extend fines from Rs.20,000 to Rs.100,000 and, in the case of a continuing offence, to create a further fine of up to Rs.20,000 for each day the offence continues. The amended provisions further provide for a minimum punishment of a three-month sentence and a Rs.20,000 fine for the exhibition of video films in contravention of the provisions of section 7(1)(a)(i) of the Act.[146]

F. *Constitutionality of Film Classification*

Classification of films results in a limitation on the breadth of the exhibition, and thereby the circulation, of cinema. Thus a system of classification of films raises the question of a restriction on the right of freedom of speech and expression of the film producer and distributor. But the Constitution sanctions this restriction, as classification imposes only such reasonable restrictions as are necessary for the protection of the interests of children and the ethical and moral standards of society. A film can exert considerable influence on the mind and in the heart of a child; its impact is more deeply and lastingly felt by a child than by an adult. A democratic state has a special interest in, and a responsibility to protect, the moral well-being of its children; India has embodied this concept in article 39(f)[147] of the Constitution.

In India, unfortunately, there are no organised public pressure groups, as found in Western countries, that are vigilant in seeing that the film industry, or the public mass media in general, conforms to certain ethical and moral standards. Occasionally some social groups or women's organisations raise a weak voice against the depiction of indecent or immoral scenes in films or of indecent cinema advertisements. Such isolated criticism hardly influences the censorial process in films, either at the production stage or at the issuance of a certificate by the Board of Film Censors to a film for public exhibition.

146 See Annexure VII.

147 INDIA CONST. art. 39(f): »The State shall, in particular, direct its policy towards securing – ... that childhood and youth are protected against exploitation and against moral and material abandonment.«

1. *The Abbas Case*

The most notable case to come before the Supreme Court challenging the constitutionality of film censorship in general, and precensorship in particular, was *K.A. Abbas v. Union of India.*[148] Mr. Abbas, a noted journalist, playwright and film producer, made a short documentary in 1968 called »Tale of Four Cities,« in which he sought to contrast the life of the rich in Calcutta, Bombay, Madras and Delhi with the squalor and destitution of the laboring masses who had helped to construct the imposing residences, factories and other industrial complexes utilised by the rich. The film explored the theme of the exploitation of the weaker section of society. A representative scene dealt with prostitution in the red-light district of Bombay, where prostitutes in short dresses stood outside the brothels enticing customers. The sequence ended on a symbolic note, with the prostitute imagining her room to be a cage and then dreaming of her life before she has embarked on a life of hustling.

Mr. Abbas applied to the Board of Film Censors for a »U« certificate, which would permit unrestricted exhibition of the film; the certificate was granted subject to the deletion of the Bombay scene from the film. Mr. Abbas then sought a writ from the Supreme Court[149] for the unrestricted exhibition of the film, alleging that the precensorship exercised by the Board of Film Censors violated the fundamental right of freedom of speech and expression, and that even if precensorship were a legitimate restraint, it had to be exercised on the basis of definite principles that preclude arbitrary action.

The Court rejected Mr. Abbas's first contention, holding that the precensorship of films was constitutionally permissible and the classification of films into »U« (universal) and »A« (restricted to adults) categories was not an unreasonable restriction within the dictates of the Constitution. Such prior

148 1971 A.I.R. 481 (S.C.). The film is in black and white and is silent, except for a song that the laborers sing while doing work and some background music and sounds for stage effect. The film, in motion sequences and still-shots, contrasts scenes of palatial buildings, hotels and factories (evidence of the prosperity of a few) with those of shanties, huts and slums (evidence of the poverty of the masses): sweating laborers toil by day to construct the buildings, yet return at night to a squalid private life. In one scene, a fat and prosperous customer is shown riding a rickshaw, pulled with difficulty by a sweating decrepit man. In a contrasing scene, the same rickshaw puller is shown riding in the rickshaw, pulled by his former customer. All the while, the statues of the leaders of the Indian Freedom Movement, from their high pedestals in front of the palatial buildings, look on helplessly at the unrelenting poverty.

149 An aggrieved party may petition the Supreme Court under article 32, and the high courts under article 226, of the Constitution for the enforcement of his or her basic right of speech and expression guaranteed by article 19(1)(a).

restraints[150] were not qualitatively different from any other form of censorship, the only distinction being the stage at which the state interposes its regulations between the individual and his freedom. The Court further noted that motion pictures, because of their unique ability to portray realism and arouse the senses, had to be treated differently than other forms of art and expression. Speaking for the Court, Chief Justice Hidayatullah said:

> The art of the cameraman, with trick photography vistavision and three dimensional representation thrown in has made the cinema picture more true to life than even the theatre or indeed any other form of representative art. The motion picture is able to stir up emotions more deeply than any other product of art. Its effect particularly on children and adolescents is very great since their immaturity makes them more willingly suspend their disbelief than mature men and women. They also remember the action in the pictures and try to emulate or imitate what they have seen. Therefore, classification of films into two categories of »U« and »A« films is a reasonable classification. It is also for this reason that motion pictures must be regarded differently from other forms of speech and expression.[151]

Mr. Abbas's second contention was that precensorship had to rest on definite principles and not be exercised arbitrarily. He argued that the guidelines contained in the directions issued by the government for censorship of cinematographic exhibition[152] were so vague as to be void, referring for authority to the »void for vagueness« doctrine evolved by the U.S. Supreme Court.[153] The Court held that the regulations and guidelines set forth in the directions to safeguard the interests of children and young persons were not uncertain or void, but were quite specific. The Court observed that the word used in the directions, such as maintaining the moral standards of the people and the country, discouraging audience sympathy with the activities of criminals or other sinners and preventing disrespect for the rules of law, were justified and within the purview of the permissible restrictions mentioned in article 19(2) of the Constitution.

150 Emerson, *The Doctrine of Prior Restriction*, 20 LAW & CONTEM. PROBS. 648 (1955). The concept of prior restraint, roughly speaking, deals with official restriction imposed upon speech or other forms of expression in advance of actual publication. Prior restraint is thus distinguished from subsequent punishment, which is a penalty imposed after the communication has been made as a punishment for having made it.

151 *K.A. Abbas*, 1971 A.I.R. at 489.

152 *See* Annexure VI.

153 Connally v. General Construction Company, 269 U.S. 385 (1926). Held, a vague law was void as it amounted to a violation of the »due process« clause. Justice Sutherland said: »[A] statute which either forbids or requires the doing of an act in terms so vague that men of common intelligence must necessarily guess at its meaning and differ as to its application violates the first essential of due process of law.«

Realising the need for the directions in limiting the discretion of the censor, the Court observed:

> The task of the censor is extremely delicate and his duties cannot be subject to an exhaustive set of commands established by prior ratiocination. But direction is necessary for him so that he does not sweep within the terms of the directions vast areas of thought, speech and expression of artistic quality and social purpose and interest.[154]

The Court said, however, that the directions did not provide for a value judgment by the censor and that this should have been included. A censor must necessarily be armed with such power in order to take into account the artistic quality of a film presented for certification. The Court stated that a censor should adopt the standard of an average man. An objectionable film depiction is not the naked portrayal of life or society, but rather one lacking the redeeming touch of art, genius or social value, such that the average man begins to feel embarrassed and disgusted when viewing such shots.

In obiter dictum, the Court remarked that the film censorship authorities should adopt principles relating to the notion of obscenity promulgated in the landmark decision of *Ranjit D. Udeshi v. State of Maharashtra.*[155] Although the *Udeshi* case involved the censorship under section 292 of the Indian Penal Code of an allegedly obscene book, the Court in *Abbas* observed that the principles that evolved therefrom »apply *mutatis mutandis* to film and other areas besides obscenity.« These principles provided, inter alia, that:

(a) Sex and nudity in art and literature cannot be regarded as evidence of obscenity without something more;
(b) Although the determination of obscenity must be predicated on a consideration of the book (film) as a whole, the allegedly obscene matter must be considered separately to ascertain whether it tends to »deprave or corrupt those whose minds are open to such immoral influences and into whose hands (or view) such material may fall«;
(c) Where obscenity and art are intermixed, art must be so preponderant as to completely overshadow the obscene matter;
(d) A determination of obscenity will not be made where the matter in question includes the propagation of ideas, opinions and information of public interest or profit; and

154 *K.A. Abbas*, 1971 A.I.R. at 498.
155 1965 A.I.R. 881 (S.C.).

(e) Obscenity is a depiction without a preponderance of social purpose or profit.

2. *Other Film Censorship Cases*

An interesting example of the use by the government of its power of review is found in *State (Delhi Administration) v. V.C. Shukla, Sanjava Gandhi and others.*[156] A member of Parliament, Amrita Nahota, produced a film called »Kissa Kursi Ka« (»A Story of Power«) in 1975. The film was »a grotesque satire,« containing a scathing criticism of the functioning of the central government. Mr. Nahata applied to the Board of Film Censors for a certificate of film on April 19, 1975. The film was viewed by the Examining Committee of the Board. While three members were of the opinion that, with drastic cuts, a certificate for exhibition should be given, the chairman and another member disagreed. Accordingly, the matter was referred to the Revising Committee, which, by a majority of six to one, granted a certificate to the film. Dissent, however, had been voiced by the chairman, and a reference was made to the central government on May 8, 1975, under rule 25(11) of the Cinematograph (Censorship) Rules of 1958. The Ministry of Information and Broadcasting finally refused certification of the film because of its objectionable nature, and the film was banned. In pursuance of the decision taken by the government, the Bombay police seized the film on August 1, 1975 and deposited the same in the godown of the Board.

In *Raj Kapoor v. State (Delhi Administration)* (Case No. 1),[157] the producers-cum-directors of a film called »Satyam Sivam Sundarm« (»Truth is God, Truth is Beauty«) were prosecuted under sections 292 and 293 of the Indian Penal Code[158] for obscene and indecent depictions. Rejecting the petitioners' contention that a criminal court could not reopen the question of obscenity when the Board of Film Censors had previously granted a certificate to a film for public exhibition, Justice Krishna Iyer of the Supreme Court said:

156 1980 A.I.R. 1382 (S.C.). The appellants V.C. Shukla, then Minister of Information and Broadcasting, and Sanjaya Gandhi were convicted of criminal conspiracy under § 120-B, read with §§ 409, 411, 414 and 435, of the Indian Penal Code for the burning of a film in the Maruti Complex in November 1975. Their convictions were overturned by the Court on the basis of insufficient direct or circumstantial evidence showing an agreement between two or more persons to commit the offence, as required by § 120-B.

157 1980 A.I.R. 258 (S.C.).

158 *See* Annexure VIII.

> [O]nce a certificate under the Cinematograph Act is issued the Penal Code, *pro tanto*, will [not] hang limp. The Court will examine the film and judge whether its public display, in the given time and clime, so breaches public morals or depraves basic decency as to offend the penal provision.[159]

The Court held that when an expert body like the Board of Film Censors decides the suitability of a film for public exhibition, after considering such relevant matters as obscenity, jurisdiction of a criminal court to decide the issue afresh effectively amounts to appellate jurisdiction. Even a civil court's decision is not conclusive proof of the matters decided in criminal cases.[160] Nevertheless, the Court advocated the exercise of restraint in intervening in such cases:

> [A] certificate granted under Section 6 of the Cinematograph Act by the Board of Censors does not provide an irrebuttable defence to accused who have been granted such a certificate, but is certainly a relevant fact of some weight to be taken into consideration by the criminal court in deciding whether the offence charged is established. Regard must be had by the Court to the fact that the certificate represents the judgment of a body of persons particularly selected under the Statute for the specific purpose of adjudicating the suitability of films for public exhibition, and that judgment extends to a consideration of the principal ingredients which go to constitute the offence under Sections 292 and 293 of the Indian Penal Code.[161]

However, in *Raj Kapoor v. Laxman* (Case No. 2),[162] the Supreme Court, without overruling its previous decision, held that in a criminal trial, a valid certificate issued by the Board did constitute a defence under section 79 of the Indian Penal Code, which reads as follows:

> Nothing is an offence which is done by any person who is justified by law, or who by reason of a mistake of fact and not by reason of a mistake of law, in good faith, believes himself to be justified by law in doing it.

159 *Raj Kapoor*, 1980 A.I.R. at 262.
160 Adi Pherozshah Gandhi v. H.M. Seervai, 1971 A.I.R. 385 (S.C.).
161 *Raj Kapoor*, 1980 A.I.R. at 263.
162 1980 A.I.R. 605 (S.C.). The complainant moved the court under § 292 of the Indian Penal Code to launch prosecution against the producers of a film. The magistrate, after examining witnesses, took cognisance of the offence and issued notices to the accused. Thereupon, the defendant petitioned the high court under § 482 of the Criminal Procedure Code to halt the prosecution on the basis of abuse of judicial process, ulterior considerations and inability to legally sustain a case against a film duly certified by the Board of Censors. The high court dismissed the defendant's petition, but he nevertheless succeeded in the instant case.

It is interesting to note that Justice Iyer, who declined to oust the jurisdiction of the criminal courts in the earlier *Raj Kapoor* decision, said:

> After having elaborately enacted such a legislation [Cinematograph Act of 1952] can it be said that a certificate granted under it by expert authority can be stultified by a simple prosecution or a shower of prosecutions for an offence under Section 292 I.P.C., driving the producer to satisfy a »lay« magistrate that, the certificate of the Board of Censors notwithstanding, the film was not offensive? The Board under Section 5B has to consider, before certification, all the points Section 292 I.P.C. prescribes.[163]

Thus the case provides immunity from prosecution under the Indian Penal Code, with respect to a decision of the Board of Film Censors, on a matter of obscenity, public morality, etc. The Cinematograph (Amendment) Act of 1981, a proviso to section 5-A of the Act of 1952, gave legislative recognition to this decision of the Court by prohibiting criminal prosecution for obscenity, in respect of any matter contained in a film for which a certificate had been granted by the Board.

G. *The Right to Privacy and State Authority to Regulate Film Viewing*

It is doubtful, in the absence of any decision to the contrary, whether the provisions of the Act of 1952 apply to the viewing of an uncertified film or its video copy in the privacy of one's home. The Supreme Court, in *Kharak Singh v. State of Uttar Pradesh*,[164] recognised the right of privacy as a fundamental right that may be infringed only upon a showing of compelling

163 *Id.* at at 607–08.

164 1963 A.I.R. 1295 (S.C.). Held, Uttar Pradesh police regulation 236(b), providing for domiciliary visits, was unconstitutional as it abridged constitutional rights embodied in article 21. *See* Wolf v. Colorado, 338 U.S. 25 (1948): Frankfurter, J. said: »[t]he security of one's privacy against arbitrary intrusion by the police is basic to a free society and that the knock at the door, whether by day or by night, as a prelude to a search, without authority of law but solely on the authority of the police, did not need the commentary of the recent history to be condemned as inconsistent with the conception of human rights in the history and the basic constitutional documents of English-speaking peoples.« *See also* Griswold v. Connecticut, 381 U.S. 479, 510 (held, a Connecticut statute making use of contraceptives a criminal offence is an unconstitutional invasion of the right of privacy of married persons); Konvitz, *Privacy and the Law: A Philosophical Prelude*, 31 LAW & CONTEM. PROBS. 272 (1966); *The Wages of Crying Wolf: A Comment on Roe v. Wade*, 82 YALE L.J. 920 (1972); European Convention on Human Rights, art. 8 (guarantees privacy and human rights); Benn, *Privacy, Freedom and Respect for Persons*, in 13 PRIVACY 15–16 (J. Pennock and J. Chapman eds.).

state interest.[165] But in recent years, courts have witnessed the legal battle between, on the one hand, proprietors of video and film industries, video libraries and restaurants and hotels – who advocate the unrestricted exhibition of video films on the television screens of the pertinent establishments or homes – and, on the other hand, the state governments, which are trying hard to control the exhibition of films in public and private through various regulatory measures, including the imposition of the technical requirements of a certified film and a license to exhibit it. It is the extent of the right of privacy that has in recent years come before the courts for adjudication.

In *Restaurant Lee v. State of Madhya Pradesh*,[166] the court held that the exhibition of movies in restaurants by the use of video cassettes, recorders (VCRs) and television screens falls within the ambit of »cinema«, as defined in the Constitution in entry 33 of list II of schedule VII (State List), and that such exhibition is governed by the regulatory provisions of the Madhya Pradesh Cinema (Regulation) Act of 1952. A license is a condition precedent, as per the provisions of section 3 of this Act, and must be procured before any such exhibitions.

The Bombay High Court, in *Dineshkumar Hanumanprasad Tiwari v. State of Maharastra*,[167] followed the *Restaurant Lee* decision and held that when a VCR was used for playing pre-recorded cassettes of movies on a television screen, it was certainly employed as an apparatus for the representation of moving pictures or a series of pictures and, as such, comes within the definition of »cinematograph«, as defined under section 2(c) of the Cinematograph Act of 1952.[168] All apparatuses, such as VCRs, that produce on viewers a discrete audio-visual effect are encompassed by the term »cinema.«

The court rejected both of the petitioner's contentions, namely, that the law governing »cinema« is the province of the federal government under entry 60 of list I of schedule VII of the Constitution and that, contrary to *Restaurant Lee*, the term »cinema« used in entry 33 of list II (State List) does not include video cassettes. The court observed that the exhibition of films on

165 *See* Govinda v. State of Madhya Pradesh, 1975 A.I.R. 1378 (S.C.). Held, the right of privacy of movement is not absolute and a law imposing reasonable restrictions upon it for compelling state interests is valid. *See also* Roe v. Wade, 410 U.S. 113 (1973) (held, the right to privacy is not absolute); Warren and Brandeis. *The Right to Privacy*. 4 HARV. L. REV. 193 (1890–91).

166 1983 A.I.R. 146 (Madhya Pradesh H.C.). *See also* Martin, *Music Video Copyright Protection: Implications for the Music Industry*, 32 UCLA L. REV. 396 (1984) for the U.S. law on the subject.

167 1984 A.I.R. 34 (Bombay H.C.).

168 § 2(c): »›Cinematograph‹ includes any apparatus for the representation of moving pictures of a series of pictures.« § 2(dc): »›film‹ means cinematograph film.«

television screens under the Video-Cassette Recorders (Regulation) Act of 1984[169] falls within entry 33, so it is not *ultra vires* for lack of legislative competence on the part of the state government.[170] The exhibition of movies in such a fashion in cafes and restaurants therefore comes within the prohibition of section 3 of the Bombay Cinema (Regulations) Act of 1953 on the exhibition by means of a cinematograph elsewhere than in a place licensed under the Act.

The Madras High Court, although following the views of the Madhya Pradesh and Bombay High Courts on the subject, held in *Entertaining Enterprises v. State of Tamil Nadu*[171] that a video library that merely rents video film to its members for their own use and does not maintain them for public exhibition need not approach the Board of Film Censors for a certificate. The Cinematograph Certification Rules of 1983 are applicable only if a video film is used for public exhibition and are not if it is used privately. The court observed that section 10(2) of the Tamil Nadu Exhibition of Films on Television Screens Through Video-Cassette Recorders (Regulation) Act of 1984, to the extent that it requires certification of a video film for exhibition in the private residences of members of a video library, is invalid and unconstitutional.

169 1984 India Cen. Act. 7.

170 INDIA CONST. art. 246. Parliament (federal government) and the state legislatures will have exclusive power to make laws with respect to any of the matters enumerated in list I (»Union List«) and list II (»State List«) respectively, and with respect to any of the matters enumerated in list III (»Concurrent List«), both Parliament and the state legislatures can make laws.

171 1984 A.I.R. 278 (Madras H.C.).

Chapter IX: Press

A. *Introduction*

The press in India dates back to 1780, when the Bengal Gazette was published at Serampore.[172] Since then, newspapers have occupied a commanding position as a medium of mass communication. The press played a vital role in India's freedom struggle, functioning as a crusading agent for the independence of the country. Today, the press continues to play an important part in creating, molding and reflecting public opinion in India.
Freedom of the press was developed in light of the Constitution through the above-discussed *Cross Road Newspaper, Organizer Newspaper* and *Bharati Press* cases (*see* Chapter VII). Beyond these cases, there is a variety of related cases and legislation that affects the freedom of the press.

B. *Related Decisions of the Supreme Court*

In *Ramji Lal Modi v. State of Uttar Pradesh*,[173] the petitioner, printer and publisher of the monthly magazine *Gaurakshak* (*Cow Protector*), was convicted under section 295A of the Indian Penal Code [174] for the publication in the magazine of an article with a proscribed content. The petitioner contended that section 295A was unconstitutional in that it was inconsistent

172 D.D. BASU, LAWS OF THE PRESS IN INDIA, 244 (1980). *See also* Ojo, *Freedom of the Press in Nigeria since 1960: A Comparative Analysis*, 18 J. INDIA L. INST. 529 (1976), and Annexures IX and X.

173 1957 A.I.R. 620 (S.C.).

174 § 295A: »Whoever, with deliberate and malicious intention of outraging the religious feelings of any class of citizens of India, by words, either spoken or written, or by signs or by visible representations, or otherwise, insults or attempts to insult the religions or the religious beliefs of that class, shall be punished with imprisonment of either description for a term which may extend to three years, or with fine, or with both.«

with articles 25 and 26 of the of the Constitution,[175] which guarantee the right of freedom of religion.[176] The Supreme Court refuted this argument and held that the impugned section was valid because it imposed a restriction in the interest of public order, i.e., it made punishable only a malicious intent to outrage the religious feeling of any class of citizens of India. The Court refused to apply the principles of the »clear and present danger« test, as laid down by the United State Supreme Court,[177] in analysing the restriction, on the ground that the framework of the Constitution of India was different from the framework of the United States constitution.

In *Express Newspapers (Private) Ltd. v. Union of India*,[178] the Supreme Court held that the Working Journalists (Conditions of Service) and Miscellaneous Provisions Act of 1955[179], which regulated certain conditions of service of its employes, was valid despite the imposition of greater financial burdens and the indirect result of the closing of marginally situated papers. These burdens would be an incidental disadvantage of extraneous consequences contemplated by the law and would, therefore, not affect its constitutionality under articles 14, 19(1)(a) and 19(1)(g) of the Constitution.

In *Sakal Newspapers (Private) Ltd. v. Union of India*,[180] the Supreme Court held unconstitutional and inoperative the Daily Newspaper (Price and Page) Order of 1960. The Order was based on section 3(1) of the Newspaper

175 INDIA CONST. art. 25(1) guarantees to every person, and not merely to citizens of India, the freedom of conscience and the right freely to profess, practice and propagate religion. However, this freedom is subject to public order, morality and health. Further, article 25(2) provides that clause (1) will not affect the operation of any existing law and thus saves the provisions of § 295A of the India Penal Code, which was enacted via the Criminal Law (Amendment) Act of 1927, 1927 India Cen. Act 25, *as amended by* 1961 India Cen. Act 45. INDIA CONST. art. 26 confers on every religious denomination or any section thereof freedom to manage their religious affairs.

176 *See* E.R.J. Swami v. State of Tamil Nadu, 1972 A.I.R. 1586 (S.C.): »The protection of these articles [articles 25 and 26] is not limited to matters of doctrine or belief; they extend also to acts done in pursuance of religion and therefore contain a guarantee for rituals and observances, ceremonies and modes of worship, which are integral parts of religion. What constitutes an essential part of a religion or a religious practice has to be decided by the courts with reference to the doctrine of a particular religion and includes practices which are regarded by the community as a part of its religion.« *See also* Durgah Committee Ajmer v. Hussain Ali, 1961 A.I.R. 1402 (S.C.); Sri Venkataramana Ajmer v. Hussain Ali, 1961 A.I.R. 255 (S.C.). *See generally* M.C. JAIN KAGZI, THE CONSTITUTION OF INDIA 572-92 (1983).

177 Dennis v. United States, 344 U.S. 494 (1952).

178 1958 A.I.R. 578 (S.C.).

179 1955 India Cen. Act 45.

180 1962 A.I.R. 305 (S.C.).

(Price and Page) Act of 1956,[181] whose pivotal provision infringed upon the liberty of the press implicit in article 19(1)(a). The Court held that the Order affected the press, because its adoption would mean either a reduction in the existing number of pages or a revision of prices. In either case, there would be a reduction in the volume or the circulation of papers and, thereby, a direct violation of the liberty of the press. Justice Mudholkar, speaking on behalf of the Court, said:

> [A]fter the commencement of the Act [on September 7, 1975] and the coming into force of the Order a newspaper which has a right to publish any number of pages for carrying its news and views will be restrained from doing so except upon the condition that it raises the selling price as provided in the schedule to the order. This would be the direct and immediate effect of the Order and as such would be violative of the right of newspapers guaranteed by Article 19(1)(a). Again, Section 3(1) of the Act in so far as it permits the allocation of space to advertisements also directly affects freedom of circulation. If the area for advertisements is curtailed the price of the newspaper will be forced up. If that happens, the circulation will inevitably go down. This would be no remote, but a direct, consequence of curtailment of advertisements.[182]

In *Bennett Coleman and Co. Ltd. v. Union of India*,[183] the Supreme Court struck down the Import Policy for Newsprint for 1972-73 as being violative of article 19(1)(a), in that the press has a right of free propagation and free circulation without restraint on publication. The freedom of speech and expression is contained not only in the volume of circulation but also in the volume of news and views. The Import Policy, along with the Newsprint Control Order of 1962, were issued under section 3 of the Essential Commodities Act of 1955 and imposed: (i) a ban on the starting of newspapers or editions by a common ownership unit, (ii) a rigid limitation of ten pages, (iii) a ban on interchangeability within a common ownership unit and (iv) an allowance of 20% page increases only to newspapers of less than ten pages. The Court, speaking through Justice Ray, said:

181 § 3 is the most important provision of this act, which empowers the central government to regulate the price of newspapers in relation to their pages and sizes if it is of the opinion that it is necessary to do so for the purpose of preventing unfair competition among newspapers, particularly those published in Indian languages. It further empowers the government to regulate the allocation of space for advertising matter. A minimum price for the given number of pages that a newspaper was entitled to publish was fixed as well.

182 1962 A.I.R. at 312–13.

183 1973 A.I.R. 106 (S.C.). § 3 of the Newsprint Control Order puts restrictions on acquisition, sale and consumption of newsprint and directs that no consumer of newsprint shall, in any licensing period, consume or use newsprint in excess of the quantity authorised by the state.

> [T]he effect and consequence of the impugned policy upon the newspapers is directly controlling the growth and circulation of newspapers. The direct effect is the restriction upon circulation of newspapers. The direct effect is upon the growth of the newsprint through pages. The direct effect is that the newspapers are deprived of their area of advertisement. The direct effect is that they are exposed to financial loss. The direct effect is that the freedom of speech and expression is infringed ... In the garb of distribution of newsprint the Government has tended to control the growth and circulation of newspapers. Freedom of the press is both qualitative and quantitative. Freedom lies both in circulation and content. The newsprint policy which permits newspapers to increase circulation by reducing the number of pages, page area and periodicity, prohibits them to increase the number of pages, page area and periodicity by reducing circulation. These restrictions constrict the newspapers in adjusting their page number and circulation.[184]

C. *Press Legislation*

The launching in 1931 of the civil disobedience movement for the attainment of independence of the country prompted the government to pass the Indian Press (Emergency Powers) Act of 1931 for better control of the press.[185] The Act imposed an obligation on the press to furnish security, which stood to be forfeited if the press published any matter that might promote hatred or contempt for the government, incite dissatisfaction with the government, incite feelings of hatred or contempt between different classes of subjects or encourage a public servant to resign or neglect his duty.

After independence of the country, the government appointed a Press Laws Enquiry Committee to review the press laws in India. The object of the review was to examine the relevance of the press laws, in view of the result that, following the enactment of the Constitution on January 26, 1950, some of the clauses of the Press (Emergency Powers) Act of 1931 were declared by the Supreme Court to be *ultra vires* under article 19(2) of the Constitution.[186]

As a result of the review, the Act of 1931 was replaced by the Press (Objec-

184 1973 A.I.R. at 120, 129, 130.

185 Executive control of the press is foreign to democratic institutions. It was a revival in India of the Star Chamber trials for press offences and of the licensing system, which the English democracy had earlier fought and gotten repealed.

186 Srinivas v. State of Madras, 1951 A.I.R. 70 (Madras H.C.): Rama Sankar v. State of Uttar Pradesh, 1954 A.I.R. 562 (Allahabad H.C.); Romesh Thappar v. State of Madras, 1950 A.I.R. 124 (S.C.); Gitlow v. New York, 268 U.S. 652 (1925); Balzae v. Puerto Rico, 258 U.S. 298 (1921).

tionable Matter) Act of 1951, and its constitutionality came to be reviewed as well.[187] The Act provided for judicial scrutiny by the sessions judge before security could be demanded from, or could be forfeited by, a printing press, and it conferred a right of appeal to the high court. The Act was of a temporary nature and was repealed in 1957.

The Press Council of India was constituted in 1966 by the government under the Press Council Act of 1965. The Council consisted of a chairman and twenty-six members drawn from various sector of the newspaper industry, members of Parliament and public persons with special knowledge in education, law, literature or culture.[188] The Press Council was an autonomous body, having such powers of a civil court as are vested under the Civil Procedure Code of 1908. The Council was authorised to warn, admonish or censure a news- paper or a news agency for any professional misconduct, any breach of the Code of Journalistic Ethics or any offence against public decency and morals. The Council's term, which expired in December 1975, was not extended, and the Press Council Act of 1965 was abolished in 1976, during the state of internal emergency that had been invoked the previous year. The Parliamentary Proceedings (Protection of Publication) Act of 1956 was also repealed.

Another step toward curbing the freedom of the press was the enactment of the Prevention of Publication of Objectionable Matters Ordinance of 1975, which provided for stringent action against the press and imposed precensorship. All of these reactionary steps were taken by the government headed by Mrs. Indira Gandhi, after the judgment of the Allahabad High Court

187 *Srinivas*, 1951 A.I.R. 70.

188 The Press Council Act of 1965, 1965 India Cen. Act 34, § 4 provided for the composition of the Council consisting of a chairman and twenty-six other members. The chairman and twenty of the members were to be nominated by a nominating committee consisting of the chairman of the Council of States (the Upper House, or Rajya Sabha), the Speaker of the House of the People (the Lower House, or Lok Sabha), and the chief justice of the Supreme Court. Thirteen of the twenty members were drawn from among working journalists, of whom six were editors of newspapers and seven were working journalists other than editors. Six persons were selected from persons who own or carry on the business of management of newspapers; of these, »big« (over 50,000 circulation), »medium« (15,000 to 50,000 circulation), and »small« (less than 15,000 circulation) newspapers each got two representatives – one from Indian languages newspapers and one from other languages newspapers. The last member nominated by the nominating committee came from news agency management. Three members of the Council were selected on the basis of special knowledge or practical experience in the fields of education, science, law, literature and culture; of these, one person was nominated by the University Grants Commission, one by the Bar Council of India and one by the Sahitya Academy. The three remaining members of the Council were drawn from members of Parliament; two were nominated by the speaker from among the House of the People and one was nominated by the chairman from among the Council of States.

holding her guilty of corrupt election practices, setting aside her election to the Lok Sabha (Lower House) of Parliament and disqualifying her from contesting any election for six years.[189] The steps were taken on the claim that the press in India had been abusing its freedom from any restrictive laws by vilifying dignitaries in office.

However, after the defeat of Mrs. Gandhi in 1977 in the sixth General Election, the combined opposition (Janta Government) that came to power restored the freedom of the press by removing all fetters that had been imposed on it during the period of emergency. The Janta Government also restored the Parliamentary Proceedings (Protection of Publications) Act of 1956 and repealed the Prevention of Publication of Objectionable Matters Ordinance of 1975.

As promised, the newly elected Janta Government revived the Press Council with the Press Council Act of 1978; its objectives were to preserve the freedom of the press and to maintain and improve the standards of newspapers and news agencies in the country. The law was also accorded constitutional protection when it was inserted into the Constitution via article 361-A,[190] making it impossible for the Parliament to deprive the privileges of the press with an ordinary law passed by a simple majority.

The Act of 1978 is basically modelled on the Press Council Act of 1965 but is different in several respects. First, the Act of 1978 boosted the number of the members of the Council from twenty-six to twenty-eight (plus a chairman)[191] by increasing the number of members drawn from Parliament from three to five.[192] Second, the Act of 1978 provided for the nomination of the chairman by a committee consisting of the chairman of the Council of the State (Rajya Sabha), the speaker of the House of the People (Lok Sabha)

189 Indira Nehru Gandhi v. Raj Narain, 1975 A.I.R. 1590 (S.C.); Indira Nehru Gandhi v. Raj Narain, 1975 A.I.R. 2299 (S.C.).

190 Article 361–A was added by the Constitutional (Forty-fourth Amendment) Act of 1978), § 42: »(1) No person shall be liable to any proceedings, civil or criminal, in any court in respect of the publication in a newspaper of a substantially true report of any proceedings of either House of Parliament or the Legislative Assembly, or, as the case may be, either House of the Legislature of a State, unless the publication is proved to have been made with malice. Provided that nothing in this clause shall apply to the publication of any report of the proceedings of a secret sitting of either House of Parliament or the Legislative Assembly, or, as the case may be, either House of the Legislature of a State. (2) Clause (1) shall apply in relation to reports or matters broadcast by means of wireless telegraphy as a part of any programmme or service provided by means of a broadcasting station as it applies in relation to reports or matters published in a newspaper. *Explanation* – In this article, ›newspaper‹ includes as news agency report containing material for publication in a newspaper.«

191 The Press Council Act of 1978, 1978 India Cen. Act 37, § 5(1).

192 *Id.* at § 5(3)(e).

and a person elected by the members of the Press Council itself.[193] The latter member of the nominating committee formerly was the chief justice of the Supreme Court under the Act of 1965. Third, the Act of 1978 empowered the central government to nominate twenty members of the Press Council: thirteen working journalists, six persons in business management and one person in news agency management.[194] The Act of 1965 provided for nomination of all members by the nominating committee outlined above. The Act of 1978 leaves unchanged the procedure for nominating the remaining eight members.[195]

D. *Official Secrets Act of 1923*

The Official Secrets Act of 1923 consists of only fifteen sections, is of a general nature and has had a great impact on the press. The Act is aimed at maintaining the security of the state against leakage of secret information, sabotage and the like. The Act deals with two kind of offences, viz., spying[196] and the wrongful communication of secret information.[197]
Section 5[198] of the Act fixes penal liability for wrongful communication on all persons who are in any way involved, either directly or indirectly, in transmitting or receiving wrongful communication of secret information. For instance, this includes any person:

(a) in possession or control of secret information;
(b) who obtains information in contravention of this Act;
(c) to whom official information has been entrusted in confidence by any person holding an office of the government; or
(d) who obtains or has access to information, due to his holding any office (present or past) or holding any government contract, or any person working under the control or supervision of any such person.

Although the terms »secret« and »official secret« were not defined in the Act, secret information extends only to official secrets and not to those of a

193 *Id.* at § 5(2).
194 *Id.* at § 5(5).
195 *Id.* at § 5(3)(d) and (e).
196 1923 India Cen. Act 19, § 3 prescribes a penalty for spying.
197 *Id.* at § 5 prescribes a penalty for wrongful communication of information.
198 *See* Annexure XI for the text of § 5.

private nature.[199] Hence, section 5 covers only secrets of a ministry or a department of the government but not those of an incorporated institution, like a university, a government company or a public corporation.[200]

A literal reading of section 5 reveals that any kind of wilful communication of secret information by anyone to any person – other than to a person to whom he is authorised to communicate it, to a person to whom it is, in the interest of the state, his duty to communicate it or to a court of law – is punishable under the Act, regardless of the purpose or impact of the communication.

Section 5 gives the executive carte blanche to prosecute anyone disclosing official information or, as per section 5(2), any person voluntarily receiving such information, knowing or having reason to believe that such information is being given to him in contravention of the Act. As in cases of other penal legislation, the burden of proof of *mens rea* rests with the prosecution.

In *Nandalal More v. State*,[201] the Punjab High Court held that budget proposals are secret documents, because their premature disclosure is not in the public interest and might cause an individual to dump goods or to speculate on the stock exchange.[202]

In a fairly recent case, *S.P. Gupta v. President of India*[203] (known as the *Judges* case), the Supreme Court took a liberal view of the disclosure of official documents under section 123 of the Evidence Act,[204] and it held that it had a right to inspect secret documents, in order to decide whether they are related to the affairs of the state and whether, on the balance, public interest justified their disclosure. The Court rejected the theory of »class documents,«[205] which would confer an absolute immunity from disclosure on all documents of the class to which demonstrably secret documents belong, irrespective of their contents. A similar liberal disclosure approach may be followed in cases of prosecution for breach of official secrecy.[206]

199 *See* S.N. JAIN, OFFICIAL SECRECY AND THE PRESS 21–22 (1982).
200 State of Kerala v. K. Balkrishna, 1961 A.I.R. 25 (Kerala H.C.).
201 1 Crim. L.J. (Punjab) 392 (1965).
202 State of Punjab v. Sodhi Sukhdeo Singh, 1961 A.I.R. 493 (S.C.); State of Uttar Pradesh v. Raj Narain, 1975 A.I.R. 865 (S.C.).
203 1982 A.I.R. 149 (S.C.).
204 § 123: »No one shall be permitted to give any evidence derived from unpublished official records relating to any affairs of State, except with the permission of the officer at the head of the Department concerned, who shall give or withhold such permission as he thinks fit.«
205 Under the »class document« heading may fall such documents as cabinet papers, minutes of discussions of heads of departments and high-level documents relating to the inner workings of the government or concerned with the framing of government policies.
206 S.N. JAIN, *supra* note 199, at 7–8.

Chapter X: Regulation of Other Media

A. *Censorship of Books*

In *Ranjit D. Udeshi v. State of Maharastra,*[207] the appellant, one of four partners in a firm which owned the »Happy Book Stall« in Bombay, was prosecuted and convicted under section 292 of the Indian Penal Code[208] for possession of an obscene book, *Lady Chatterley's Lover* (unexpurgated edition). Dismissing the appeal and upholding both the conviction and the constitutionality of section 292, the Supreme Court held that the opinions of literary or other experts were not relevant to the question of whether a publication is obscene. The Court adopted the test of obscenity laid down by Chief Justice Cockburn in *Regina v. Hicklin:*[209]

> The test of obscenity is this, whether the tendency of the matter charged as obscenity is to deprave and corrupt those whose minds are open to such immoral influences, and into whose hands a publication of this sort may fall ... it is quite certain that it would suggest to the minds of the young of either sex, or even to persons of more advanced years, thoughts of a most impure and libidious character.

In *Amar Nath Bali v. State of Punjab,*[210] the Chief Commissioner of Delhi ordered the banning of a book, entitled *Now It Can Be Told,* on the ground that it contained matters contrary to section 4(1)(h) of the Press (Emergency Powers) Act of 1931.[211] The book described events that took place following the partition of India, including riots in West Punjab where Muslims attacked Sikhs and Hindus; the book also allegedly contained matters hostile to the Dominion of Pakistan and the Muslim League. But as no aspersions were cast on the Muslim citizens of India and as the book contained no matters that would promote feelings of enmity or hatred between

207 1965 A.I.R. 881 (S.C.)
208 *See* Annexure VIII.
209 [1868] 3 Q.B. 360.
210 1951 A.I.R. 18 (Punjab H.C., Special Bench).
211 § 4(1)(h): »Whenever it appears to the State Government that any printing press is used for the purpose of printing or publishing any book containing any words, signs or visible representations, which tend, directly or indirectly, to promote feelings of enmity or hatred between different classes of the citizens of India, the State Government may declare all copies of such book, wherever found in India, to be forfeited to the Government.«

different classes of Indian citizens, the book did not come within section 4(1)(h) and the order was rescinded. The court further held that section 4(1)(h) was *ultra vires*, since it restricted the freedom of speech and expression guaranteed by article 19(1)(a) of the Constitution but did not fall within one of the interests enumerated in article 19(2).[212]

B. *Censorship of Dramatic Performances*

Madan Lal Kapur v. State of Rajasthan[213] arose out of the censorship of a dramatic performance. Madan Lal staged a play in which a target carrying different colors was shot at with a pistol. The performance was banned under section 3(c) of the Rajasthan Dramatic Performance Ordinance 29 of 1949[214] on the ground that it tended to »deprave« and »corrupt« the audience. The petitioner contended before the high court that his fundamental right under article 19(1)(g) of the Constitution »to practice any profession, or to carry on any occupation, trade or business« had been violated.

In allowing the petition, the court held that the restrictions in the banning order were not reasonable as they did not give the aggrieved party an opportunity to be heard and to show that the act of shooting did not in any way deprave or corrupt the audience. Unreasonableness makes the order defective under article 19(6)[215] as well as article 19(1)(g) of the Constitution.

In *State of Uttar Pradesh v. Bagoo Lal*,[216] the defendant had staged a play,

212 *See supra* pp. 78–79.

213 1953 A.I.R. 162 (Rajasthan H.C.).

214 § 3(c): »Whenever the District Magistrate is of the opinion that any play, pantomime, or other drama or entertainment or any part thereof performed or held in a public place is ... likely to deprave and corrupt persons present at the performance or entertainment [,] ... such Magistrate may by order prohibit the performance or entertainment or any part thereof.«

215 INDIA CONST. art. 19(6): »Nothing in sub-clause (g) of the said clause shall affect the operation of any existing law in so far as it imposes, or prevents the State from making any law imposing, in the interest of the general public, reasonable restrictions on the exercise of the right conferred by the said sub-clause, and, in particular, nothing in the said sub-clause shall affect the operation of any existing law in so far as it prescribes or empowers any authority to prescribe, or prevents the State from making any law prescribing or empowering any authority to prescribe, the professional or technical qualifications necessary for practising any profession or carrying on any occupation, trade or business.« This clause was later amended by § 3 of the Constitutional (First Amendment) Act of 1951.

216 1956 A.I.R. 571 (Allahabad H.C.). The case was referred by the additional district magistrate of Lucknow, under § 432 of the Criminal Procedure Code of 1898, to the high court for a decision on a point of law whether the Dramatic Performance Act of 1876, 1876 India Cen. Act 19, had become void in view of article 19 of the Constitution.

entitled *IDGAH*, written by the famous novelist Prem Chand. The defendant was prosecuted under sections 3 and 10 of the Dramatic Performance Act of 1876.[217] The court dismissed the action, holding:

> [T]he Dramatic Performance Act is *ultra vires* of the Constitution of India, because its procedural part imposes such restrictions on the right of freedom of speech and expression which cannot be covered by the saving clause in Article 19(2). By leaving the matter entirely to the subjective determination of the District Magistrate, it has denied the essential minimum requirements of natural justice, namely the right to be heard before final condemnation and the right to have the order reviewed and objectively determined by a higher tribunal, judicial or otherwise.[218]

C. *Video Piracy of Films and Broadcasts*

Although piracy of books, printed materials, works of fiction, art and literature[219] has been a continuing problem, piracy of films in India is a relatively new development that is causing great concern to both film producers and the government. The rapid proliferation of video-cassette recorders and the tremendous growth of the video-viewing public in India in recent years has posed serious problems of video piracy and infringement of copyright,[220] as well as the states' authority to regulate and control the exhibition of films. Video cassettes of films and TV programmes are reproduced and distributed on a massive scale, without any remuneration for the authors, performing artists, publishers or producers concerned or any taxes to the state, seriously threatening the very survival of the film industry in

217 § 3: »Whereas the provincial Government is of the opinion that any play, pantomime or other drama performed or about to be performed in a public place is (a) of a scandalous or defamatory nature, or (b) likely to excite feelings of disaffection to the Government established by law in British India, or (c) likely to deprave or corrupt persons present at the performance, the Provincial Government ... may by order prohibit the performance.« § 10 prescribes the procedure for the enforcement of these restrictions.

218 1956 A.I.R. at 575.

219 Piracy technically means robbery on the high seas and was the first internationally acknowledged crime that could be tried by a municipal court where the accused was caught. However, piracy in the case of copyright means the unlawful reproduction or fraudulent sale or distribution of intellectual works in violation of legal rights; this has damaging consequences on the various parties, such as the author, the publishing industry, the producer of the audiovisual material and the broadcaster.

220 Bhattacharya, *Piracy of Films, Broadcasts and Books*, 19 COMMUNICATOR 17 (1984).

India. It is alleged in many cases that even before a film is released in the country, its cassettes are illegally produced and exported. Consequently, producers are losing revenue, and the government is losing substantial foreign-exchange earnings and revenue. For instance, there was a sharp increase in foreign-exchange earnings in India from film export from the early 1970s through 1977-78, when revenues reached U.S.$ 19.5 million; thereafter, there has been a sharp decline both in the number of films exported and in earnings. The table below illustrates this

Year	*Number of Films Exported*	*Earnings in US$ Million*
1977-78	1697	195
1978-79	1559	117
1979-80	1338	104
1980-81	1075	94
1981-82	905	60

It should be further noted that during the same period, the gross revenues earned by theatres in foreign countries showing Indian films also dwindled. A large number of theatres showing Indian films in the U.K., U.S., Canada and the Middle East countries have been closed.

To combat the trend in video piracy and its adverse effect on the growth of the film industry, a number of steps have been taken on the basis of representations received from various film organisations and associations. Some of the important measures that have been taken in this regard are as follows:

(a) The Cinematograph Act of 1952 has been amended with a view to discouraging the exhibition of uncertified video films. The Cinematograph (Amendment) Act of 1984, which came into force on August 27, 1984, provides in section 7 for enhanced punishment for the exhibition of uncertified films, including video films. A minimum punishment has also been prescribed for offences relating to the exhibition of uncertified video films.[221]

(b) The Cinematograph (Certification) Rules of 1983, which came into force on March 1, 1984, have been amended to provide that video films shall be certified separately by the Board of Film Censors, even though the films might have already been certified.[222]

221 *See* Annexure VII.

222 *See supra* note 137.

(c) The Copyright (Amendment) Act of 1984, which came into force on October 8, 1984, provides for enhanced punishment for different kinds of offences under the Act, so as to make punishment a deterrent.

D. *Audio-Visual Technology and the Transfer of Goods and Services*

It is interesting to note that neither the enactment of punitive anti-smuggling laws nor the imposition of a high rate of duty on imported items[223] has been able to check the rapid flow into India of foreign electronics goods, such as video-cassette recorders, video cameras, color televisions and other electronic articles. Markets all over the country are swamped with electronic goods. This has resulted in an unabated transfer of goods and services from the outside world. This large-scale smuggling and importation into India of communications technology has meant the establishment of fresh links among the »elites« of several countries, and people in India have started watching foreign tele-films and recorded programmes more than Indian television. Further importation of the lastest electronic equipment and hardware and software through Indians living abroad has quickened this process of establishing emotional ties with the outside world.

Likewise, India is exporting a very substantial number of recorded video cassettes of Indian films and music to the Middle East and neighboring Western countries to satisfy the needs of those Indians living abroad. In fact, Indian movies and music are very common in those countries and are viewed with great interest. Fascination for Western films, programmes and music in India and the attraction of Indian films and music abroad will go a long way toward helping increase the exchange of information and the sharing of cross-cultural experiences.

The broad exchange of media products has been made possible by the audio and video technology developments in recent years. But the masses in India are still unaware of this information explosion. There is an immense effort underway to secure wider participation by the public in programming and programme productions, as well as in media management communication.

223 The Customs Act of 1962, 1962 India Cen. Act 52, in §§ 132–140 provides for prosecution of individuals, companies and customs officials who commit offences proscribed under the Act. The punishment for evasion of duties or prohibitions may extend to imprisonment for five years and a fine, subject to a minimum of six months of imprisonment. The Custom Tariff Act of 1975, 1975 India Cen. Act 51, and the relevant rules thereunder provide for duties as high as 240% to 340% *ad valorem* on goods imported into India.

Even so, attempts are made to deprive the general public of the benefits of new technology and innovations, regardless of whether it is in the public interest to so deprive. Just such an issue came before the Monopolies and Restrictive Trade Practices Commission recently in the case of *In re* All-India Film Producers' Council of Bombay.[224] The case centered on a circular issued by the respondent All-India Film Producers' Council on April 14, 1980 and on a Council notice in the August 22, 1981 issue of the Film and Trade Guide and Film Information, both of which had sought to draw the attention of all of India's film producers to the fact that they should not in their own interest, as well as in the interest of the trade, assign any rights in respect of video cassettes of Indian films for distribution in India. They had been asked to retain their rights because if the exhibition of motion pictures through video tapes were allowed, theatrical exhibition of pictures in cinema halls would be considerably affected. The Council had warned the producers that, in the event of non-compliance with this request, they would be subject to expulsion from the membership of the Council and to fines.

Western Electronics Ltd. of Delhi challenged the action of the Council and lodged a complaint on August 29, 1981 with the Monopolies and Restrictive Trade Practices Commission, on the ground that the action of the Council amounted to a restrictive trade practice and that such practices were against public policy.

The Commission, after instituting an enquiry under section 10(a)(i) of the Monopolies and Restrictive Trade Practices Act of 1969,[225] held that the directions issued by the respondent, prohibiting film producers from selling or assigning video rights, amounted to a restrictive trade practice and were against the public interest within the meaning of section 2(o) of the Act,[226] as they restricted the rights of the Council's members. The Commission observed that one of the major, if not the only, activities of the

224 A copy of the judgment has been procured with the courtesy of the chairman of the Monopolies and Restrictive Trade Practices Commission of Delhi.

225 § 10(a)(i): »The commission may inquire into – (a) any practice – ... upon its own knowledge or information.«

226 *Id.* at § 2(o): »›Restrictive trade practice‹ means a trade practice which has, or may have, the effect of preventing, distorting or restricting competition in any manner and in particular: (i) which tends to obstruct the flow of capital or resources into the stream of production, or (ii) which tends to bring about manipulation of prices, or conditions of delivery or to effect the flow of supplies in the market relating to goods or services in such manner as to impose on the consumers unjustified costs or restrictions.«

video-cassette industry in India is the recording onto video cassettes of Indian motion pictures whose rights have been assigned by the producers of the motion pictures. Hence, if the film producers were restrained from assigning or selling video rights, the entire industry for the manufacturing and recording of video cassettes would be crippled and its long-term growth strangled. This judgment will go a long way toward regulating the law of the transfer of goods and services technology in the field of telecommunications.

Chapter XI: Radio Broadcasting

A. *Propagation of Radio Transmissions*

Radio transmissions are effectuated through the employment of one of three carrying »bands«: medium frequency, or the medium-wave (mw) band; high frequency, or the short-wave (sw) band; or very-high frequency, or the VHF band. As a general principle, the first two bands support the amplitude modulation (AM) transmission systems. Frequency modulation (FM) transmissions, because of bandwidth considerations, are confined only to the VHF band.

The basic distinction between the bands results from differences in the mode of propagation. Medium frequencies travel along the ground and tend to hug the earth's surface. At night, they are also reflected by the ionosphere enveloping the earth and reach longer distances. Services transmitted in the medium frequency are generally stable and are therefore preferred for domestic service.

High frequencies are propagated solely by the reflection of the radiated beam off of the ionospheric layers 60 to 400 km above the earth's surface. Since the existence of these layers is a result of the action of solar radiation on the atmosphere, their characteristics are susceptible to diurnal and seasonal variations. Significant and usually predictable changes also occur with the cyclical variations in solar activity, of which the Sunspot Number is a good index. Because of the resulting instability, high-frequency transmissions provide only a second-quality service and require continual management for optimisation. The advantage, of course, is that they reach very long distances and provide broadcasters with the ability to establish international programme services.

In the VHF band, propagation is essentially limited to the line of sight and requires the use of high antenna towers. The chief advantages of VHF transmissions are higher fidelity and lower susceptibility to interference and noise. The disadvantage, apart from the necessity of high tower structures, is the relatively greater cost of reception equipment.

B. *Broadcasting Before Independence: All-India Radio*

The history of broadcasting[227] in India is closely linked with the history of a momentous era, one that witnessed the Indian struggle for independence, the attainment of freedom and the beginning and the advancement of the process of rapid economic and social development.[228]

India is among the earliest countries in the world to have adopted broadcasting. Broadcasting came to India as early as 1923, with the establishment of a radio club in Calcutta, which broadcast its first programme in November 1923. This was followed by the establishment of radio clubs in Bombay, Madras, Karachi and Rangoon. Experimental transmission had, however, commenced as early as August 1921, when the Times of India, in collaboration with the Posts and Telegraph Department, broadcast a special programme of music at the request of the Governor of Bombay, Sir George Lloyd, who heard it in Poona.[229]

However, it was not until 1927 that a private concern, the Indian Broadcasting Company (IBC), started a regular broadcasting service in India, inaugurating the Bombay Broadcasting Station in July and a Calcutta station in September. Due to the heavy losses it had accumulated, the company could not continue for long and went into liquidation after a short span of three years. To rectify the resulting absence of broadcasting and to satisfy public demands, the Government of India took over the assets of the IBC on April 1, 1930.

Broadcasting thus came into the hands of the government. It was placed under the Department of Industries and Labor in 1932 and began operating as a governmental medium as the Indian State Broadcasting Service (ISBS).

227 Broadcasting is a form of communication employing radio waves as a carrier and is unlike telecommunications, which is point to point; broadcasting, as the very name suggests, is omnidirectional and public. The information communicated in sound radio is the spoken word, while in television a visual image is transmitted in addition to the sound. The broadcast system consists of studio centres, where the programmes are produced and presented in a form suitable for the medium transmitters, relay centres that radiate the programmes and networking arrangements that enable the audio centres to feed the sets of transmitters distributed over a region or country. *See* THE WORKING GROUP ON AUTONOMY FOR AKASHVANI AND DOORDARSHAN, 2 REPORT 18 (1978). *See also* Copyright (Amendment) Act of 1983, 1983 India Cen. Act 23, § 2(dd), which defines »broadcast« as »communication to the public (i) by any means of wireless diffusion, whether in any one or more of the forms of signs, sounds or visual images; or (ii) by wire, and includes a rebroadcast.«

228 U.L. BARUAH, »THIS IS ALL-INDIA RADIO« 1–14 (1983).

229 1 REPORT, *supra* note 227, at 3–5. The first regular broadcast service started in Pittsburgh (U.S.) in 1920, closely followed by the Radio Corporation of America and British Broadcasting Corporation in 1922.

The Indian Wireless Telegraph Act of 1933 was enacted to regulate broadcasting services in India, and it continues to do so today. Another statute, the Government of India Act of 1935, empowers the federal government under section 129 to frame rules and regulations for broadcasting in the country.[230]

In view of the growing importance of broadcasting, the government finally decided in 1935 to place the ISBS on a more permanent footing, and an independent department, called All-India Radio (AIR), was constituted (in 1957, AIR was itself officially redesignated as »Akashvani«, or »voice from the sky,« which is a Hindi synonym of All-India Radio). The administration of broadcasting, initially with the Department of Industries and Labor, was transferred to Department of Communication in 1937 and then to the Ministry of Information and Broadcasting in 1941. AIR was made a separate department of the Ministry of Information and Broadcasting. By this time, the International Frequency Registration Board had alloted to India the call sign »VU,« and the Colaba Observatory »time pips« were introduced over AIR.[231]

A 1939 report on the progress of broadcasting in India recommended both the establishment of basic short-wave service, in order to provide the whole of India with at least a second-grade service, and the supplementaion of this service with a first-grade, medium-wave service at important centres. As a result, a number of short-wave transmitters were commissioned in the country.

The first 10-kW short-wave transmitter was commissioned at Bombay on February 4, 1938. There followed stations in Lucknow (5 kW mw) on April 2, 1938, in Delhi (5 kW sw) on June 1, 1938, in Madras (5 kW mw and 10 kW sw) on June 16, 1938 and in Calcutta (10 kW) on August 16, 1938. With this foundation, the first interstation relays between Bombay and Delhi on short wave could begin in early 1939. The same year saw the opening of 5-kW mw stations at Tiruchirapalli on May 16 and at Dacca on December 16.[232] At this time, evasion of licensing began to be noticed, and, accordingly, the first organised anti-piracy drive was launched early in 1939.

The real break for broadcasting in India came with World War II: the war made it necessary for the government to expand the broadcasting organisa-

230 This includes the construction and use of transmission apparatuses in the provinces or states and the regulation of fees in respect of the construction or use of transmitters and the use of receiving apparatuses in the provinces or states.

231 2 REPORT, *supra* note 227, at A–8.

232 U.L. BARUAH, *supra* note 228, at 7.

tion to meet the requirements of its war efforts. At the outbreak of the war, the centralised broadcast of news bulletins originated in Delhi. These were initially in Indian languages, such as Tamil, Telugu, Gujarati, Marathi and Pushto, in addition to the existing bulletins in English, Hindustani and Bengali, making twenty-seven news bulletins a day. The first external broadcast, a Pushto transmission, occurred on October 1, 1939 and opened the gate for further transmissions to foreign countries. The Germans as well began broadcasting a series of programmes in Indian languages. Alarmed by this propaganda inroad, the British government responded by opening an Indian Section within the BBC.

The end of the war witnessed momentous political developments in the country. The transfer of power to India by the British at midnight on August 14–15, 1947 was broadcast live over AIR. At the time of Independence, there were nine AIR stations, of which six – Delhi, Calcutta, Bombay, Madras, Lucknow and Tiruchi – went to India. The Lahore, Peshawar and Dacca stations went to Pakistan. With the integration of the princely states into India, a number of native stations in Hyderabad, Aurangabad, Trivendrum, Baroda and Mysore had become part of AIR by 1950.

C. *Broadcasting After Independence: Expansion of AIR*

After independence of the country in 1947, the Constitution (which came into operation on January 26, 1950) placed broadcasting in the Union List, making the federal government directly responsible for broadcasting.[233] It had become apparent that broadcasting, constituting in its reach, impact and dimensions the most powerful and potent medium of mass communication, had to be expanded. Its significance as a source of information and education was particularly great in a vast and developing country like India, where 85% of its 700 million people lived in over half a million villages and where the reach of the print media was limited. Against this background, expansion of broadcasting was brought within the ambit of planned development in 1951, when India's first Five-Year Plan (1951–56) was inaugurated. At the end of the plan, All-India Radio numbered twenty-six stations, whose twenty-nine mw and seventeen sw transmitters possessed 741.35 kilowatts of power.

233 INDIA CONST. schedule VII, list I (Union List), entry 31 authorises the federal government to make laws for posts, telegraphs, telephone, wireless broadcasting and other like forms of communication. The control of the manufacture and the licensing would fall under entry 31 as other forms of communication.

The third Five-Year Plan (1961–66) continued the pace of development with a medium-wave expansion programme, whereby a number of auxiliary centres were provided with limited studio facilities directly on the transmitter premises. Frequencies for these transmitters had been allocated in 1959 at the World Administrative Radio Conference, held in Geneva under the auspices of the International Telecommunication Union (ITU). The centres were more or less conceived of as relaying stations, as they were equipped with facilities for the playback of tapes prerecorded at parent stations found mainly in state capitals. These auxiliary centres were thus set up in Tirunelveli, Bikaner, Cuddapah, Visakhapatnam, Sambalpur, Raipur and Sangli in 1963; in Gwalior, Jeypore and Jabalpur in 1964; in Bhadrawati, Jodhpur and Rampur in 1965; and in Culbarga, Coimbatore and Siliguri in 1966. They were mostly of 20-kW power, with the exception of a few 10-kW centres in Gwalior, Gulbarga and Coimbatore. Visakhaptnam and Jodhpur were provided with 100-kW transmitters.

During 1963, independent radio stations in Kohima, Imphal and Port Blair were set up with low-power, medium-wave transmitters that were later upgraded; a 20-kW short-wave transmitter had already been commissioned at Kurseong to provide service in Nepali, Sikkimese and Bhutanese to North Bengal and adjoing areas. At this time, twenty-six Vividh Bharati transmitters were installed in existing AIR stations and in two new centres in Kanpur and Chandigarh. A radio station to cover the Kutch region of Gujarat was commissioned at Bhuj on October 10, 1965. The following year, on March 6, 1966, a low-power radio station was commissioned at Passighat as part of a scheme to cover the all-important administrative centre of Arunachal Pradesh (the northeast frontier area, know as NEFA with such radio stations).

D. *AIR Expansion During the VIth Five-Year Plan (1981–1985)*

The All-India Radio network, originally six radio stations in 1947, now consists of ninety-eight radio stations following the completion of the VIth Five-Year Plan (1981–1985).[234] The 142 medium-wave transmitters possess 8,245 kW of power; the 40 short-wave transmitters, 2,865 kW; and the four VHF transmitters, 60 kW (see Map I). In addition, fifty-six AIR sta-

234 MINISTRY OF INFORMATION AND BROADCASTING, ANNUAL REPORT (1983–84) 85. *See* Annexure XII.

tions have been provided with single terminals to receive quickly the signals from INSAT-IB, [235] and this has brought about considerable improvement in the quality of centrally organized programmes from Delhi. AIR serves about 95% of India's population spread over 86% of the country, including such difficult locations as Leh and Trarwang and such distant areas as the Andamanan Nicobar and Lakshdweep Islands.

E. *AIR Expansion Proposals for the VIIth Five-Year Plan (1986–1990)*

The VIIth Five-Year Plan (1986–1990) envisages a large-scale expansion of the AIR network throughout the country. By 1990, the country is to have 203 broadcasting stations, 150 medium-wave transmitters with 10,856 kW of power, 54 short-wave transmitters with 7,293 kW of power, and 104 VHF transmitters with 3,270 kW of power. It is estimated that by that time, 97–98% of the population and 91% of the country will be within the day-time ambit of the radio signals emanating from AIR stations.[236]

F. *Frequency Management via International Regulation*

To avoid the overlapping of assigned frequencies and the resulting interference, each radio station must operate on a particular predetermined frequency and must not drift beyond a very small permissible tolerance. There are a limited number of frequency channels available for assignment. But since the number of transmitters in operation greatly exceeds the number of available channels, multiple use of common frequencies is unavoidable. It is necessary, therefore, that the use of the same frequency by more than one staion be made in a perfectly compatible manner. This requires close coordination between various countries, especially those neighboring one another. The essence of this coordination is the spacing of transmitters operating on the same or adjacent frequencies at distances sufficiently far apart so that, in any service area, the unwanted, or interfering, signal is lower (by a prescribed minimum value) than the wanted signal.

The best international frequency coordination is evidently achieved by the allocation of frequency assignments under mutually agreed plans. This need

235 *See infra* pp. 138–39.
236 ANNUAL REPORT, *supra* note 234, at 17.

for international discipline was recognised by the establishment of the International Frequency Registration Board (IFRB), which is one of the organs of the ITU. It is the responsibility of the IFRB to ensure that radio transmissions emanating from the territories of its member-countries are compatible with other transmissions and do not cause mutual interference. In the case of the medium-frequency band, an agreement was reached at an international conference convened by the ITU in 1975 that regulates the use of this band until 1989. The ITU has also resolved to convene planning conferences for the high-frequency and VHF bands, on global and regional bases respectively.

In India and other countries of the Asia and Pacific regions, the frequencies assigned to broadcasting stations are from one of the following bands:

(a) medium-frequency band(mw):	525–1605 kHz (kilohertz);
(b) high-frequency band(sw):	3–30 MHz (megahertz);
(c) very-high-frequency band(VHF):	87–108 MHz.

In 1977, the ITU assigned frequencies in the 12-GHz (gigahertz) band. The Radio Regulations of the ITU allocate the frequency bands 11.7–12.2 GHz, 41–43 GHz and 84–86 GHz to the Broadcasting Satellite Service; the frequency band 2.5–2.699 GHz is restricted to the community-reception mode, which will require the use of somewhat complex receiving terminals. In addition, the possibility of allocating a frequency band in the vicinity of 1 GHz is being internationally explored.

G. *AIR Code*

Perhaps the most important development of 1967 was the introduction of the nine-point AIR Code for individual broadcasters. The Code prohibits the broadcasting by individuals on All-India Radio of:

(a) criticism of friendly countries;
(b) an attack on religion or communities;
(c) anything obscene or defamatory;
(d) an incitement to violence or anything disturbing the maintenance of law and order;
(e) anything amounting to contempt of court;
(f) an aspersion against the integrity of the president, the governors or the judiciary;

(g) an attack on a political party by name;
(h) hostile criticism of any state or the central government; and
(i) anything showing disrespect for the Constitution or advocating a change in the Constitution by violent means (advocating changes in a constitutional manner is not barred).

With the proclamation of internal emergency by the government of Mrs. Indira Ghandi on June 25, 1975, AIR was brought under stricter control, and the AIR Code was discarded as obsolete. It was again restored after the general election in March 1977, when the opposition Janta Party came to power.

H. *AIR Programmes*

In the home services, AIR broadcasts programmes in twenty-one major languages and forty-six tribal and other dialects. The programmes put out by AIR stations can be categorised as follows:

(a) news and programmes broadcast from Delhi of nationwide interest;
(b) news and cultural programmes broadcast from state capitals, catering to the needs and interests of their respective states;
(c) regional services broadcast by individual stations, catering to the needs and interests of their respective areas; and
(d) programmes broadcast for listeners in foreign countries.

The principal ingredients of the AIR programme output are music, talk shows, interviews and discussions, newscasts, plays, features and documentaries, educational broadcasts for specific audience groups (rural listeners, industrial workers, women, children, youth, the armed forces, tribal people, etc.), sports and outside broadcasts. But along with the expansion of broadcasting in terms of the number of radio stations, transmitters and listeners, there has also been a significant reorientation of programmes. They are now more field based and the accent is on agriculture, hygiene, health and family welfare, in addition to the above-mentioned programmes. Immediacy, authenticity and objectivity are the claimed guiding principles in all of these broadcasts.

In addition, All-India Radio supplies recorded-music, spoken-word and other programmes to about 150 countries and other foreign broadcasting organisations, under cultural exchange agreements and AIR's programme exchange agreements.

AIR is also participating on the so-called INSAT mission for the country-wide distribution of such centrally or regionally originated programme services as news bulletins. AIR has recognised the possibility that, at some future point, it might become desirable to establish direct satellite-based services in the individual-reception mode, permitting direct-to-home broadcasting.

I. *Programme Output and Pattern*

391,246 hours of programmes in the home (general) service and 142,381 hours in the Vivdh Bharati (commercial) service were broadcast by AIR's eighty-three stations in 1980. The corresponding figures for 1965, as reported by the Chanda Committee, were 118,657 hours and 10 minutes in the home service and 54,482 hours in the Vividh Bharati service. Thus, during that fifteen-year period, the programme output more than doubled. The average daily output in 1980 was more than 1000 hours in the home service and over 390 hours in the Vividh Bharati service. The number of hours broadcast in the home service during the last few years are as follows:

1977: 354,240 hours, 09 minutes
1978: 367,272 hours, 07 minutes
1979: 370,561 hours, 40 minutes
1980: 391,246 hours, 00 minutes

Of the total number of programmes broadcast, the amount of music broadcasts has stabilised at around 40%; news, at 23%; spoken-word, at 10%; drama, at 3%; and rural and other special-audience broadcasts, at 24%. The situation for five of the seven AIR stations in 1939 – Delhi, Calcutta, Bombay, Madras and Lucknow – amounted to 72.79% music (Indian music: 58.85%; European music: 13.94%), 6.25% spoken-word, 4.22% drama, 10.84% news and 6.30% rural programmes. A decline in the quantum of music and an increase in the number of spoken-word broadcasts and special programmes for rural listeners are significant trends.

These figures reveal the increased stress that has been placed on information and education for development. AIR has been under constant pressure to increase the amount to developmental information, and this has resulted in a step-up in the number of news and spoken-word broadcasts, as well as in the number of programmes for special audiences, like farmers, industrial workers and linguistic and ethnic minorities. This restructuring has been mainly at the cost of music programmes. Reduction in the level of entertainment programmes in the regional services has been a matter of concern to station authorities, and an effort has been made to check further erosion and maintain the existing proportions.

J. *Local Radio*

The VIth Five-Year Plan (1981–85) had identified thirty places for local radio stations of 1 kW and twenty-nine places for VHF transmitters; however, on account of a constraint on resources, only six transmitters were installed in the following regions:

Adilabad:	uncovered tribal area in Andhra Pradesh.
Diphu:	uncovered tribal area in Assam.
Keonjhar:	uncovered tribal area in Orissa.
Kota:	headquarters, chambal command area development project.
Nagarcoil:	uncovered district in Tamilnadu.
Schlarpur:	uncovered district in Maharashtra.

In addition, the ITU has allocated 352 low-power transmitters for every district of India, but each district is too large for coverage by either a low-power medium-wave or VHF transmitter. AIR therefore prefers to call these transmitters »local radio transmitters« rather than »district transmitters.« A local radio station is expected to have one multipurpose recording studio with dubbing facilities and a transmission booth for the broadcasting of a transmission of about 7.5 hours, including some three hours of local origination. The question of whether some of these sites could not be given medium-power transmitters, where allocations are available, is being further explored.

K. *External Services*

The External Services division of India's Ministry of External Affairs, is responsible for the country's external publicity. The External Services broadcasts aim to project a true and objective image of the country to listeners abroad and to explain the country's point of view on matters of national and international importance. This is done through daily commentary, press reviews and news bulletins. These broadcasts also try to acquaint foreign listeners with the workings of the democratic system in India and stimulate interest abroad in the rich heritage of India's art, culture and traditions. The programmes highlight the progress that is being achieved in the industrial, economic and social fields. The news bulletins are broadcast in twenty-five languages – seventeen foreign and eight Indian – for over fifty-six hours daily, reaching listeners in widely scattered areas of the world; the press reviews and commentary are broadcast in most of these languages.

Chapter XII: Television

A. *Growth of Television in India*

Television, which is perhaps the only genuine revolution in the realm of human communication since Gutenberg's invention of the printing press, began modestly in India in the late 1960s. Although the first television centre was established in Delhi on September 15, 1959, it was basically a pilot project aided by UNESCO for education and development; regular transmission soon followed. Telecasts were in black and white, and, as the range was only 40 km, viewing was limited to rural and urban areas in and around Delhi. Community viewing television sets were provided by the Ford Foundation, with programmes directed toward school and rural audiences. The service remained experimental until 1965, when regular programmes were introduced in the evening transmission. A second television centre was founded in Bombay, after a gap of some fifteen years, on October 2, 1972 and was followed by the opening of television centres in other metropolitan cities and important towns, such as Srinagar und Jullandhar in 1973 and Calcutta, Madras and Lucknow in 1975, making a total of seven television centres in the country. With the advent of satellite-based television in India, beginning with SITE (Satellite Instructional Television Experiment) in 1975–76 and continuing with the present INSAT-IB (Indian Satellite IB), television services have been extended to cover a vast area of the population.

In fact, a momentous burst of Indian television growth came on the eve of the Ninth Asian Games, held in Delhi in November 1982, when forty-one low-power transmitters were installed in various state capitals and important towns. This led to the development of television in the country on an unprecedented scale. At present, Indian television has seven main, full-fledged centres, eighteen relay centres and three »upgrah« (remote) centres, with eight transmitters for rural coverage and 185 low-power transmitters (see Map II).[237] Of these twenty-eight centres, twenty are equipped with programme-production facilities; the other centres use programmes made in

237 *See* Annexure XIII.

nearby base production centres. The rapid expansion of a television network in the country has increased the reach of television to about 70% of the total population. It is hoped that by 1990, multichannel television broadcasts will reach every home and become an integral part of the daily life of the people.[238] Such a rapid expansion of television on a mass scale in a mere three and a helf years since November 1982 is one of the most unique and remarkable television achievements in the world. To make television more accessible to the people, the federal government has as well done away with the license fee, initially Rs.50 per set, as of April 1, 1985.

B. *Broad Objectives of Radio and Television*

The activities of radio and television in India have been enormously expanded in range and scope during their years of existence. They operate broadly under the following main objectives:

(a) to act as a catalyst for social change;
(b) to promote national integration;
(c) to stimulate a scientific temper in the minds of the people;
(d) to disseminate the message of family planning as a means of population control and family welfare;
(e) to provide essential information and knowledge in order to stimulate greater agricultural production;
(f) to promote, and help preserve, an environmental and ecological balance;
(g) to highlight the need for social welfare measures, particularly those for the welfare of women, children and the less-privileged;
(h) to promote interest in games and sports; and
(i) to create artistic and cultural heritage values.

C. *The SITE Project*

In 1955, India set up its first experimental satellite communications earth

238 However, the actual access to television will depend on the number of those who can buy television sets. It has been found that more than 95% of television sets are concentrated in metropolitan and other cities; less than 5% are located in rural areas, where 80% of India's population lives.

station, with the assistance of the United Nations Development Programme (UNDP). The possibility of using a satellite for instructional television was envisaged by the Indian Space Scientists in 1959, and an agreement was signed between the Indian Space Research Organisation (ISRO) and the United States National Aeronautics and Space Administration (NASA) to undertake a cooperative experiment in instructional television via satellite. The overall conception, planning, organising and financing of the operation were the joint responsibility of NASA, ISRO and the UNDP. As a result of the agreement, a unique, one-year Satellite Instructional Television Experiment (SITE), a joint AIR and ISRO project, was begun in August 1975, arousing wide international interest.[239]

The hardware for the project consisted of a NASA ART-6 (Application Technology Satellite) provided by the United States. The satellite served as a reflector of messages sent from the earth: it concentrated and magnified the signals it received and relayed them back to earth. India provided the prime earth station, located at Ahemadabad, and other supporting earth stations at Delhi, Amritsar and Nagpur, with each station transmitting in its own regional language. The powerful signals could then be picked up with a three-metre-diameter, chicken-mesh antenna located in each of nearly 2400 villages in the six states of Andhra Pradesh, Bihar, Karnataka, Madhya Pradesh, Orissa and Rajasthan (400 villages in each state).[240] The villages were thus provided with television programmes through direct reception from the satellite. Each village was provided with a television set located in a public building, usually a school, accessible to all members of the village community. The television sets were operated by a teacher-custodian.

The capsule programmes transmitted by the satellite to the selected villages were produced at three core production centres in Delhi, Cuttack and Hyderabad. The national programmes were broadcast from the earth station located in Delhi and the other programmes from Ahmedabad, with the transmitter at Pij. As a follow-up to SITE, television centres were set up in 1977 in Jaipur, Raipur, Gulberge and Hyderabad.

Some of the main objectives of the experiment were:

239 *See The SITE Experience*, UNESCO (No. 91), p. 7 (Paris 1983). The satellite was lifted into space in May 1974. It had a 30 decron mesh antenna and was positioned 35,680 km above the equator at 94 degrees longitude above the Galapagos Islands. For the purposes of SITE, the satellite was moved from 94 degrees to 35 degrees West.

240 *Id.* at 7–10. The selection of the villages was made partly on the basis of satellite location and partly for reasons of economic backwardness.

(a) to gain experience in the development, testing and management of a satellite-based instructional television system, particularly in the rural areas, and to demonstrate optimal system performance;
(b) to demonstrate the potential value of satellite technology in the rapid advancement of effective mass communication in developing countries;
(c) to demonstrate the potential value of satellite-broadcast television in the practical instruction of village inhabitants; and
(d) to stimulate national development in India, with important managerial, economic, technological and social implications.

The project also had certain specific objects, such as contributions to family planning, national integration, general school and adult education, a teacher training programme and improvement of occupational health and hygiene and agricultural practices.
The five major departments involved in the project were: Posts and Telegraph, Agriculture, Health and Family Planning, Education and Information and Broadcasting. Educational institutes, like the Indian Institute of Technology at Kanpur, the Community Science Centre at Ahemedabad and the Homi Bhabha Centre at Bombay, provided science education programmes. All-India Radio and the National Council of Educational Research and Training (NCERT) also participated in the project.

D. *Impact of SITE*

The total telecast duration was four hours per day. The ninety-minute transmission in the morning between 10:00 and 11:30 was meant for primary school children and teachers and focused largely on science education.[241] The two and a half hours of transmission in the evening, commencing at 6:00, was aimed at general village viewing. Out of this transmission, one half-hour was devoted to the National Programme in Hindi, common to all

241 *Id.* at 11–18. The programmes were produced partly by the Space Application Centres in Ahemdabad and Bombay and partly by the Delhi Television Studio in collaboration with the National Council of Education Research and Training.

the village clusters, and thirty to forty minutes of special language programmes direted at each cluster separately.[242]

The SITE project was an experiment in many respects. SITE, on the one hand, was an experiment in the viability of satellite-based mass television as an instrument of instruction and social change; on the other hand, it was a test of India's scientific and technological manpower, including social researchers, in meeting the challenge of providing the hardware and the software for such a gigantic experiment in a remarkably short period of time. The challenges were met, and the project was a decided success.

The various studies undertaken to assess the impact that SITE had in the villages where it operated can be summarised as follows:

(a) SITE programmes reached remote rural areas, and even though the novelty effect wore off after the first few weeks, these programmes were able to command a daily audience of around 100 persons per set, or about 250,000 persons in the six cluster areas. Television reached more viewers in each experimental village than all other forms of mass media put together.

(b) While entertainment programmes were enjoyed by all, there was also a considerable demand for instructional programmes; in fact, some data suggest that the villagers, on the whole, wanted more instructional programmes than were provided.

(c) Television programmes often led to discussions among the viewers.

(d) SITE programmes were viewed by a fairly large number of women, though never a majority of the viewers. The programmes were viewed by an even larger number of small farmers and agricultural workers, who constituted a majority of the viewing group, despite having been less well represented in the programmes than the upper strata and school-educated segments of the population.

(e) SITE programmes led to significant benefits for viewers in the areas of health and agriculture.

(f) SITE programmes consistently led to significant gains in general awareness and knowledge among individuals who viewed the programmes frequently, in comparison with the control groups.

(g) SITE programmes stimulated curiosity and interest in school children and led them to ask their parents and teachers questions.

242 *Id.* at 13. This programme was produced by the television wing of All-India Radio, later called Doordarshan. The regional programmes were produced mainly at base production centres located in four cities – Hyderabad, Cuttack, Ahmedabad and Delhi.

(h) SITE programmes led at least large farmers into greater contact with extension agents.
(i) SITE programmes succeeded in getting persons of different castes and social strata to sit together to view a common programme.
(j) Two studies indicate that SITE programmes had the effect of bridging the gap between progressive and backward villages and the gap, within a village, between advanced and backward caste villagers.
(k) From the point of view of social science research, SITE had a spin-off effect, in that it has generated considerable interest in the study of mass communication and media research. It also gave social researchers the experience of working as a team in comparatively large groups. As many as seventy-eight social scientists from the SAC-ISRO organisations were engaged in the studies from the planning phase to the data-collection phase.[243]

SITE was also extremely useful in pointing out some of the steps that need to be taken if large-scale, rural-oriented telecasts are to be undertaken again.
The fear that satellite television will become increasingly monopolised by urban elite groups and that it will transmit not developmental but light, film-based entertainment programmes to the rural areas is one that has been expressed by many. The way to combat that possibility is not to prevent the emergence of rural television altogether, but instead to ensure, through the building-up of public opinion, that the policy makers and programme managers will be sensitised to this danger and will be forewarned that their performance will be judged in terms of the contribution they make towards creating a developmental awareness in the countryside. As the SITE experiment has shown, the rural population is not averse to the instructional message. In fact, it has asked for a greater share of the instructional message in relation to the entertainment message.[244]

E. *Television is Doordarshan*

When television initially came to India in 1959, it was linked with All-India Radio; later it was thought desirable to separate it from radio for its proper

243 *Id.* at 55–56.
244 *Id.* at 57.

functioning and expansion in the country. Accordingly, television was divested from AIR on April 1, 1976 under the name of Doordarshan, a Hindi synonym of television. A directorate was established for administration and logistical planning and for execution of media activities. The directorate is housed at Mandi House in Delhi and coordinates the activities of all television and transmission centres in the country.

Within the broad objectives of entertainment, education and information, the organisational credo of Doordarshan entails its being a catalyst for the instigation of social change, for the promotion of national integration, for the stimulation of scientific temper, for the provision of guidance for family welfare, for the promotion of the production of agriculture, for the development of healthy habits, for the creation of positive attitudes regarding the welfare of children and the weaker sections of society and for the instillation of a spirit for games, sports and cultural heritage among its viewers.

F. *Television Through Satellite: INSAT-IB*

Following the success of SITE, the Government of India approved in mid-1977 a proposal for a first-generation, multipurpose Indian National Satellite (INSAT) system of her own. Accordingly, INSAT-IA was launched by a NASA Delta booster rocket on April 8, 1982 and became operational on August 15, 1982. Unfortunately, it was declared unusable on September 6, 1982, due mainly to depletion of satellite fuel.

Work began soon thereafter on a similar satellite, INSAT-IB. It was launched on August 30, 1983 with the U.S. space shuttle Challenger from Kennedy Space Centre in Florida (U.S.) and became fully operational on October 15, 1983. INSAT-IB reached its predetermined, 36,000-km-high, geostationary orbit above the earth at 74° East longitude, where it is expected to remain some seven years. Its capabilities include: nationwide television coverage by direct telecast to low-cost community receiver sets; television and radio programme distribution and networking; relay of hydrological, meteorological and oceanographic data from unattended land- and ocean-based data transmission platforms; and disaster warning transmissions.

INSAT-IB is a unique joint venture of the Department of Space, the Posts and Telegraphs Department (now the Department of Telecommunications), the Meteorological Department of the Ministry of Tourism and Civil Aviation and Doordarshan and AIR of the Ministry of Information and Broadcasting. While the Department of Space has the responsibilities of hardware establishment and operation and maintenance of the space segment, other concerned departments have been entrusted with preparation of their respective ground segments. For example, Doordarshan produces television software for rural communities and other target groups. The Government of India has constituted a high-level committee of departmental secretaries, known as the INSAT Coordination Committee, which maintains interagency coordination during the implementation and operation phases of the system.[245] Plans for the launching of INSAT-IC by mid-1986 have also been approved.

G. *INSAT Television in Rural Areas*

In addition to one-step, nationwide television coverage, INSAT-IB has also made it possible to provide national networking of all existing transmitters in order to facilitate programme exchange between different television centres. Thus, INSAT television provided two distinct features: direct telecast and nationwide networking using existing terrestrial transmitters. With this arrangement, important events could be covered and distributed live to all parts of the country. The major advantage of this system, moreover, was the ability to provide television service to those remote, rural and backward areas of the country where developmental efforts require mass-media support. With this new communication tool in hand, the government targeted undeveloped clusters of the country for coverage.[246]

The selection of these clusters was made in such a way that the widest possible range of experience from the project, that is, in different cultural and linguistic settings, would be obtained for use in the future expansion into other parts of the country. Initially, in the first phase in Orissa and Andhra Pradesh, 800 rural villages received programmes directly from the satellite with the help of a ruggedised TV set – one augmented by a 12-foot-diametre, parabolic antenna of chicken mesh and a front-end converter – known as a Direct-Reception Set (DRS). In addition, VHF sets were covered by terrestrial transmitters at Hyderabad and Sambalpur (both SITE continuity

245 B.K. Khurana, Doordarshan: INSAT-IB Basic Information 10 (1985).

246 Three districts each in the six states of Andrha Pradesh, Orissa, Maharastra, Bihar, Gujarat and Uttar Pradesh were identified for coverage and selected on the basis of backwardness of the area, availability of suitable physical and developmental infrastructures and utilisation of existing television programme production facilities.

areas) and by a 10-kW terrestrial transmitter at Nagpur. In the second phase in August 1984, new 10-kW terrestrial transmitters were installed at Rajkot (Gujarat), Ranchi (Bihar), Gorakhpur (Uttar Pradesh) and Nagpur (Maharashtra). The programmes fed through the satellite were received by 300 DRSs in each state, as well as by VHF sets in the selected districts. In all, 2000 DRSs and 2000 VHF sets were installed in the six states for community viewing in rural areas.

H. *Mechanism of Utilisation*

INSAT-IB has two »S«-band transponders for use by radio and television. Two uplinks for these transponders are presently in operation. In view of the rapid expansion of television to 70% of the total population, one of the available »S«-band transponders is being used exclusively for the National Programme/Network; the other »S«-band transponder is utilised for primary schools and programmes for higher education being organised by the University Grants Commission. In addition, a »C«-band transponder is currently being utilised by Doordarshan through the uplink at the ISRO earth station in Delhi. Since programmes are uplinked from Delhi in the initial stages, capsuled programmes are sent well in advance to Delhi from the programme production centres established at different clusters.

Programmes are broadcast daily for eighty-five minutes for each cluster – forty-five minutes of transmission in the morning hours and forty minutes in the evening – in addition to the ninety-minute National Programme at 9:00 PM. The morning transmission is devoted to school education, with twenty minutes for children five to eight years, twenty minutes for children nine to eleven years and five minutes for the transition between lessons. Once a week, a separate programme with hints for teachers is telecast. Presently these programmes are produced jointly by Doordarshan and the Centre for Educational Technology of the Ministry of Education; ultimately, the entire responsibility for planning and production of these programmes will be entrusted to the Centre.

The evening, forty-minute, area-specific programmes are produced by Doordarshan with the active help and participation of such various user-ministries as Food and Agriculture, Rural Development, Health and Family Welfare, etc. The main focus of the evening transmission is on agriculture, family welfare, health and hygiene, formal and informal education, as well as general entertainment and weather forecasts. Topical programmes, like news and current affairs, are covered by the National Programme. The programmes are area-specific relevant to the prevailing culture and are based primarily on the needs and requirements of the local people, as determined and assessed through specific studies on target audience.

An additional, one-hour daily programme for higher education, sponsored by the University Grants Commission, is telecast in the afternoon through INSAT-IB. It is an enrichment programme rather than syllabus oriented, which will help in the improvement of the quality of higher education in the country. The programme is directed at students, at teachers for guidance, and at the educated public at large. In order to give impetus to the scheme, a communication cell has been set up by the University Grants Commission, the National Council of Educational Research and Training Centre, and the Audio-Visual Research Centres to facilitate the production and utilisation of these programmes and to identify different universities and national institutions that would derive benefits from such facilities in improving the standards of education through media. A large number of TV sets have been provided at these institutions. Initially, the programmes were in English and were comprised of short items not exceeding twenty minutes in duration. Preproduction and feed-forward research studies are already underway.

I. *Satellite Communication Technology: An Appraisal*

The Asia-Pacific Seminar on Utilisation of Satellite Technology for Mass Communication was held in Delhi in April 1984. Some of the important suggestions to come from the seminar are summarised below:

(a) Technology should be applied for the fabrication of hardware appropriate for the realisation of a country's communications objectives. Software technology should lead, not follow, hardware.

(b) Research should be promoted through the cooperative effort of countries and the findings widely shared. One advantage of this cooperation would be the maximal use of, and the reduced expenditure on, the satellite transponders that disseminate both the sound and picture signals. Possibilities include the utilisation of one transponder for conveying two television signals and the use of spot beams for transmitting area-specific programmes to limited areas. The latter would be of special importance to countries with wide linguistic, ethnic or other diversity.

(c) In planning satellite systems, consideration must be given to ensuring that a proper balance is struck between the cost and complexity of the space segment and that of the earth segment to meet national communications objectives. For example, higher-power satellites, using higher-frequency bands (like ku) that operate in spot beams, permit signals to be received via relatively small and less costly earth stations.

(d) For direct reception, especially in the context of community viewing, a reduction can be achieved in the cost of disc antennas in the central service area of the satellite by reducing their diametre; larger-diametre antennas may still be necessary in the fringe areas.

(e) Possibilities for the reduction of the cost of building earth stations for the uplinking of programmes should be explored.

(f) Considering the higher cost of TV receivers, as opposed to those for radios, there should be widespread provision for interactive community viewing of TV.

(g) Great care should be taken in the selection of foreign programmes for telecast in developing countries. While it is useful to borrow educative programmes, the projection of foreign lifestyles and entertainment not only serves no purpose, but it can also be socially disorienting. It was noted in this connection that the Islamic Republic of Iran and Indonesia have strongly reduced the number of imported TV programmes.

(h) Locally produced entertainment programmes of a trivial nature and those depicting sex and violence, particularly commercial films, can be as harmful as ill-chosen foreign programmes.

(i) It is not enough that TV programmes be indigenously produced; they should be attractive enough to hold the viewers' interest. Examples cited included the experience of some African countries, where the indigenous content of TV programmes had been very high but did not attract adequate viewer interest.

(j) As regards quality programming, emphasis was placed on the importance of the proper training of TV programme producers. It was noted that, in many developing countries, this aspect had been neglected. As a result, the low quality of programmes, combined with the high cost of indigenous production, led to reliance on imported and irrelevant software and amounted to a self-invited cultural invasion.

(k) The recording and playback abilities of video tape should be exploited to spur local interest and to assist development-promoting programmes for specific districts or other small administrative units. Reference was made in this connection to the use in Indonesia of 300 mobile vans equipped with VCRs and wide screens for community viewing by large numbers of people. In this way, locally made programmes, including traditional social drama, could be made readily available to their audiences.

(l) As in the case of radio, the television medium should be used for programmes of national, regional and local interest, utilising the appropriate satellite-microwave, single-station or video mode. Proper use of television should encourage communication of people among themselves, from the people to their authorities and from political leaders and development experts to the people. Feedback is of the utmost importance in relevant programming for developing countries, which are not, unlike more affluent countries, extensively served by telecommunications. News and current affairs programmes in many countries tend to be under greater governmental constraints than entertainment programmes. Even with these constraints, programmes can still be more professional in their treatment and presentation.

J. *Advancements in Television*

To supplement black-and-white transmission, Doordarshan introduced color programming on August 15, 1982, and it presently telecasts nearly 95% of its programmes in color. In national programmes, all transmissions are in color. With color TVs and VCRs selling briskly, close-circuit television being increasingly employed by large companies and department stores, and teleconferencing and mini-computers becoming the latest corporate demand, the indigenous television industry is mushrooming. The scope of the expansion in electronics has also widened, for India forms the world's second-largest potential TV viewing market and consumer market for other electronic products. To meet the rapidly increasing demand for TV sets, the federal government has approved the installation of plants that are capable of producing one million picture tubes a year.

Within the next ten years, the government envisages the initiation of a three-channel system for television. Each centre, apart from SITE continuity centres, will have two channels – one each for urban and rural viewers – with a third commercial channel. In conformity with this proposal, a second channel already has been started in Delhi and Bombay. Plans for the opening of a second channel at other centres have been finalised.

Doordarshan is aiming during the VIIth Five-Year Plan (1986–1990) to provide a three-tier TV service, comprising (i) primary service in each major state to be available in the language of that state, (ii) national service to be available throughout the country and to be based on programmes produced at Delhi, as well as on programmes of national relevance originating from other centres, and (iii) local service to be available for a limited duration from the local transmitters, with provisions for separate channels at the metropolitan centres. Doordarshan's proposals also envisage, inter alia, greater availability of facilities for local production in each state or union territory and more intensive TV coverage of the border areas.

Several important developments followed the recommendations of the 1978 Working Group on Autonomy for Akashvani and Doordarshan.[247] A considerable number of commercial advertisements and sponsored programmes were included in transmissions, resulting in a substantial increase in revenues. More telecast time also began being devoted to commercial feature films and film-based programmes. These developments showed that the indigenous development of software was at the heart of television's future in India.

A serious complaint, though, ensued about the commercial telecasts, in that there had been a shift away from the original intent and purpose of introducing television, namely, to use it for educational and developmental purposes. The complaint appears to have some merit, as there is today but a symbolic use of terrestrial centres and satellite technology for rural audiences.

K. *Software: A Review*

It is the message content and form of desired software that should dictate the choice of communications hardware, and not the other way around.[248]

247 The Ministry of Information and Broadcasting appointed in 1977 a working group, consisting of 10 members with B.G. Verghese as its chairman, to examine the functional and legal aspects of the proposal that would give full autonomy to AIR (»Akashvani«) and Doordarshan. It would have to be consistent with the accountability to Parliament and should draw on the experience in the matters of broadcasting of the different forms of autonomous organisations existing in other democratic countries. The working group submitted a comprehensive, two-volume report to the government in February 1978, suggesting autonomous status for AIR and Doordarshan. *See supra* note 227. In the meantime, the general elections took place in the country, and Mrs. Indira Gandhi again returned to power; her government did not accept the recommendations for the autonomy for AIR or Doordarshan.

248 Bhagat, *Communication in India: Prospects and Policy*, 28 COMMUNICATOR 53 (1983).

Realising the importance of software, the Ministry of Information and Broadcasting appointed a working group on television software on December 6, 1982.[249] Two of the objectives of the group were to examine the need for acquiring a multicomposite of rural and urban viewers and to recommend a programme pattern, taking into account the existing programme production facilities, that would provide development of television in the proper direction.

The committee opined that the audio-visual media should serve a larger, national purpose. It would be a calamity, said the committee, if the use of communications technology were not properly applied as an aid to socio-economic transformations and to growth with social justice. Unless the importance of software is realised, cautioned the committee, the TV expansion plan would stand condemned as the greatest communications aberration in the history of the Third World.

Reflecting a genuine fear among the committee that, under pressure from vested interests, India will fail to adapt TV technology to indigenous needs and innovative uses, their report outlined the existing handicaps – some organisational and managerial, others political – and recommended various measures to improve services. Pointing to the structure and administration of television, the report noted that good TV programmes require creativity at every stage.[250]

As stated above, the committee stressed that the key to TV effectiveness lies in the right kind of software. The model producer is one who is a communications activist in an egalitarian society. He must love outdoor life, and, for programmes devoted to play and recreation, he should turn to the world of nature. The challenge to him is to produce problem-oriented, people-oriented, development-oriented and entertainment-cum-enrichment-oriented programmes suited to a developing country. Given two major assumptions – the revolutionary relevance of communications technology in a developing society and a nearly universal access to TV – whose production style is intimately related to the common man's problems, needs and feelings – television will grow into an institution of the people. While admitting that governmental planning of software carries its own dangers, the committee expected that a wider social vision and a deeper social consciousness will direct the work of the TV communicator.

It is out of such challenges that a democratic society is spurred toward an

249 The working group was headed by P.C. Joshi, director of the Institute of Economic Growth. The committee submitted its report to the government on January 18, 1985.

250 Desai, *A New Doordarshan*, The Statesman, January 18, 1985.

idealised culture that would allow honest work and happy living. Through varied telecasting – song, dance, and music; traditional theatre and folk arts; programmes derived from classical and tribal heritage – the monotony of television should dissipate, leaving behind a more meaningful frame for other programmes.

L. *National Programming*

The National Programme is a ninety-minute transmission that serves to keep the public informed about cultural, social and economic progress in various parts of the country, to bring home the message of unity and to foster a spirit of national integration in the country. The programme is telecast between 9:00 PM and 10:30 PM and includes two fifteen-minute news bulletins, one in Hindi and the other in English.

The National Programme was introduced on August 15, 1982 for simultaneous telecast by all transmitters throughout the country. The programmes are produced at various centres and broadly reflect themes like national integration, communal harmony, family welfare, India's cultural heritage (including art and dance), world literature and India's struggle for independence, science programmes and current affairs. An element of light entertainment and several new serials are also included within this broad spectrum.

It has been noted and renoted in various quarters that television has become an indiscriminate distributor of feature-film entertainment and screen materials that are in poor taste. Taking heed of this widespread disapproval and public criticism, Doordarshan has completely retailored the National Programme. Effective March 10, 1985, telecasts started at 8:30 PM and began with sponsored programmes, such as »Hum Log« (»We People«) and »Yeh Jo Hai Zindagi« (»It is the Life«). A special, fortnightly programme – »Janwani« (»Voice of the People«) – invites people from all over the country to send in their grievances on matters of public interest to the programme coordinator; the minister of the concerned department then replies to the complaints and questions and explains the government's point of view on those matters. »Janwani«, a Hindi programme, has its English counterpart, entitled »Panorama.« The first programme aired March 19, 1985 and discussed the problem of spurious drugs. »Janwani« and »Panorama« are telecast on alternate Tuesdays, and representative audiences are invited from various parts of the country. Two additional programmes, the Hindi »Paksh aur Vipaksh« (»For and Against«) and the English »Point-Counterpoint,« are telecast once a month. Their basic objective is to present the views of the ruling party and the opposition on subjects of great national significance.

All of these programmes have been designed to open the government-controlled media and to provide maximum freedom to focus on issues of general concern and common interest. The meetings of ministers with the affected public will inculcate a sense of responsibility and accountability among public servants.

Doordarshan has also dubbed into Hindi a variety of educational programmes, such as »Living Heritage,« »Wildlife« and »Living Planets.« Interesting foreign programmes are also regularly broadcast, which appeal to viewers from all sections of society, increase comprehension and information and upgrade general awareness standards.

Commercials were introduced on television on January 1, 1976. At present, all the main television centres telecast commercial spots, as well as sponsored programmes; these are also yielding good revenues for the exchequer. But with the spate of newly-introduced sponsored programmes, they also provide much fun, frolic, jest and zest, as well as advertisement for the sponsors. The sponsored era, with a lot of entertainment, has arrived.

Nevertheless, after sitting through sponsored programmes, one wonders whether a welfare state's monopolistic mass medium of television were not advocating commercialism and consumerism. All the charming and colorful faces appearing on the screen to buy toiletries, costly fabrics and artificial food do not exactly correspond with a welfare state's ideology. Although it may be accepted that all of the enticing advertisements will only be of relevance to those who have enough hard cash to buy the products, one must still ask about the 70% of those in India who do not get even two square meals a day and who have no use whatsoever for Max Factor cosmetics or sophisticated kitchen appliances. It is not satisfactory to say that those who cannot buy the advertised poducts still benefit from the entertainment the advertisers bring. This is rather like giving a glimpse of a steaming bowl of rice to a starving person from a distance and then allowing him to starve.[251]

251 Hindustan Times, March 18, 1985, at 5.

M. *Foreign Programmes*

Foreign feature films are procured from the U.S.'s M.P.E.A.A. (Motion Picture Export Association of America) and from the Soviet Export Film Agency. Foreign films are telecast from all centres except Gulburga (Maharastra), Sambalpur (Orissa) and Muzzafarpur (Bihar); area-specific programmes are telecast instead at those locations. Television documentaries and serials are obtained from the British Broadcasting Corporation (BBC) and Transtel, among others. Some of the popular serials include »Yes, Minister,« »The Lucy Show,« »Are You Being Served?,« »Target,« »Sorry« and »Different Strokes«.

N. *Quality Improvement in Production and Programming*

The government has undertaken several measures to improve the quality and content of production and programmes. Doordarshan has its own in-house Audience Research and Evaluation Organisation, with units located at each satellite-television centre. These units have developed special feedback mechanisms, called »tele-clubs,« through which data is collected from rural areas. The work of these units is supervised and controlled at Doordarshan by the director of Audience Research. Apart from this mechanism, there are a number of committees that monitor, advise and guide television programming. Some of these committees are: the Task Force for Commercial Programmes; the Central Advisory Committee for Utilisation of INSAT; the Programme Advisory Committee of Television Centres; and the Media Advisory Committee.

O. *Cable Television*

Cable television in India has not yet become as popular as in Western countries; it is confined almost to a few cities, to big business houses and to institutions. But in November 1982, India's first Cable Service Project was started by the Rourkela Steel Plant, and it has emerged as a top entertainment service among the plant's workers. The Rs.1,000,000 project was undertaken in order to establish better communication with workers and to close the gaps between various types of laborers; the service reaches an estimated 20,000 people.

News, features, films and documentaries are transmitted twenty-one hours each week from a central control station, located in one of the community service centres in the steel plant township, to twelve other community centres interspersed throughout the city and linked by underground cables. The station is equipped with a video transmission device, a camera and other accessories. The shows are produced by the plant's public relations department, and the plant's electronics department maintains the cables. The Programme Committee, headed by the deputy general manager of the plant, looks after the quality of programmes telecast.

The cable service got a boost during the IXth Asian Games, when cassettes began being air-lifted daily from Delhi to show major events. The biggest attraction for viewers is, however, the usual forte of Hindi and English films shown twice a week. Nevertheless, plant news and documentaries on steel making comprise a good quota of the transmissions, and these serve to place the activities of the plant in proper perspective, to improve productivity, to highlight the need for safety, to further congenial labor relations and to deliver social-welfare messages. The use of amateur talent culled from the employes, their children and officials is also encouraged. Enterprising and good-looking boys and girls are auditioned and given camera tests; some are then asked to handle regular newscasts and announcements. They love every bit of this exposure, getting an opportunity to try to show their talents.

Chapter XIII: Penal Laws Applicable to the Press

A. *Defamation*

Defamation, an injury to a person's reputation, is both a crime and a civil wrong.[252] The law of civil defamation, as in common-law countries, is uncodified in India; it is largely based on case law. The law of criminal defamation is codified in the Indian Penal Code. Section 499 of the IPC states when an act of imputation amounts to defamation, using terms that expressly require *mens rea*; the section provides defences that include almost all the traditional defences to proceedings for defamation.[253]

Section 500 prescribes punishment for crimes of defamation with simple imprisonment for a term that may extend to two years, with a fine or with both. Sections 501[254] and 502[255] punish the act of printing or engraving matters known to be defamatory and the sale of printed or engraved substances containing defamatory matters.[256]

In a civil action for defamation, truth is a defence, but in a criminal action, the accused must prove both the truth of the matter and that its publication was for the public good. The defence of truth is not satisfied merely by proving that the publisher honestly believed the statement to be true; he must prove that the statement was in fact true.

In *Sabib Singh Mehra v. State of Uttar Pradesh*,[257] the appellant was prosecuted under section 500 of the IPC for publishing an article entitled »Ulta chor Kotwal Ko Dante« (»Thief Reprimands Police Officer«) in the Aligarh paper *Kaliyug* dated September 23, 1960. The relevant English-translated version of the article reads:

> How the justice stands at a distance as a helpless, spectator of the show as to the manner in which the illicit bribe money from plaintiffs and defendants enters into

252 *See* WINFIELD, LAW OF TORTS 245 (1971).
253 *See* Annexure VIII.
254 *Id.*
255 *Id.*
256 *See* K.D. GAUR, CRIMINAL LAW: CASES AND MATERIALS 637, 648 (1985); LAW COMMISSION OF INDIA, 42ND REPORT ON THE INDIAN PENAL CODE 430–32 (1971).
257 1965 A.I.R. 1451 (S.C.).

> the pockets of the Public Prosecutors and Assistant Public Prosecutors and the extent to which it reaches and to which use it is put.[258]

The Supreme Court held that the impugned remarks were per se defamatory of the group of persons referred to. There was nothing on the record to establish that the defamatory remarks were made in good faith and after due care and attention as to their truth; nor was there anything to indicate that the statements were made for the protection of the interest of the person making it or of any other person, or for the public good, attracting the provisions of exception 3 or exception 9 of section 499 of the IPC.[259]
Rejecting the appellant's argument for a lenient punishment, the Court said:

> The Press has great power in impressing the minds of the people and it is essential that persons responsible for publishing anything in newspapers should take good care before publishing anything which tends to harm the reputation of a person. Reckless comments are to be avoided. When one is proved to have made defamatory comments with an ulterior motive and without the least justification motivated by self-interest, he deserves a deterrent punishment.[260]

In *Harbhajan Singh v. State of Punjab*,[261] the Supreme Court overturned the conviction of the appellant, who had been prosecuted and convicted under section 500 of the IPC. Surinder Singh Kairon, the son of Sri Pratap Singh Kairon, then chief minister of the State of Punjab, had complained that the appellant had published a statement in *Blitz*, a monthly magazine of Bombay, on July 23, 1957. Extracts from it, which were given publicity in a number of papers, were highly defamatory of Mr. Kairon. The statement read:

> [T]he son of our Chief Minister is not only a leader of smugglers but is responsible for a large number of crimes being committed in the Punjab. But because the culprit happens to be the Chief Minister's son, the cases are always shelved.[262]

In setting aside the conviction, the Court said that, as the impugned statement was for the public good, the appellant was entitled to claim the protection of exception 9 of section 499 of the IPC.[263]

258 *Id.* at 1452.
259 *See* Annexure VIII.
260 1965 A.I.R. at 1454.
261 1966 A.I.R. 97 (S.C.).
262 *Id.* at 99.
263 *See* Annexure VIII.

B. *Incitement to an Offence*

»Incitement to an offence,« as stated before, was added to article 19(2) of the Constitution by the Constitution (First Amendment) Act of 1951 in order to sanction laws punishing incitement to, or abetment of, offences not necessarily involving violence.
In *Indulak K. Yagnik v. State of Maharastra*,[264] section 3 of the Police (Incitement to Disaffection) Act of 1922[265] was challenged as contrary to article 19(1)(a) of the Constitution. The Bombay High Court held that an inducement or attempted inducement of a police officer, punishable under section 3, amounted to an incitement to an offence; thus, the section was saved by article 19(2), which allows the state to reasonably restrict incitements to offences, since the restriction imposed by section 3 was reasonable in view of its circumscribed scope.

C. *Contempt of Court*

Contempt of court has been defined by Lord Russell in *R. v. Gray* as an act done or writing published to bring a court or a judge into disrepute or to obstruct or interfere with the due course of justice or lawful process of the court.[266] The object of a contempt proceeding is to ensure a fair trial and to prevent the bringing into disrepute of the authority and the administration of law. These principles have been followed in India for a long time and are now contained in the Contempt of Court Act of 1971. The Constitution also empowers the Supreme Court and the high courts to punish for contempt.

264 1960 A.I.R. 399 (Bombay H.C.).

265 § 3: »Whoever intentionally causes or attempts to cause, or does any act which he knows is likely to cause, disaffection towards the Government established by law in India amongst the members of a police force, or induces or attempts to induce, or does any act which he knows is likely to induce, any member of a police force to withhold his service or to commit a breach of discipline shall be punished with imprisonment which may extend to six months, or with fine which may extend to two hundred rupees, or with both. *Explanation*: Expressions of disapprobation of the measures of the Government with a view to obtaining their alteration by lawful means, or of disapprobation of the administration or other actions of the Government, do not constitute an offence under this section unless they cause or are made for the purpose of causing or are likely to cause disaffection.«

266 [1900] 2 Q.B. 36, 40. The accused, an author, was held liable for contempt of court; he had published an article containing personal scurrilous abuse of a judge for his observations in an earlier indecency proceeding.

Section 2 of the Act of 1971 defines contempt of court as both civil contempt and criminal contempt. Civil contempt means the wilful disobedience of any order or other process issued by a court or the wilful disobedience of any undertaking given to a court. Criminal contempt includes any act or statement scandalising or tending to scandalise, or lowering or tending to lower, the authority of any court; prejudicially interfering or tending to interfere with the due course of any judicial proceeding; or obstructing or tending to obstruct the administration of justice in any manner. However, an innocent publication does not amount to contempt of court. The Act further makes it clear that any publication with respect to a matter that is not pending in a court and that is a fair criticism of judicial acts does not amount to contempt of court. Thus, a reflection upon the conduct of a judge may not always be contempt, and even a scurrilous attack on a judge will amount to contempt only when it is calculated to obstruct or interfere with the administration of justice or proper administration of law.

An analysis of the following cases will reveal that the courts have attempted to expand the law on the freedom of the press and the authority of the judiciary to ensure the due administration of justice.[267]

In *E.M.S. Namboodiripad v. T.N. Nambiar*,[268] the appellant, then chief minister of the State of Kerala, made various critical remarks against the judiciary at a press conference held in November 1967. He referred to the judiciary as »an instrument of class oppression,« and he accused judges of being »guided and dominated by class hatred, class interests and class prejudices, instinctively favouring the rich against the poor« and of often acting against their conscience. He further said that, as part of the ruling class, the judiciary »works against workers, peasants and other sections of the working classes« and »the law and the system of judiciary essentially serve the exploiting classes.«[269]

267 SECOND PRESS COMMISSION, REPORT 52 (1982) explained the role of the press as having »the right, which is also its professional function, to criticise and advocate. The whole gamut of public affairs including the administration of justice is the domain for fearless and critical comment. But the public function which belongs to the press makes it an obligation of honour to exercise this function only with the fullest sense of responsibility. Without such a lively sense of responsibility a free press might readily become a powerful instrument of injustice. The competing claims of the court to maintain its authority and of the freedom of the press to comment on matters of public interest must be reconciled. Without a free press there can be no free society. Freedom of the press, however, is not an end in itself, but a means to an end of a free society.«

268 1970 A.I.R. 2015 (S.C.).

269 *Id.* at 2020.

The appellant argued that the statement was protected by article 19(1)(a), as it was merely an expression of his belief in the Marx-Engels philosophy and, further, it was fair commentary on the state of the judicial system in the country. The Court rejected the argument and said that, while it is intended that there should be freedom of speech and expression, it is also intended that, in the exercise of the right, contempt of court shall not be committed. Such remarks are a direct attack on the judicial system and amount to contempt of court. Chief Justice Hidayatullah, speaking on behalf of the Court, said:

> No doubt the Courts, while upholding the laws and enforcing them, do give support to the State but they do not do so out of any impure motives. They do not range themselves on the side of the exploiting classes and indeed resist them when the law does not warrant an encroachment. To charge the judiciary as an instrument of oppression, the Judges as guided and dominated by class hatred, class interests and class prejudices instinctively favouring the rich against the poor is to draw a very distorted and poor picture of the judiciary. It is clear that it is an attack upon the judges which is calculated to raise in the minds of the people a general dissatisfaction with and distrust of all judicial decisions. It weakens the authority of law and law courts.[270]

C.K. Daphtary v. O.P. Gupta[271] demonstrated the limits to which the judiciary may be criticised. The defendant, a former judge whose suit for wrongful dismissal was denied by the Supreme Court, published and circulated a pamphlet criticising the adverse decision that had been delivered by a senior justice of the Court, using such terms as »dishonest judgment,« »open dishonesty«, »deliberately and dishonestly« and »utter dishonesty.« The pamphlet alleged that the justice had cleverly asked a junior justice to deliver the judgment and that the junior justice had toed the line and had written what the senior justice had told him to write. The defendant was convicted on a finding that the remarks made against the justice in the pamphlet were wholly unjustified.[272]

The defendant had argued that even a scurrilous attack on a judge does not affect the administration of justice, and, even if such an attack were to have an adverse effect on the administration of justice, it must be balanced against the harm that could ensue if such criticism were stopped. The Court, in refuting this contention, said:

270 *Id.* at 2024.
271 1971 A.I.R. 1132 (S.C.).
272 *Id.* at 1145.

> This sort of attack in a country like ours has the inevitable effect of undermining the confidence of the public in the Judiciary. If confidence in the Judiciary goes, due administration of justice definitely suffers.[273]

Perspective Publications v. State of Maharastra[274] involved an article entitled »Story of a Loan and Blitz Thackersey Libel Case,« published in the weekly periodical *Mainstream*. The author of the article made a clear imputation of impropreity, lack of integrity and oblique motives against Justice Tarkunde of the Bombay High Court for his decision in the »Thackersey Blitz Case«; the justice had awarded damages of Rs.300,000 in favor of one Krishnaraj Thackersey against the weekly newspaper *Blitz* and its editor. In the instant case, the Court held that the article constituted contempt of court:

> It is open to anyone to express fair, reasonable and legitimate criticism of any act or conduct of a judge in his judicial capacity or even to make a proper and fair comment on any decision given by him because »justice is not a cloistered virtue and she must be allowed to suffer the scrutiny and respectful though outspoken comments of ordinary men.« A distinction must be made between a mere libel or defamation of a judge and what amounts to a contempt of court. The test in each case would be whether the impugned publication is a mere defamatory attack on the judge or whether it is calculated to interfere with the due course of justice or the proper administration of law by his court. It is only in the latter case that it will be punishable as contempt. Alternatively the test will be whether the wrong is done to the judge personally or it is done to the public. . . . the publication of a disparaging statement will be an injury to the public if it tends to create an apprehension in the minds of the people regarding the integrity, ability or fairness of the judge or to deter actual or prospective litigants from placing complete reliance upon the court's administration of justice or if it is likely to cause embarassment in the mind of the judge himself in the discharge of his official duties.[275]

273 *Id.* at 1144. *See also* R.C. Cooper v. Union of India, 1970 A.I.R. 1318 (S.C.); Jagdish Prasad Saxena v. State of Madhya Bharat, 1961 A.I.R. 1070 (S.C.).

274 1971 A.I.R. 221 (S.C.). The article alleged that architects Khare-Tarkunde Private Ltd. of Nagpur got a loan facility of Rs.100,000 from the Bank of India through its directors Thackersey and Jaisinh Vithaldas, a relative of Thackersey. The partners of Khare-Tarkunde included the father, two brothers and other relatives of Justice Tarkunde, who awarded damages of Rs.30,000 against *Blitz* in favor of Thackersey. The decision and the sanction of the loan occured almost simultaneously.

275 *Id.* at 230. *See also* Brahma Prakash Sharma v. State of Uttar Pradesh, 1954 A.I.R. 10 (S.C.); In re Editor, Printer and Publisher of the Times of India, 1953 A.I.R. 75 (S.C.); Debi Prasad Sharma v. King Emperor, 1943 A.I.R. 202 (P.C.); Aswani Kumar v. Arabinda Bose, 1952 A.I.R. 369 (S.C.).

In *In re S. Mulgaokar*,[276] the Supreme Court held that criticisms of the judiciary must be strictly rational and sober and must proceed from the highest of motives, without being colored by partisan spirit or tactics. The judiciary cannot be immune from criticism; to criticise a judge fairly, albeit fiercely, is not a crime but a necessary right.[277] But if the criticism is based on an obvious distortion or gross misstatement of facts and is made in a manner that is designed to lower the prestige and reputation of the judiciary and destroy public confidence in it, it cannot be tolerated.[278]

In a fairly recent case, *National Textile Workers' Union v. P.R. Ramakrishnan*,[279] the accused made serious allegations, later published in a newspaper, against the judges of the Madras High Court. The gist of the allegations was that certain judgments given by the four judges of the high court proceeded from corrupt motives. Holding the contemner guilty under section 12 of the Contempt of Courts Act of 1971, the Court observed that the power to punish for contempt is granted to the Court not because the judges need protection but because the citizens need an impartial and strong judiciary. The conduct and writings of the contemner constituted serious interference with the administration of justice, since his sole objective in giving publicity to the defamatory allegations against the judges was to deter them from deciding cases against him or against those with whom he had an interest.[280]

On the role of the press in a democracy, the Court said that while commenting on matters pending in courts, the press should bear in mind that the parties to a case have as much right to redress at the hands of a court uninfluenced by external pressure as the press has to publish news and com-

276 1978 A.I.R. 727 (S.C.). The dispute arose out of an article in the December 13, 1977 edition of the *Indian Express*, where a holding of the Supreme Court in the so-called *Habeas Corpus* case (Additional District Magistrate of Jabalpur v. S. Shukla, 1976 A.I.R. 1207 (S.C.)) was allegedly distorted to serve ulterior objectives. The following sentence criticised a supposed Code of Judicial Ethics, wrongly assumed to have been drafted by some of the justices of the Supreme Court: »So adverse has been the criticism that the Supreme Court Judges, some of whom had prepared the draft Code, have disowned it.« In reality, the chief justice of the Supreme Court had suggested to the chief justices of the high courts that they meet to draft a code of ethics so as to prevent possible lapses from the path of rectitude and propreity on the part of judges. The contempt proceedings against the accused were later dropped by the Court.

277 E.S. VENKATARAMIAH, *supra* note 89, at 44–45; Dhavan Rajeev, *On the Law of the Press in India*, 26 J. INDIA L. INST. 288 (1984).

278 1978 A.I.R. at 733–34, 736–38.

279 1983 A.I.R. 759 (S.C.).

280 *Id.* at 760–61.

ments. While fair criticism, even if strong, may not be actionable, the attributing of improper motives without justification to judges that tends to bring them into ridicule, hatred or contempt is actionable because courts, as institutions of national importance, must be able to discharge their duties prescribed by the Constitution and the law without fear and favor.

In a recent case, *Vincent Panjkulangara v. Justice Krishna Iyer*,[281] the Kerala High Court observed that a judge's criticism, which prima facie appeared to be vitriolic, did not amount to contempt of court. The statement was not designed to lower the prestige and image of judiciary but rather had the laudable object of improving the workings of the administration of justice.

281 1983 Kerala Law Times 823. Justice Iyer, an activist judge on the Supreme Court, made some critical observations regarding the judiciary at a conference of advocates that he attended following his retirement; contempt proceedings ensued from his remarks.

Chapter XIV: National and International Copyright

A. *Copyright Act of 1957*

The Copyright Act of 1957[282] was enacted to consolidate the earlier laws relating to copyright and to make their provisions more effective. Coming into effect on January 21, 1958, the brief Act has as its primary object the protection from annexation and infringement by others[283] of the fruits of an author's labor, skill or intellect, through the creation of a proprietary and statutory right that the author[284] acquires in his work.[285] The author of the work shall be the first owner of the copyright, subject to the provisions of section 17 of the Act, and he will have the sole right to produce the work in any material form he likes. Being the sole owner of the work, the author: (i) may assign to any person the copyright in an existing or future work,[286] upon his signature in writing;[287] (ii) may relinquish all or any of the rights comprised by the copyright by giving notice in the prescribed form to the Registrar of Copyrigths;[288] and (iii) may grant to any person an interest in any existing or future work by license in writing signed by him or by his duly authorised agent.[289]

282 1957 India Cen. Act 14. The Copyright Act of 1847, 1847 India Cen. Act 20, was the earliest Indian law on the subject. In 1914, the Indian Copyright Act was passed, incorporating the English Copyright Act of 1911. To consolidate the law on the subject, the Copyright Act of 1957 was passed. *See* Annexure XIV.

283 Piracy of books and printed materials has become a major threat to the stability of the world book trade and a barrier to the development of an efficient and economical book publishing industry. The pirate is able to make quick money and to avoid paying taxes to the state and royalties to the author.

284 Copyright Act of 1957, § 2(d): »›author‹ means (i) in relation to a literary or dramatic work, the author of the work; (ii) in relation to a musical work, the composer; (iii) in relation to an artistic work other than a photograph, the artist; (iv) in relation to a photograph, the person taking the photograph; (v) in relation to a cinematograph film, the owner of the film at the time of its completion; and (vi) in relation to a record, the owner of the original plate from which the record was made, at the time of the making of the plate.«

285 *Id.* at § 2(y): »›work‹ means any of the following works, namely (i) a literary, dramatic, musical or artistic work; (ii) a cinematograph film; (iii) a record.«

286 *Id.* at § 17.

287 *Id.* at § 19.

288 *Id.* at § 21.

289 *Id.* at §§ 30, 31, 32.

The Copyright (Amendment) Act of 1983[290] and the Copyright (Amendment) Act of 1984[291] have extensively amended the Act of 1957, seeking to include within its purview the modern media of communication, such as »video films,«[292] »duplicating equipment,«[293] »compilations and computer programmes,«[294] etc., and to make punishment for infringement of copyright more harsh.[295]

B. *Infringement of Copyright*

Infringement of copyright is a trespass on a private domain owned and occupied by the owner of the copyright and is therefore punishable by law.[296] In other words, the infringement of copyright is in the nature of an invasion of a right in property; the intention of the infringer is immaterial, provided there is an infringement.

A copyright will be deemed to be infringed only when an act is done without the consent of the owner of the copyright. For an infringement of a copyright to be actionable in a court of law, there must be a »substantial infringement of the work«; fair appraisal and dealing with a work will not come within the scope of the Copyright Act.[297]

Section 51 of the Copyright Act specifies the acts that would, without a license from the owner of the copyright or statutory authority or in contravention of the terms thereof, amount to an infringement of the copyright in the work.[298] Section 52 enumerates the acts that would not constitute infringement of copyright, since such acts are arguably done in the public

290 1983 India Cen. Act 23.

291 1984 India Cen. Act 65.

292 *Id.* at § 2(f): »›Cinematograph film‹ includes the soundtrack, if any, and ›cinematograph‹ shall be construed as including any work by any process analogous to cinematography. *Explanation*: ›Video films‹ shall also be deemed to be work analogous to cinematography.«

293 *Id.* at § 2(hh): »›Duplicating equipment means any mechanical contrivance or device used or intended to be used for making copies of any work.«

294 *Id.* at § 2(o): »›Literary work‹ includes tables and compilations and computer programmes, that is to say, programmes recorded on any disc, tape, perforated media or other information storage device, which, if fed into or located in a computer or computer-based equipment, is capable of reproducing any information.« *See* Dhar, *Computer, Software and Copyright Protection: Indian Dilemma*, 1985 A.I.R. JOURNAL 50.

295 Copyright (Amendment) Act of 1984, §§ 63 and 63A.

296 *See* G. WILLIAMS, TEXT BOOK OF CRIMINAL LAW 637–38, 686–87 (1978).

297 S.K. Dutt v. Law Book Co., 1954 A.I.R. 570 (Allahabad H.C.).

298 *See* Annexure XIV.

interest.[299] Section 52A prescribes the particulars to be included in records and video films so as to identify the true owner and the authority under which the work had been produced.[300]
Protection against the infringement of copyright is not infinite. It is limited to the author's lifetime plus fifty years after his or her death, measured from the beginning of the calendar year next following the year in which such author dies. The same rule of fifty years is applicable in cases where the government is the owner of the copyright.[301] Since the infringement of copyright is not only a civil wrong but also a criminal wrong, the Act provides for both civil and criminal action in the case of an encroachment of the copyright of the owner.[302] An aggrieved owner of a copyright may institute the necessary civil or criminal proceedings in the appropriate court of law for enforcement of his right.

C. *Civil Liability for Infringement of Copyright*

The civil remedies for infringement of copyright are provided in Sections 54 to 62 of the Copyright Act. They include: (i) damages, (ii) an injunction, (iii) an accounting,[303] (iv) recovery of possession of infringing copies[304] and (v) damages for conversion, since the proceeds from the sale of the infringing copies are the owner's property converted by the infringer to his own use.
In *R.G. Ananad v. Messrs. Delux Films*,[305] the appellant's suit for violation of copyright in his drama *Hum Hindustani* was dismissed by the Supreme Court, which said that, since a violation of copyright amounts to an act of

299 *See* Messrs. Blackwood and Sons Ltd. v. A.N. Parasuraman, 1959 A.I.R. 410 (Madras H.C.).
300 *See* Annexure XIV.
301 Copyright Act of 1957, §§ 22–29.
302 *Id.* at §§ 54–70.
303 *Id.* at § 55(1). See Associated Publishers (Madras) Ltd. v. Bashyam alias »Arya«, 1961 A.I.R. 114 (Madras H.C.) (held, copyright is a right of property and any injury caused to such right will give rise to a claim for damages); Dharam Dutt v. Ram Lal, 1957 A.I.R. 161 (Punjab H.C.) (held, it is well settled that damages for conversion in a copyright case are to be calculated at the time of conversion, which takes place when a party deals with goods in manner inconsistent with the right of the owner).
304 Copyright Act of 1957, § 58. *See* Gopal Das v. Jagannath Prasad, 1938 A.I.R. 266 (Allahabad H.C.) (held, the owner of the copyright, being the absolute master of the property in copyright, has a right to recover the possession of the infringing copies unsold and the price of the copies sold, such infringing copies being regarded as the property of the owner).
305 1978 A.I.R. 1613 (S.C.).

piracy, the violation must be proved by clear and cogent evidence. Where the same ideas are being developed in different manners, it is manifest that, the source being common, similarities are bound to occur. Violation of copyright exists when the similarities are on fundamental or substantial aspects of the mode of expression and are nothing but a basic imitation, with few variations, of the copyrighted work. One of the surest and safest tests for violation of copyright, said the Court, is whether the reader, spectator or viewer, after having read or seen both of the works, is clearly of the opinion that the subsequent work appears to be a copy of the original. The Court further held that there cannot be a copyright in an event that has actually taken place. There is a distinction between the materials upon which one claiming copyright has worked and the product of the application of one's skill, judgment, labor and talent; the former are common property and are not subject to copyright.

The Judicial Committee of the Privy Council, in the case of *Macmillan and Co. Ltd. v. K. and J. Cooper*,[306] held that piracy of a copyright occurs when the original has been either substantially copied or so imitated as to be a mere evasion of the copyright.

In *K.R. Venugopala Sarma v. Sangu Ganesan*,[307] the Madras High Court held that an infringement of copyright is complete even though the reproduction was not exact, because the effect on the mind of the spectator by seeing the two pictures was that the defendant's picture was nothing but a copy of the plaintiff's picture. The court observed:

> [T]he degree of resemblance between the two pictures, which is to be judged by the eye, must be such that the person looking at the [defendant's] picture must get the suggestion that it is the [plaintiff's] picture. One picture can be said to be a copy of another picture only if a substantial part of the former picture finds a place in the reproduction.[308]

In the case of *N.T. Raghunathan v. All-India Reporter Ltd.*,[309] the Bombay High Court held that since the defendant had copied the ideas and

306 1924 A.I.R. 25 (P.C.).

307 1972 Crim. L.J. 1098 (Madras H.C.).

308 *Id.* at 1100.

309 1971 A.I.R. 48 (Bombay H.C.). *See also* Romesh Choudhary v. Ali Mohamad Nosheri, 1965 A.I.R. 101 (Jamma and Kashmir H.C.) (held, in order to be actionable, the infringement must be a colorable imitation of the original with the purpose of deriving profit); Daily Calendar Supplying Bureau v. United Concern, 1967 A.I.R. 381 (Madras H.C.); Cunniah and Co. v. Balraj and Co., 1961 A.I.R. 111 (Madras H.C.); Mohendra Chundra Nath Ghosh v. Emperor, 1928 A.I.R. 359 (Calcutta H.C.); Mohini Mohan Singh v. Sita Nath, 1931 A.I.R. 233 (Calcutta H.C.).

style of an abridgement, the expression of those ideas and the form in which they were expressed, a case for violation of copyright had been made out.

In *Indian Performing Right Society Ltd. v. Eastern India Motion Picture Association,*[310] the Supreme Court held that an author (composer) of a lyric or musical work who has authorised a film producer to appropriate his work for the soundtrack of a cinemtographic film cannot restrain the film owner from screening the film in public for profit, from making any record from the soundtrack associated with the film or from communicating or authorising the communication of the film by radio diffusion.[311] In such cases, said the Court, the owner of the film cannot be said to wrongfully appropriate anything that belongs to the composer of the lyric or musical work. The copyright (comprising a bundle of exclusive rights mentioned in section 14(1)(c) of the Copyright Act) vests in a cinematographic film on its completion, which is said to take place when the visual and audible portions are synchronised.

D. *Criminal Liability for Infringement of Copyright*

Sections 63 to 70 of the Copyright Act provide punishment for various types of criminal offences committed in relation to or connected with the infringement of copyright. The provisions are quite exhaustive and cover various types of infringement. For instance, section 63 makes infringement of copyright or other rights conferred by the Act an offence and provides for punishment that may extend to three years of imprisonment and a fine of up to Rs.200,000, with a minimum of not less than six months of imprisonment and not less than Rs.50,000. Section 63A, which had been inserted by the Copyright (Amendment) Act of 1984, provides for an enhanced penalty in cases of second and subsequent convictions.[312]

Section 63 requires the ingredient of *mens rea* on the part of the accused for conviction under the Act. That is to say, the accused must be shown to have knowingly infringed the copyright in a work or violated a right conferred by the Act. The court must thus consider whether there was an infringement of the copyright in the work concerned and whether such infringement was with the requisite *mens rea.*[313]

310 1977 A.I.R. 1443 (S.C.).

311 *See* Annexure XIV.

312 *Id.*

313 A. Susiah v. Muniswamy, 1966 A.I.R. 175 (Madras H.C.); J.N. Bogga v. All-India Reporter Ltd., 1969 A.I.R. 302 (Bombay H.C.).

Section 64 of the Act empowers a police officer not below the rank of sub-inspector to seize and produce before a magistrate as soon as possible all copies of the work, wherever found, if he is satisfied that an offence has been committed in respect of the infringement of copyright.

Additional offences under the Act include: possession of plates for the purpose of making infringing copies,[314] making false entries in the Register of Copyrights or producing or tendering false entries,[315] making false statements for the purpose of deceiving any authority or officer[316] and offences by companies (in such cases, the company and its officers are equally liable for infringement).[317]

In view of the technical nature of the offence, only a first class magistrate or a presidency magistrate can try offences under the Act.[318] Regardless of whether an alleged offender is convicted, the magistrate may order all copies of the work or all plates in possession of the alleged offender be delivered to the owner of the copyright.

E. *International Copyright Applicability in India*

The Copyright Act, in sections 40 to 43, has incorporated the provisions relating to international copyright. Section 40 empowers the central government to extend copyright to foreign works.[319] Section 41 authorises the government to specify the publications of international organisations that are to enjoy copyright under the Act. The International Organisation Order of 1958 was then promulgated, specifying the United Nations and its agencies and the Organisation of American States as organisations to which section 41 shall be applicable. Section 42 authorises the central government to restrict the rights in the work of foreign authors first published in India if it appears to the government that a foreign country does not give or has not undertaken to give adequate protection to the works of Indian authors. Section 43 provides for the laying of orders made by the central government before both houses of Parliament for their approval.

314 *See* Annexure XIV at § 65.
315 *Id.* at § 67.
316 *Id.* at § 68.
317 *Id.* at § 69.
318 Copyright Act of 1957, § 70.
319 *See* Annexure XIV.

ANNEXURES

ANNEXURE I

GROWTH OF TELECOMMUNICATION SERVICES FROM 1948 TO 1984

ITEM	1948	1978	1979	1980	1983	1984
1. Switching equipment capacity (millions of lines)	.100	2.017	2.188	2.336	2.827	3.053
2. Underground cables (million pair km)	N/A	9.988	10.782	11.748	14.580	15.707
3. Direct exchange lines (millions)	.082	1.777	1.868	2.016	2.465	2.667
4. Telephones connected to telephone systems* (millions)	.168	2.247	2.423	2.615	3.215	3.462
5. Telephone exchange	321	6238	6866	7430	9288	9978
6. Trunk automatic exchanges	–	17	17	18	24	28
7. Trunk automatic exchange lines	–	30,450	34,000	40,300	54,520	80,620
8. Stations connected to trunk automatic exchanges	–	77	108	125	205	237
9. Subscriber trunk dialing routes (point-topoint)	–	114	131	137	189.5	201
10. Telegraph offices, including combined offices	3824	17,905	21,711	24,457	30,761	34,334
11. Telex exchanges	–	101	117	136	170	176
12. Telex subscribers	–	14,641	16,447	17,983	21,496	22,552
13. Telex capacity (lines)	–	19,865	212,025	22,015	26,100	29,844
14. Long-distance public call offices	328	8730	11,732	13,830	18,999	21,083

* Around 1.15 million telephone connections were added to the network during the VIth Five-Year Plan (1981–1985). About 800,000 potential subscribers, or 25% of the number of working connections, are waiting for connections.

Source: MINISTRY OF INFORMATION AND BROADCASTING, INDIA 1985 474 (Table 23.1).

ANNEXURE II

COMPARATIVE STATEMENT OF ANNUAL GROSS INVESTMENT IN TELECOMMUNICATIONS IN DEVELOPED AND DEVELOPING COUNTRIES (IN NATIONAL CURRENCIES AT CURRENT PRICES)

	Investment in Millions			Ratio of Investment to GDP			Ratio of Investment to Gross Fixed Capital Formation		
	1969	1974	1978	1969	1974	1978	1969	1974	1978
A. Developed Countries									
1. Australia	297.7	561.1	937.3	1.10	1.11	1.03	4.1	4.7	4.49
2. Belgium	6302.0	12,633.0	15,567.0	0.547	0.659	N/A	2.394	2.696	N/A
3. Fed. Rep. Germany	3481.1	6355.7	6280.1	0.758	1.01	0.60	2.183	2.945	2.157
4. Canada	693.0	1520.0	2101.0	0.979	1.149	1.00	4.02	4.43	4.03
5. France	3448.0	9932.0	19,890.0	0.491	0.777	1.06	2.10	3.195	4.66
6. Japan	603,853.0	1,219,405.0	1,671,743.0	0.934	1.04	0.857	2.615	2.822	2.867
7. Norway	449.0	922.0	2204.0	0.725	0.805	1.165	2.63	2.32	3.38
8. Sweden	136,426.0	219,338.0	352,519.0	0.47	0.42	0.41	1.86	1.68	1.90
9. United Kingdom	372.0	696.0	845.0	0.44	0.73	0.86	1.92	3.22	4.16
10. United States	6426.0	11,749.0	15,904.0	0.76	0.92	0.82	0.49	0.60	0.48
B. Developing Countries									
1. Afghanistan	14.0	15.6	75.4	—	0.021	—	—	—	—
2. Argentina	270.2	1093.1	211,464.6	0.38	0.31	N/A	1.72	1.48	N/A
3. Burma	4.68	2.73	162.17	0.047	0.024	0.053	0.435	0.205	0.785
4. Brazil	N/A	5847.0	28,206.0	—	0.81	0.82	—	3.35	3.68
5. Mexico	1071.0	3291.0	9299.0	0.286	0.404	—	1.47	1.79	—
6. India	360.0	919.0	2273.0	—	0.17	0.49	—	1.03	1.31
7. Bangladesh	—	—	303.35	—	—	0.246	—	—	1.51
8. Sri Lanka	15.3	—	115.0	0.14	—	0.39	0.67	—	2.47
9. Singapore	24.1	—	177.8	0.49	—	1.19	2.50	—	3.38
10. Korea	13,384.0	43,370.0	204,816.0	0.56	1.13	1.47	2.42	2.47	3.90

Source: MINISTRY OF COMMUNICATIONS, TELECOMMUNICATIONS – VIth FIVE-YEAR-PLAN (1981-1985) 228-29.

ANNEXURE III

COUNTRIES SERVICED BY OCS TELEX

Destinations to which fully automatic,
subscriber-dialed telex service is available
(December 31, 1984)

Afghanistan
Alaska (U.S.)
Algeria
Angola
Anguila
Antigua
Argentina
Australia
Austria
Bahamas
Bahrain
Barbados
Belgium
Benin
Bermuda
Bolivia
Botswana
Brazil
Brunei
Bulgaria
Burma
Camaroon
Canada (CNP & TWX)
Cayman Islands
Central African Republic
Chad
Chile
China (PRC)
Columbia
Cook Island
Congo
Costa Rica
Cuba
Cyprus
Czechoslovakia
Denmark
Djibouti
Dominica
Dominican Republic
Ecuador
El Salvador
Ethiopia
Falkland Islands (U.K.)
Faeroe Islands (Denmark)
Fiji
Finland
France
Gabon
Gambia
Germany (G.D.R.)
Germany (F.R.G.)
Ghana
Gibraltar (U.K.)
Greece
Greenland
Grenada
Guadeloupe (France)
Guam
Guatemala
Guinea
Guyana
Haiti
Hawaii (U.S.)
Honduras
Hong Kong
Hungary
Iceland
Indonesia
Iran
Iraq
Ireland
Israel
Italy
Ivory Coast
Jamaica
Japan
Jordan
Kenya
Korea (South)
Kuwait
Lebanon
Lesotho
Liberia
Libya
Luxemburg
Macao (Portugal)
Malagasy Republic
Malawi

Malaysia
Maldives
Malta
Mariana Islands
Marshall Islands
Martinique (France)
Mauritania
Mauritius
Mexico
Montserrat (U.K.)
Morocco
Mozambique
Nauru
Nepal
Netherlands
Netherlands Antilles
New Caledonia (France)
New Zealand
Niger
Nigeria
Nicaragua
Norfolk Island
Norway
Oman
Pakistan
Panama
Papua New Guinea
Paraguay
Peru
Phillipines (Philcom, ITT, GM, ETPI)
Poland
Portugal
Puerto Rico
Qatar
Réunion (France)
Roumania
Samoa (U.S.)
Samoa (Western)
San Marino
Saudi Arabia
Senegal
Seychelles (U.K.)
Sierra Leone
Singapore
Solomon Islands
Somalia
South Africa
Spain
Sri Lanka
St. Christopher
St. Lucia
St. Pierre and Miquelon (France)
St. Vincent
Surinam
Swaziland
Sweden
Switzerland
Sudan
Syria
Taiwan
Tanzania
Thailand
Tonga
Trinidad and Tobago
Tunisia
Turkey
Turks and Caicos Islands
United Arab Emirates
Uganda
Union of Soviet Socialist Republics
United Kingdom
United States (RCA, ITT, TWC, WUL, WUD, FTC and TRT)
Uruguay
Vanuatu
Vatican City
Venezuela
Virgin Islands (U.K.)
Virgin Islands (U.S.)
Yemen (P.D.R.)
Yemen Arab Republic
Yugoslavia
Zaire
Zambia
Zimbabwe

Source: MINISTRY OF COMMUNICATIONS, REPORT 1984-1985 68-69.

ANNEXURE IV

ORGANISATION CHART OF THE MINISTRY OF INFORMATION AND BROADCASTING

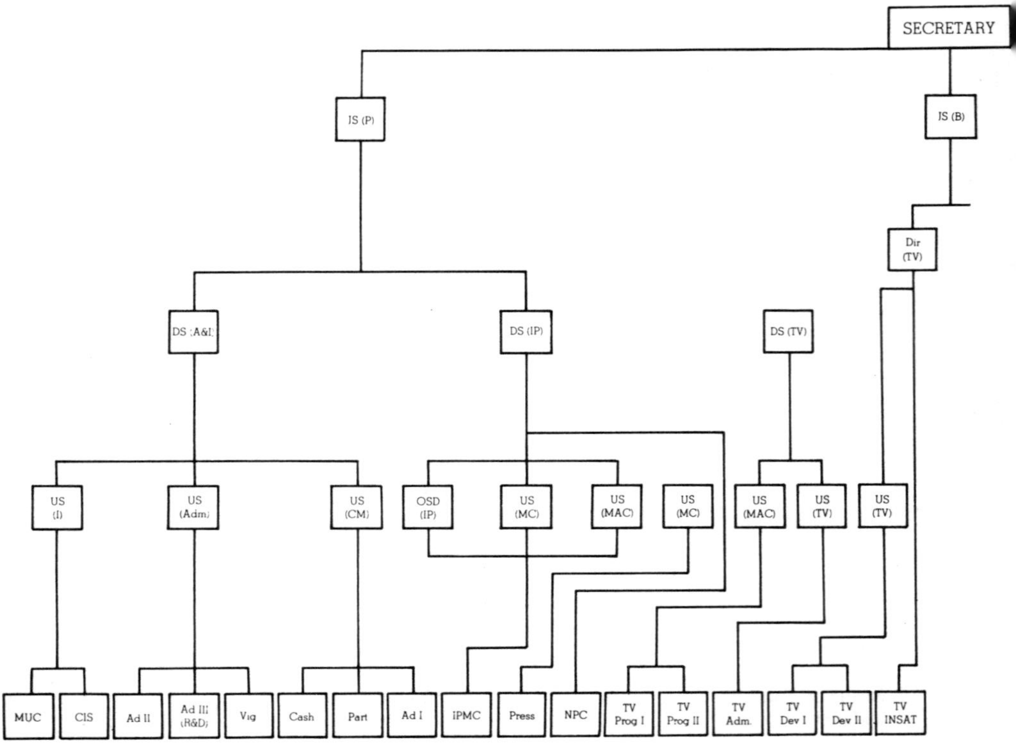

LEGEND

1. J.S. (P) — Joint Secretary (Policy)
2. J.S. (B) — Joint Secretary (Broadcasting)
3. J.S. (F) — Joint Secretary (Films)
4. J.S. (FA) — Joint Secretary (Financial Adviser)
5. C.C.A. — Chief Controller of Accounts
6. Dir. (TV) — Director (TV)
7. Dir. (A.I.R.) — Director (All India Radio)
8. Dy. Secy. (T.V.) — Deputy Secretary (Television)
9. D.S. (A & I) — Deputy Secretary (Administration & Information)
10. D.S. (I.P.) — Deputy Secretary (Information Policy)
11. D.S. (D) — Deputy Secretary (Films)
12. D.S. (F) — Deputy Secretary (Films)
13. D.S. (Fin.) — Deputy Secretary (Finance)
14. FFO — Facilities Officer (Films)
15. U.S. (I) — Under Secretary (Information)
16. U.S. (A) — Under Secretary (Administration)
17. U.S. (CM) — Under Secretary (Career Management)
18. U.S. (MC) — Under Secretary (Media Coordination)
19. U.S. (MAC) — Under Secretary (Media Advisory Committee)
20. U.S. (B) — Under Secretary (Broadcasting)

21. U.S. (BP) — Under Secretary (Broadcasting Policy)
22. U.S. (TV) — Under Secretary (Television)
23. U.S. (Fin.)-I — Under Secretary (Finance)-I
24. U.S. (PC & Fin.)-II — Under Secretary (Plan Coordination & Finance)-II
25. U.S. (Fin.)-III — Under Secretary (Finance)-III
26. O.S.D. (IP) — Officer on Special Duty (Information Policy)
27. S.A. (WM) — Senior Analyst (Work Measurement)
28. S.A. (O & M) — Senior Analyst (Organisation & Methods)
29. D.D. (OL) — Deputy Director (Official Language)
30. D.C.A. (HQR) — Deputy Controller of Accounts (Headquarters)
31. D.C.A. (IC) — Deputy Controller of Accounts (Internal Check)
32. D.C.A. (IRLA) — Deputy Controller of Accounts (Internal Running Ledger Accou
33. Admn. I — Administration I Section
34. Admn. II — Administration II Section
35. Admn. III (R & D) — Administration III Section
36. Cash — Cash Section
37. Parl. Cell — Parliament Cell
38. M.U.C. — Media Unit Cell
39. Press — Press Section
40. Vigl. — Vigilance Section

(As on January 1, 1986)

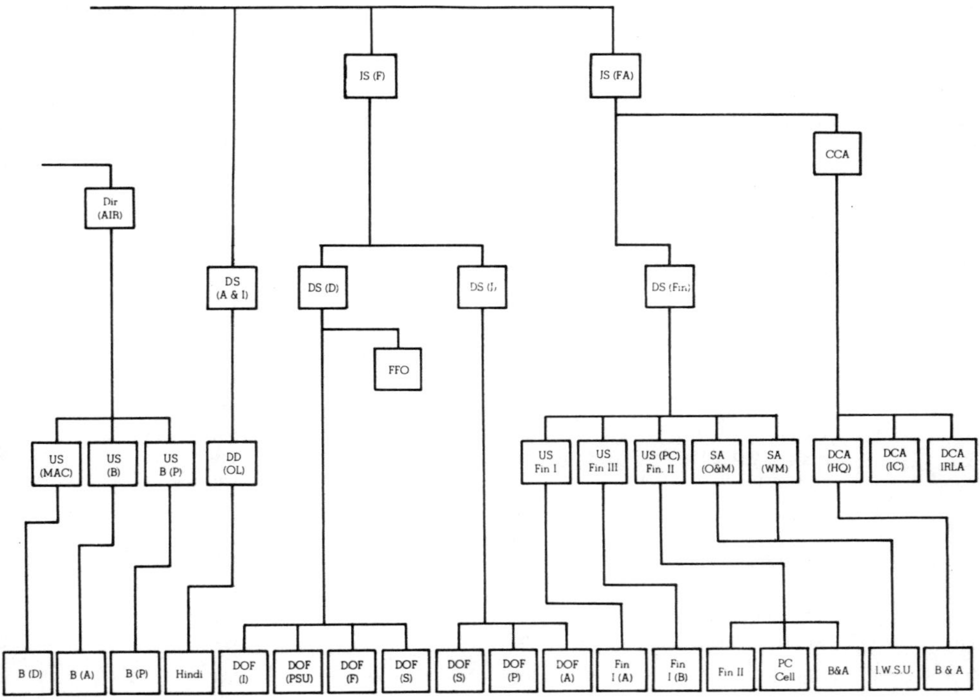

41. I.P. & M.C. — Information Policy and Media Coordination Section
42. N.P.C. — News Pool Cell
43. T.V. — Television Section
44. B (D) — Broadcasting (Development) Section
45. B (A) — Broadcasting (Administration) Section
46. B (P) — Broadcasting (Policy) Section
47. Hindi — Hindi Section
48. D.O.F. (I) — Desk Officer, Film (Industry)
49. D.O.F. (PSU) — Desk Officer, Film (Public Sector Undertakings)
50 D.O.F. (F) — Desk Officer, Film (Festivals)
51. D.O.F. (P) — Desk Officer, Film (Production)
52. D.O.F. (S) — Desk Officer, Film (Societies)
53. D.O.F. (A) — Desk Officer, Film (Administration)
54. B & A — Budget and Accounts
55. Fin. I (A) — Finance I (A) Section
56. Fin. I (B) — Finance I (B) Section
57. Fin. II — Finance II Section
58. P.C. Cell — Plan Coordination Cell
59. I.W.S.U. — Internal Work Study Unit
60. C.I.S. — Central Information Service Section

ANNEXURE V

ENTERTAINMENT TAX, INCLUDING SURCHARGE

(As of January 3, 1979)

State	Basic Admission Rate (Paise)	Total Tax (%)	Gross Admission Rate (Paise)
1. Andhra Pradesh	100	55	155
	200	65	330
	300	65	495
2. Assam	100	80	180
	200	100	400
	300	100	600
3. Bihar	100	100	200
	200	100	400
	300	100	600
4. Delhi	100	60	160
	200	60	320
	300	60	480
5. Gujarat	100	50	150
(cities of 100,000+	200	52.5	305
residents)	300	57	470
6. Gujarat	100	47.5	147.5
(cities of 50,000 –	200	50	300
100,000 residents)	300	54	462.5
7. Gujarat	100	45	145
(cities of less than	200	47.5	295
50,000 residents)	300	52	455
8. Karnataka	100	60	160
	200	70	340
	300	70	510
9. Madhya Pradesh	100	40	140
	200	50	300
	300	50	450
10. Maharashtra (Bombay, Pune,	100	42.5	142.5
Nagpur and Sholapur	200	56	312.5
	300	62.5	487.5
11. Maharashtra (other cities)	100	37.5	137.5
	200	50	300
	300	57	470
12. Himachal Pradesh	100	75	175
	200	75	350
	300	75	525

State	Basic Admission Rate (Paise)	Total Tax (%)	Gross Admission Rate (Paise)
13. Jammu and Kashmir	100	60	160
	200	60	320
	300	60	480
14. Haryana	100	100	200
	200	100	400
	300	100	600
15. Chandigarh	100	100	160
	200	60	320
	300	60	480
16. Orissa	100	40	140
	200	60	320
	300	60	480
17. Punjab	100	100	200
	200	125	450
	300	125	675
18. Rajasthan	100	60	160
	200	100	400
	300	100	600
19. Tamil Nadu	100	76	176
	200	95	390
	300	93	580
20. Uttar Pradesh	100	125	225
	200	125	450
	300	117	650
21. West Bengal (black and white)	100	70	170
	200	95	390
	300	123	670
22. West Bengal (color)	100	110	210
	200	132	465
	300	157	770

In Kerala, the tax is levied by the respective local authorities. The rate levied is to be not less than 15% and not more than 30%. A surcharge of 60% is also levied on the entertainmant tax amount. In Punjab, a 100% tax is levied on the first 40% of the seats and a 125% tax on the remainder.

Source: WORKING GROUP ON NATIONAL FILM POLICY, REPORT 115-17 (1980).

ANNEXURE VI

GUIDELINES FOR FILM CERTIFICATION

In the exercise of the powers conferred by sub-section (2) of Section 5B of the Cinematograph Act of 1952, the Central Government hereby directs that, in sanctioning films for public exhibition, the Board of Film Censors shall be guided by the following principles:

(1) The objectives of film censorship will be to ensure that:
- (a) the medium of film remains responsible and sensitive to the values and standards of society;
- (b) artistic expression and creative freedom are not unduly curbed; and
- (c) censorship is responsive to social change.

(2) In pursuance of the above objectives, the Board of Film Censors shall ensure that:
- (a) anti-social activities, such as violence, are not glorified or justified;
- (b) the *modus operandi* of criminals or other visuals or words likely to incite the commission of any offence are not depicted;
- (c) pointless or avoidable scenes of violence, cruelty and horror are not shown;
- (d) scenes which have the effect of justifying or glorifying drinking are not shown;
- (e) human sensibilities are not offended by vulgarity, obscenity and depravity;
- (f) visuals or words depicting women in ignoble servility to men or glorifying such servility as a praiseworthy quality in women are not presented;
- (g) the sovereignty and integrity of India is not called in question;
- (h) the security of the State is not jeopardised or endangered;
- (i) friendly relations with foreign States are not strained;
- (j) public order is not endangered; and
- (k) visuals or words involving defamation or contempt of court are not presented.

(3) The Board of Film Censors shall also ensure that the film:
- (a) is judged in its entirety from the point of view of the overall impact, and
- (b) is examined in the light of contemporary standards of the country and the people to which the film relates.

(4) Films that meet the above-mentioned criteria but are considered unsuitable for exhibition to non-adults shall be certified for exhibition to adult audiences only.

Source: Notification from the Ministry of Information and Broadcasting, *Extraordinary Gazette of India*, July 1, 1978, part II(3)(ii)

ANNEXURE VII

§ 7 OF THE CINEMATOGRAPH (AMENDMENT) ACT OF 1984

(1) If any person –

(a) exhibits or permits to be exhibited in any place –

(i) any film other than a film which has been certified by the Board as suitable for unrestricted public exhibition or for public exhibition restricted to adults or to members of any profession or any class of persons and which, when exhibited, displays the prescribed mark of the Board and has not been altered or tampered with in any way since such mark was affixed thereto;

(ii) any film which has been certified by the Board as suitable for public exhibition restricted to adults, to any person who is not an adult; or

(iii) any film which has been certified by the Board as suitable for public exhibition restricted to any profession or class of persons, to a person who is not a member of such profession or who is not a member of such class; or

(b) without lawful authority (the burden of proving which shall be on him), alters or tampers with in any way any film after it has been certified; or

(c) fails to comply with the provisions contained in section 6A^{+} or with any order made by the Central Government, or by the Board in the exercise of any of the powers or functions conferred on it by this Act or the rules made thereunder,

he shall be punishable with imprisonment for a term which may extend to three years, or with fine which may extend to 100,000 rupees or with both, and in the case of a continuing offence with a further fine which may extend to 20,000 rupees for each day during which the offence continues.

Provided that a person who exhibits or permits to be exhibited in any place video film in contravention of the provisions of sub-clause (i) of the clause (a) shall be punishable with imprisonment for a term which shall not be less than three months, but which may extend to three years and with fine which shall not be less than 20,000 rupees, but which may extend to 100,000 rupees, and in the case of a continuing offence with a further fine which may extend to 20,000 rupees for each day during which the offence continues.

Provided further that a court may, for adequate and special reasons to be mentioned in the judgement, impose a sentence of imprisonment for a term of less than three months or a fine of less than 20,000 rupees.

+ § 6A reads: »Any person who delivers any certified film to any distributor or exhibitor shall . . . notify . . . the title, the length of the film, the number and the nature of the certificate granted in respect thereof and the conditions, if any, subject to which it has been so granted … .«

ANNEXURE VIII

SELECTED PROVISIONS OF THE INDIAN PENAL CODE

§ 292: Sale, etc. of Obscene Books, etc.

(1) For purposes of sub-section (2), a book, pamphlet, paper, writing, drawing, painting, representation, figure or any other object shall be deemed to be obscene if it is lascivious or appeals to the prurient interest or if its effect, or (where it comprises two or more distinct items) the effect of any one of its items, is, if taken as a whole, such as to tend to deprave and corrupt persons who are likely, having regard to all relevant circumstances, to read, see or hear the matter contained or embodied in it;

(2) Whoever –

(a) sells, lets to hire, distributes, publicly exhibits or in any manner puts into circulation, or for purposes of sale, hire, distribution, public exhibition or circulation, makes, produces or has in his possession any obscene book, pamphlet, paper, drawing, painting, representation or figure or any other obscene object whatsoever; or

(b) imports, exports or conveys any obscene objects for any of the purposes aforesaid, or knowing or having reason to believe that such object will be sold, let to hire, distributed or publicly exhibited or in any manner put into circulation; or

(c) takes part in or receives profits from any business in the course of which he knows or has reason to believe that any such obsene objects are, for any of the purposes aforesaid, made, produced, purchased, kept, imported, exported, conveyed, publicly exhibited or in any manner put into circulation; or

(d) advertises or makes known by any means whatsoever that any person is engaged or is ready to engage in any act which is an offence under this section, or that any such obscene object can be procured from or through any person; or

(e) offers or attempts to do any act which is an offence under this section, shall be punished on first conviction with imprisonment of either description for a term which may extend to two years, and with fine which may extend to two thousand rupees, and, in the event of a second or subsequent conviction, with imprisonment of either description for a term which may extend to five years, and also with fine which may extend to five thousand rupees.

Exception – This section does not extend to –

(a) any book, pamphlet, paper, writing, drawing, painting, representation or figure –

(i) the publication of which is proved to be justified as being for the public good on the ground that such book, pamphlet, paper, writing, drawing, painting, representation or figure is in the interest of science, literature, art, or learning or other objects of general concern, or

(ii) which is kept or used *bona fide* for religious purposes;

(b) any representation sculptured, engraved, painted or otherwise represented on or in –

(i) any ancient monument within the meaning of the Ancient Monuments and Archaeological Sites and Remains Act of 1958 (24 of 1958), or

(ii) any temple, or any car used for the conveyance of idols, or kept or used for any religious purpose.

§ 293: Sale, etc. of Obscene Objects to Young Persons

Whoever sells, lets to hire, distributes, exhibits or circulates to any person under the age of twenty years any such obscene object as is referred to in the last preceding section, or offers or attempts so to do, shall be punished on first conviction with imprisonment of either description for a term which may extend to two thousand rupees, and, in the event of a second or subsequent conviction, with imprisonment of either description for a term which may extend to seven years, and also with fine which may extend to five thousand rupees.

§ 294: Obscene Acts and Songs

Whoever, to the annoyance of others,
(a) does any obscene act in any public place, or
(b) sings, recites or utters any obscene songs, ballads or words, in or near any public place,
shall be punished with imprisonment of either description for a term which may extend to three months, or with a fine or with both.

§ 499: Defamation

Whoever by words either spoken or intended to be read, or by signs or by visible representations, makes or publishes any imputation concerning any person intending to harm, or knowing or having reason to believe that such imputation will harm the reputation of such person, is said, except in the cases hereinafter excepted, to defame that person.
Explanation 1. – It may amount to defamation to impute anything to a deceased person, if the imputation would harm the reputation of that person if living, and is intended to be hurtful to the feelings of his family or other near relatives.
Explanation 2. – It may amount to defamation to make an imputation concerning a company or an association or collection of persons as such.
Explanation 3. – An imputation in the form of an alternative or expressed ironically may amount to defamation.
Explanation 4. – No imputation is said to harm a person's reputation, unless that imputation directly or indirectly, in the estimation of others, lowers the moral or intellectual character of that person, or causes it to be believed that the body of that person is in a loathsome state, or in a state generally considered as disgraceful.
First Exception. – It is not defamation to impute anything which is true concerning any person, if it be for the public good that the imputation should be made or published. Whether or not it is for the public good is a question of fact.
Second Exception. – It is not defamation to express in good faith any opinion whatever respecting the conduct of a public servant in the discharge of his public functions, or

respecting his character, so far as his character appears in that conduct, and no further.
Third Exception. – It is not defamation to express in good faith any opinion whatever respecting the conduct of any person touching any public question, and respecting his character, so far as his character appears in that conduct, and no further.
Fourth Exception. – It is not defamation to publish a substantially true report of the proceedings of a Court of Justice, or of the result of any such proceedings.
Explanation. – A Justice of the peace or other officer holding an enquiry in open Court preliminary to a trial in a Court of Justice, is a Court within the meaning of the above section.
Fifth Exception. – It is not defamation to express in good faith any opinion whatever respecting the merits of any case, civil or criminal which has been decided by a Court of Justice or respecting the conduct of any person as a party, witness or agent, in any such case, or respecting the character of such person, as far as his character appears in that conduct, and no further.
Sixth Exception. – It is not defamation to express in good faith any opinion respecting the merits of any performance which its author has submitted to the judgment of the public, or respecting the character of the author so far as his character appears in such performance, and no further.
Explanation. – A performance may be submitted to the judgment of the public expressly or by acts on the part of the author which imply such submission to the judgment of the public.
Seventh Exception. – It is not defamation in a person having over another authority, either conferred by law or arising out of lawful contract made with that other, to pass in good faith any censure on the conduct of that other in matters to which such lawful authority relates.
Eighth Exception. – It is not defamation to prefer in good faith an accusation against any person to any of those who have lawful authority over that person with respect to the subject-matter of the accusation.
Ninth Exception. – It is not defamation to make an imputation on the character of another, provided that the imputation be made in good faith for the protection of the interest of the person making it, or of any other person, or for the public good.
Tenth Exception. – It is not defamation to convey a caution, in good faith, to one person against another, provided that such caution be intended for the good of the person to whom it is conveyed, or of some person in whom that person is interested, or for the public good.

§ 500: Punishment for Defamation

Whoever defames another shall be punished with simple imprisonment for a term which may extend to two years, or with fine, or with both.

§ 501: Punishment for Defamation

Whoever prints or engraves any matter, knowing or having good reason to believe that such matter is defamatory of any person, shall be punished with simple imprisonment for a term which may extend to two years, or with fine, or with both.

§ 502: Punishment for Defamation

Whoever sells or offers for sale any printed or engraved substance containing defamatory matter, knowing that it contains such matter shall be punished with simple imprisonment for a term which may extend to two years, or with fine, or with both.

ANNEXURE IX

NUMBER OF NEWSPAPERS IN INDIA (1981)

State/Territory	Dailies	Tri-/Bi-weeklies	Weeklies	Others	TOTAL
1. Andra Pradesh	62	2	377	627	1068
2. Assam	6	4	66	89	165
3. Bihar	43	4	304	263	614
4. Gujarat	36	2	165	449	652
5. Haryana	12	–	134	222	368
6. Himachal Pradesh	1	–	21	55	77
7. Jammu and Kashmir	25	–	111	38	174
8. Karnataka	105	4	213	621	943
9. Kerala	103	2	135	765	1005
10. Madhya Pradesh	102	9	357	223	691
11. Maharashtra	166	25	642	1727	2560
12. Manpur	30	2	3	40	75
13. Meghalaya	1	4	23	22	50
14. Nagaland	–	–	4	2	6
15. Orissa	11	–	40	262	313
16. Punjab	34	1	210	355	600
17. Rajasthan	87	3	414	527	1031
18. Tamil Nadu	104	6	147	959	1216
19. Tripura	13	1	42	11	67
20. Uttar Pradesh	178	18	1342	1164	2702
21. West Bengal	57	7	464	1587	2115
22. Arunachal Pradesh	–	–	–	–	–
23. Andaman and Nicobar Islands	4	–	5	8	17
24. Chandigarh	11	–	33	123	167
25. Dadra and Nagar Haveli	–	–	1	–	1
26. Delhi	48	2	342	1933	2325
27. Goa, Daman and Diu	8	–	9	30	47
28. Lakshadweep	–	–	–	–	–
29. Mizoram	17	1	14	12	44
30. Pondicherry	–	1	6	44	51
TOTAL	1264	98	5624	12,158	19,144

Source: MINISTRY OF INFORMATION AND BROADCASTING, INDIA 1983: A REFERENCE MANUAL 159–60.

ANNEXURE X

NUMBER AND CIRCULATION OF NEWSPAPERS, BY LANGUAGE

Language		Dailies	Tri-/Bi-weeklies	Weeklies	Others	TOTAL
1. Hindi	N	470	27	2709	2730	5936
	C	3684	32	4672	5596	13,984
2. English	N	123	13	428	3276	3840
	C	3355	7	1849	5828	11,039
3. Assamese	N	3	3	26	52	84
	C	62	41	90	56	249
4. Bengali	N	44	8	417	1113	1582
	C	1059	6	927	1307	3299
5. Gujarati	N	40	5	174	510	729
	C	1145	4	680	711	2540
6. Kannada	N	85	3	161	406	655
	C	556	4	661	687	1888
7. Kashmiri	N	–	–	1	–	1
	C	–	–	–	–	–
8. Malayalam	N	112	–	121	607	840
	C	1386	–	1481	1260	4127
9. Marathi	N	127	17	370	617	1131
	C	1399	17	647	820	2883
10. Oriya	N	14	–	40	245	299
	C	178	–	26	211	415
11. Punjabi	N	24	1	184	243	452
	C	231	–	447	350	1028
12. Sanskrit	N	2	–	4	25	31
	C	2	–	5	4	11
13. Sindhi	N	6	–	20	39	65
	C	20	–	5	13	38
14. Tamil	N	106	4	129	618	857
	C	956	2	2050	1494	4502
15. Telugu	N	37	2	162	382	583
	C	439	11	508	598	1556
16. Urdu	N	148	6	672	552	1378
	C	734	8	891	621	2254
17. Bilingual	N	33	15	373	1220	1641
	C	32	8	310	670	1020
18. Multilingual	N	9	1	66	279	355
	C	6	2	7	132	177

Language		Dailies	Tri-/Bi-weeklies	Weeklies	Others	TOTAL
19. Others	N	40	3	65	191	299
	C	11	–	34	47	92
	N	1423	108	6122	13,105	20,758
	C	15,255	142	15,290	20,405	51,102

Note: All circulation figures x 1000.
Source (numbers): MINISTRY OF INFORMATION AND BROADCASTING, INDIA 1985 201
Source (circulation): MINISTRY OF INFORMATION AND BROADCASTING, INDIA 1983 159-60

ANNEXURE XI

§ 5 OF THE OFFICIAL SECRETS ACT OF 1923: WRONGFUL COMMUNICATION, ETC. OF INFORMATION

(1) If any person having in his possession or control any secret official code or password or any sketch, plan, model, article, note, document or information which relates to or is used in a prohibited place or relates to anything in such a place, or which is likely to assist, directly or indirectly, an enemy or which relates to a matter the disclosure of which is likely to affect the sovereignty and integrity of India, the security of the State or friendly relations with foreign States or which has been made or obtained in contravention of this Act, or which has been entrusted in confidence to him by any person holding office under Government, or which he has obtained or to which he has had access owing to his position as a person who holds or has held office under the Government or as a person who holds or has held a contract made on behalf of the Government, or as a person who is or has been employed under a person who holds or has held such an office or contract –

(a) wilfully communicates the code or password, sketch, plan, model, article, note, document or information to any person other than a person to whom he is authorised to communicate it, or a Court of Justice or a person to whom it is, in the interests of the State, his duty to communicate it; or

(b) uses the information in his possession for the benefit of any foreign power or in any other manner prejudicial to the safety of the State; or

(c) retains the sketch, plan, model, article, note or document in his possession or control when he has no right to retain it, or when it is contrary to his duty to retain it, or wilfully fails to comply with all directions issued by lawful authority with regard to the return or disposal thereof; or

(d) fails to take reasonable care of, or so conducts himself as to endanger the safety of the sketch, plan, model, article, note, document, secret official code or password or information, he shall be guilty of an offence under this section.

(2) If any person voluntarily receives any secret official code or password or any sketch, plan, model, article, note, document or information, knowing or having reasonable ground to believe at the time when he receives it that the code, password, sketch, plan, model, article, note, document or information is communicated in contravention of this Act, he shall be guilty of an offence under this section.

(3) If any person having in his possession or control any sketch, plan, model, article, note, document or information, which relates to munitions of war, communicates it, directly or indirectly to any foreign power or in any other manner prejudicial to the safety or interests of the State, he shall be guilty of an offence under this section.

(4) A person guilty of an offence under this section shall be punishable with imprisonment for a term which may extend to three years, or with fine or with both.

ANNEXURE XII

AIR STATION LOCATIONS, BY STATE AND UNION TERRITORY (As of January 1, 1986)

I. *By State*

1. Andhra Pradesh
   - Hyderabad
   - Vijayawada
   - Visakhapatnam
   - Cuddapah
2. Assam
   - Guwahati
   - Silchar
   - Dibrugarh
3. Bihar
   - Patna
   - Ranchi
   - Bhagalpur
   - Darbhanga
4. Gujarat
   - Ahmedabad
   - Baroda
   - Bhuj
   - Rajkot
   - Vadodara
5. Haryana
   - Rohtak
6. Himachal Pradesh
   - Shimla
7. Jammu and Kashmir
   - Srinagar
   - Jammu
   - Leh
8. Karnataka
   - Bangalore
   - Bhadrawati
   - Dharward
   - Gulbarga
   - Mangalore/Udipi
   - Mysore
9. Kerala
   - Alleppey
   - Calicut
   - Trichur
   - Trivandrum
10. Madhya Pradesh
    - Ambikapur
    - Bhopal
    - Chatarpur
    - Gwalior
    - Indore
    - Jabalpur
    - Jagdalpur
    - Raipur
    - Rewa
11. Maharashtra
    - Aurangabad
    - Bombay
    - Jalgaon
    - Nagpur
    - Parbhani
    - Pune
    - Ratnagiri
    - Sangali
12. Manipur
    - Imphal
13. Meghalaya
    - Shillong
    - Tura
14. Nagaland
    - Kohima
15. Orissa
    - Cuttack
    - Sambalpur
    - Jeypore
16. Punjab
    - Jalandhar
17. Rajasthan
    - Jaipur
    - Ajmer
    - Bikaner
    - Udaipur
    - Jodhpur
    - Suratgarh
18. Sikkim
    - Gangtok

19. Tamil Nadu
   - Coimbatore
   - Madras
   - Tiruchirapalli
   - Tirunelveli
   - Nagercoil

20. Tripura
   - Agartala

21. Uttar Pradesh
   - Lucknow
   - Allahabad
   - Varanasi
   - Rampur
   - Kanpur
   - Mathura
   - Garakhpur
   - Najibabad

22. West Bengal
   - Calcutta
   - Kuresong
   - Siliguri

II. *By Union Territory*

1. Andaman and Nicobar Islands
   - Port Blair

2. Arunchal Pradesh
   - Pasighat
   - Tawang
   - Tezu

3. Chandigarh
   - Chandigarh

4. Delhi
   - Delhi

5. Goa, Daman and Diu
   - Panaji

6. Pondicherry
   - Pondicherry

7. Mizoram
   - Aizawl

8. Laccadive and Minicoy Islands
   - none

9. Dardar and Nagarhaveli
   - none

Note: The list does not include the 2-megawatt transmitters at Rajkot and Calcutta or the shortwave transmitters at Aligarh and Delhi, which are mainly utilised for the external/internal news linkups, etc.

Source: MINISTRY OF INFORMATION AND BROADCASTING, ANNUAL REPORT (1983–1984) 85–86

ANNEXURE XIII

TV CENTRE LOCATIONS

(As of March 1, 1986)

State/Union Territory	Existing Centres		Centres Under Construction	
	HPT Centre+	LPT Centre++	HPT Centre+	LPT Centre++
1. Assam				
	Guwahati	Tezpur	Dibrugarh	Diphu
		Silchar	Silchar	Jorhat
		Dibrugarh		
2. Andra Pradesh				
	Hyderabad	Warangal	Visakhapatnam	Prodattur
	Vijayawada	Rajamundry	Vijayawada	
		Kakinada		
		Visakhapatnam		
		Nellore		
		Nizamabad		
		Kurnool		
		Anantpur		
		Tirupati		
		Adoni		
		Cuddapah		
		Mebboobnagar		
		Karimnagar		
3. Bihar				
	Patna	Dhanbad		Bettiah
	Muzaffarpur	Jamshedpur		
	Ranchi	Gaya		
		Bhagalpur		
		Munger		
		Purnea		
		Darbhanga		
4. Delhi				
	Delhi			
5. Gujarat				
	Ahmedabad	Surat		Bhuj
	Rajkot	Vadodara		
	Dwarka	Bhavnagar		
		Bharuch		
		Patna		
		Navasari		
6. Haryana				
		Hissar		
		Bhiwani		

State/Union Territory	Existing Centres		Centres Under Construction	
	HPT Centre[+]	LPT Centre[++]	HPT Centre[+]	LPT Centre[++]
7. Karnataka				
	Bangalore	Dharwad		
	Gulbarga[1]	Mysore		
		Mangalore		
		Belgaum		
		Bellary		
		Devangare		
		Bhadravati		
		Bijapur		
		Raichur		
		Gadeg Betagari		
		Hospet		
8. Kerala				
	Trivandrum	Calicut		
	Cochin	Cannanore		
		Palghat		
9. Madhya Pradesh				
	Bhopal	Jabalpur		
	Indore	Gwalior		
	Raipur[1]	Ratlam		
		Sagar		
		Burhanpur		
		Rewa		
		Murwara		
		Bilaspur		
		Singrauli		
		Korba		
		Khandwa		
10. Maharashtra				Satara
	Bombay	Sholapur		
	Nagpur	Nasik		
	Pune	Kolhapur		
		Aurangabad		
		Sangli		
		Amravati		
		Malagaon		
		Akola		
		Dhula		
		Nanded		
		Ahmednagar		
		Jalgaon		
		Jalna		
		Bhusawal		
		Chandrapur		
		Lutur		
		Parbhani		
		Gondiya		
11. Manipur				
		Imphal		Imphal[1]
		Ukhrul		

State/Union Territory	Existing Centres		Centres Under Construction	
	HPT Centre⁺	LPT Centre⁺⁺	HPT Centre⁺	LPT Centre⁺⁺
12. Orissa				
	Sambalpur[1]	Rourkela	Cuttack	Bhavanipatna
	Cuttack	Berhampur		
		Koraput		
13. Rajasthan				
	Jaipur	Jodhpur		
		Ajmer		
		Kota		
		Bikaner		
		Udaipur		
		Alwar		
		Ganganagar		
		Bhilwara		
		Khetri		
		Jaiselmer		
		Barmer		
		Suratgarh		
14. Punjab				
	Amritsar		Pathankot	
	Jalandhar			
	Bhatinda			
15. Tamil Nadu				
	Kodaikanal		Salem	
	Madras		Tiruchirapalli	
			Vellore	
			Kumbakonam	
			Coimbatore	
			Neyveli	
16. Uttar Pradesh				
	Allahabad		Bareily	
	Agra		Deoria	
	Gorakhpur		Moradabad	
	Lucknow		Aligarh	
	Mussoorie		Jhansi	
	Kanpur		Sultanpur	
	Varanasi		Rai-Bereli	
			Faizabad	
			Etawah	
			Behraich	
			Sahjahanpur	
			Rampur	
			Pauri	
			Farukhabad	
			Nainital	
			Pithoragarh	
			Sambhal	

State/Union Territory	Existing Centres		Centres Under Construction	
	HPT Centre+	LPT Centre++	HPT Centre+	LPT Centre++
17. West Bengal				
	Asansol		Kharagpur	Kurseong
	Calcutta		Malda	
	Murshidabad		Bardhaman	
	Kuresong[1]		Balurghat	
			Shantiniketan	
18. Himachal Pradesh				
	Kasauli		Kulu	
			Shimla	
19. Jammu and Kashmir				
	Srinagar		Kargil	Poonch
	Poonch[1]		Jammu	
	Jammu		Leh	
20. Meghalaya				
			Tura	Tura
			Shillong	Shillong[1]
21. Pondicherry				
			Pondicherry	
22. Nagaland				
		Kohima		
			Kohima[1]	Dimapur
				Tuensong
23. Mizoram				
		Aizwal	Aizwal[1]	
24. Sikkim				
			Gangtok	
25. Tripura				
			Agartala	
26. Andaman and Nicobar Islands				
			Port Blair	
			Car Nicobar	
27. Arunachal Pradesh				
			Itanagar	Tezu
28. Goa, Daman and Diu				
	Panaji[1]			Passighat
				Panji

Source: MINISTRY OF INFORMATION AND BROADCASTING, ANNUAL REPORT (1985–86) 77–80

+: HPT = high-power transmission center

++: LPT = low-power transmission center

1: HPT Centre with 1.0-kW transmitter

ANNEXURE XIV

SELECTED PROVISIONS OF THE COPYRIGHT ACT OF 1957

§ 14: Meaning of Copyright

(1) For the purpose of this Act, »copyright« means the exclusive right, by virtue of, and subject to the provisions of this Act:

(a) in case of a literary, dramatic or musical work, to do and authorise the doing of any of the following acts, namely:
- (i) to reproduce the work in any material form;
- (ii) to publish the work;
- (iii) to perform the work in public;
- (iv) to produce, reproduce, perform or publish any translation of the work;
- (v) to make any cinematograph film of or record in respect of the work;
- (vi) to communicate the work by radio-diffusion or to communicate to the public by a loud speaker or any other similar instrument the radio-diffusion of the work;
- (vii) to make any adaptation of the work;
- (viii) to do in relation to a translation or an adaptation of the work any of the acts specified in relation to the work in clauses (i) to (vii),

(b) in the case of an artistic work, to do or authorise the doing of any of the following acts, namely:
- (i) to reproduce the work in any material form;
- (ii) to publish the work;
- (iii) to include the work in any cinematograph film;
- (iv) to make any adaptation of the work;
- (v) to do in relation to an adaptation of the work any of the acts specified in relation to the work in clauses (i) to (iii);

(c) in the case of a cinematograph film, to do or authorise the doing of any of the following acts, namely:
- (i) to make a copy of the film;
- (ii) to cause the film, in so far as it consists of visual images, to be seen in public and, in so far as it consists of sounds, to be heard in public;
- (iii) to make any record embodying the recording in any part of the soundtrack associated with the film by utilising such soundtrack;
- (iv) to communicate the film by radio-diffusion;

(d) in the case of a record, to do or authorise the doing of any of the following acts by utilising the record, namely:
- (i) to make any other record embodying the same recording;
- (ii) to cause the recording embodied in the record to be heard in public;
- (iii) to communicate the recording embodied in the record by radio-diffusion.

(2) Any reference in sub-section (1) to the doing of any act in relation to a work or a translation or an adaptation thereof shall include a reference to the doing of that act in relation to a substantial part thereof.

§ 40: Power to Extend Copyright to Foreign Works

The Central Government may, by order published in the official Gazette, direct that all or any provisions of this Act shall apply –

(a) to works first published in any territory outside India to which the order relates in like manner as if they were first published within India;
(b) to unpublished works, or any class thereof, the authors whereof were at the time of the making of the work, subjects or citizens of the foreign country to which the order relates in like manner as if the authors were citizens of India;
(c) in respect of domicile in any territory outside India to which the order relates in like manner as if such domicile were in India;
(d) to any work of which the author was at the date of the first publication thereof, or in a case where the author was dead at that date, was at the time of his death, a subject or citizen of a foreign country to which the order relates in like manner as if the author were a citizen of India; and thereupon, subject to the provisions of this Chapter and of the order, this Act shall apply accordingly.

§ 51: When Copyright Infringed

Copyright in a work shall be deemed to be infringed –

(a) when any person, without a licence granted by the owner of the copyright or the Registrar of Copyrights under this Act or in contravention of the conditions of the licence so granted or of any condition imposed by a competent authority under this Act –
(i) does anything, the exclusive right to do which is by this Act conferred upon the owner of the copyright, or
(ii) permits for profit any place to be used for the performance of the work in public where such performance constitutes an infringement of the copyright in the work unless he was not aware and had no reasonable ground for believing that such performance would be an infringement of copyright, or
(b) when any person –
(i) makes for sale or hire, or sells or lets for hire, or by way of trade displays or offers for sale or hire, or
(ii) distributes either for the purpose of trade or to such an extent as to affect prejudicially the owner of the copyright, or
(iii) by way of trade exhibits in public, or
(iv) imports into India any infringing copies of the work.
Explanation: For the purposes of this section, the reproduction of a literary, dramatic, musical or artistic work in the form of a cinematograph film shall be deemed to be an »infringing copy.« Provided that nothing in sub-clause (iv) shall apply to the import of two copies of any work, other than a cinematograph film or record for the private or domestic use of the importer.

§ 52A: Particulars to be Included in Records and Video Films

(1) No person shall publish a record in respect of any work unless the following particulars are displayed on the record and on any container thereof, namely:

(a) the name and address of the person who has made the record;
(b) the name and address of the owner of the copyright in such work; and
(c) the year of its publication.

§ 63: Offence of Infringement of Copyright or Other Rigthts Conferred by this Act

Any person who knowingly infringes or abets the infringement of –
(a) the copyright in a work, or
(b) any other right conferred by this Act,
shall be punishable with imprisonment for a term which shall not be less than six months but which may extend to three years and with fine which shall not be less than fifty thousand rupees but which may extend to two lakh (200,000) rupees;
Provided that the court may, for adequate and special reasons to be mentioned in the judgment, impose a sentence of imprisonment for a term of less than one year or a fine of less than one lakh (100,000) rupees.

§ 63A: Enhanced Penalty on Second and Subsequent Convictions

Whoever having been already convicted of an offence under section 63 is again convicted of any such offence shall be punishable for the second and for every subsequent offence, with imprisonment for a term which shall not be less than one year but which may extend to three years and with fine which shall not be less than one lakh (100,000) rupees but which may extend to two lakh (200,000) rupees.
Provided that the court may, for adequate and special reasons to be mentioned in the judgment, impose a sentence of imprisonment for a term of less than one year or a fine of less than one lakh (100,000) rupees.

§ 65: Possession of Plates for Purpose of Making Infringing Copies

Any person who knowingly makes, or has in his possession, any plate for the purpose of making infringing copies of any work in which copyright subsists shall be punishable with imprisonment which may extend to two years and shall also be liable to fine.

§ 67: Penalties for Making False Entries in Register, etc. or Producing or Tendering False Entries

Any person who –
(a) makes or causes to be made a false entry in the Register of Copyrights kept under this Act, or
(b) makes or causes to be made a writing falsely purporting to be a copy of any entry in such register, or
(c) produces or tenders or causes to be produced or tendered as evidence any such entry or writing, knowing the same to be false, shall be punished with imprisonment which may extend to one year, or with fine, or with both.

§ 68: Penalty for Making False Statements for the Purpose of Deceiving or Influencing any Authority or Officer

Any person who –
(a) with a view to deceiving any authority or officer in the execution of the provisions of this Act, or
(b) with a view to procuring or influencing the doing or omission of anything in relation to this Act or any matter thereunder makes a false statement or representation knowing the same to be false, shall be punishable with imprisonment which may extend to one year, with fine, or with both.

§ 69: Offence by Companies

Where any offence under this Act has been committed by a company, every person who at the time the offence was committed was in charge of, and was responsible to the company for, the conduct of the business of the company, as well as the company, shall be deemed to be guilty of such offence and shall be liable to be proceeded against and punished accordingly.

Source: Gazette of India, Extraordinary Part II, sec. 3, p. 167 (1958).

MAP I

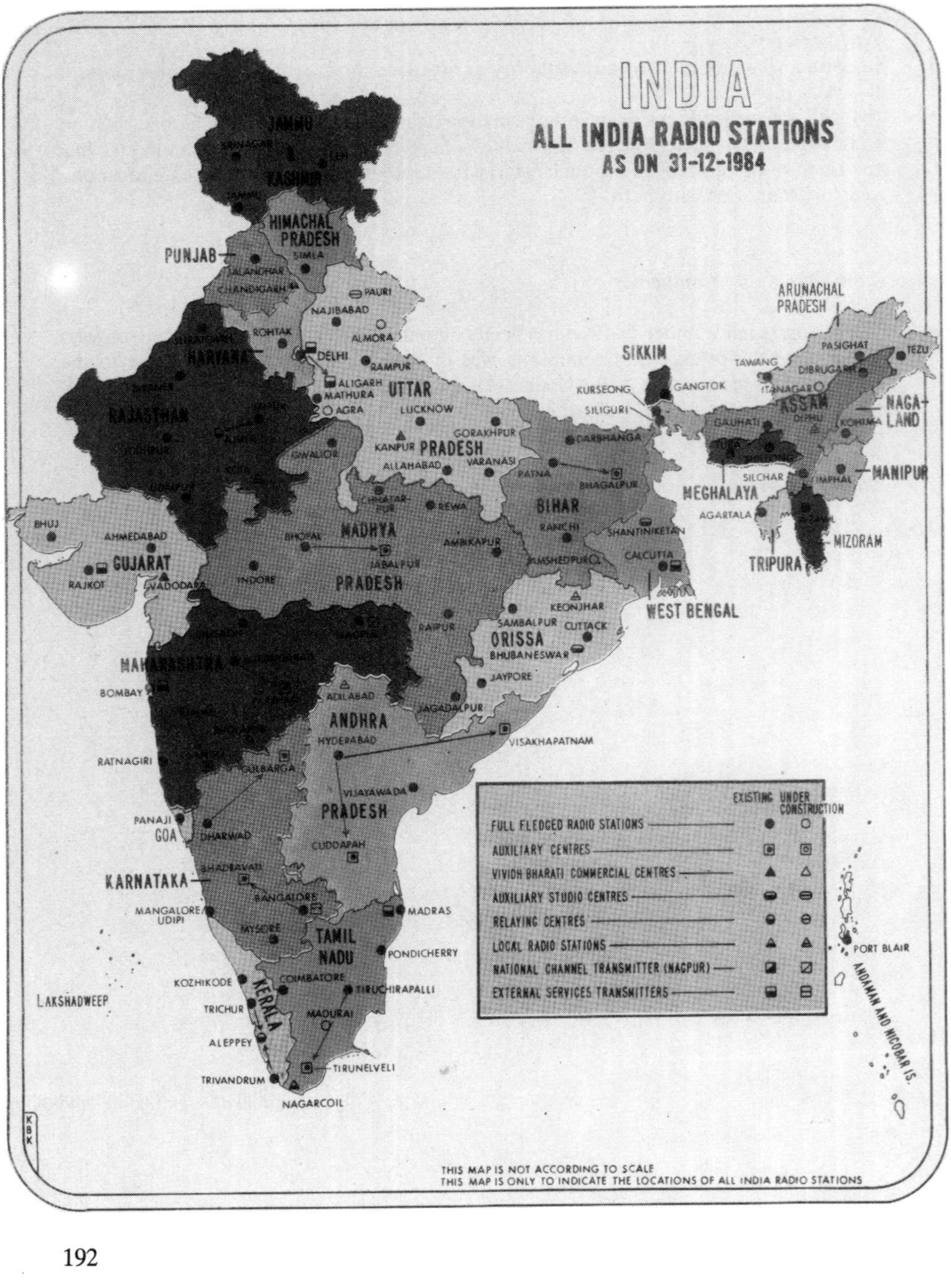
INDIA
ALL INDIA RADIO STATIONS
AS ON 31-12-1984
JAMMU
KASHMIR
SRINAGAR
LEH
JAMMU
HIMACHAL PRADESH
SIMLA
PUNJAB
JALANDHAR
CHANDIGARH
PAURI
NAJIBABAD
ALMORA
ROHTAK
HARYANA
DELHI
RAMPUR
ALIGARH
MATHURA
AGRA
UTTAR
PRADESH
LUCKNOW
GORAKHPUR
KANPUR
ALLAHABAD
VARANASI
RAJASTHAN
JODHPUR
GWALIOR
KOTA
UDAIPUR
REWA
BHOPAL
MADHYA
PRADESH
JABALPUR
AMBIKAPUR
INDORE
RAIPUR
BHUJ
AHMEDABAD
GUJARAT
RAJKOT
VADODARA
ARUNACHAL PRADESH
PASIGHAT
TEZU
TAWANG
DIBRUGARH
ITANAGAR
SIKKIM
GANGTOK
KURSEONG
SILIGURI
ASSAM
NAGA-LAND
GAUHATI
DIPHU
KOHIMA
DARBHANGA
PATNA
BHAGALPUR
SHILLONG
SILCHAR
IMPHAL
MANIPUR
MEGHALAYA
AGARTALA
MIZORAM
BIHAR
RANCHI
SHANTINIKETAN
JAMSHEDPUR
CALCUTTA
TRIPURA
WEST BENGAL
KEONJHAR
SAMBALPUR
CUTTACK
ORISSA
BHUBANESWAR
JAYPORE
MAHARASHTRA
NAGPUR
BOMBAY
ADILABAD
JAGADALPUR
ANDHRA
HYDERABAD
VISAKHAPATNAM
RATNAGIRI
GULBARGA
VIJAYAWADA
PRADESH
PANAJI
GOA
DHARWAD
CUDDAPAH
KARNATAKA
BHADRAVATI
BANGALORE
MANGALORE/UDIPI
MADRAS
MYSORE
TAMIL NADU
PONDICHERRY
KOZHIKODE
COIMBATORE
TIRUCHIRAPALLI
KERALA
LAKSHADWEEP
TRICHUR
MADURAI
ALEPPEY
TIRUNELVELI
TRIVANDRUM
NAGARCOIL
PORT BLAIR
ANDAMAN AND NICOBAR IS.
EXISTING
UNDER CONSTRUCTION
FULL FLEDGED RADIO STATIONS
AUXILIARY CENTRES
VIVIDH BHARATI COMMERCIAL CENTRES
AUXILIARY STUDIO CENTRES
RELAYING CENTRES
LOCAL RADIO STATIONS
NATIONAL CHANNEL TRANSMITTER (NAGPUR)
EXTERNAL SERVICES TRANSMITTERS
KBK
THIS MAP IS NOT ACCORDING TO SCALE
THIS MAP IS ONLY TO INDICATE THE LOCATIONS OF ALL INDIA RADIO STATIONS

MAP II

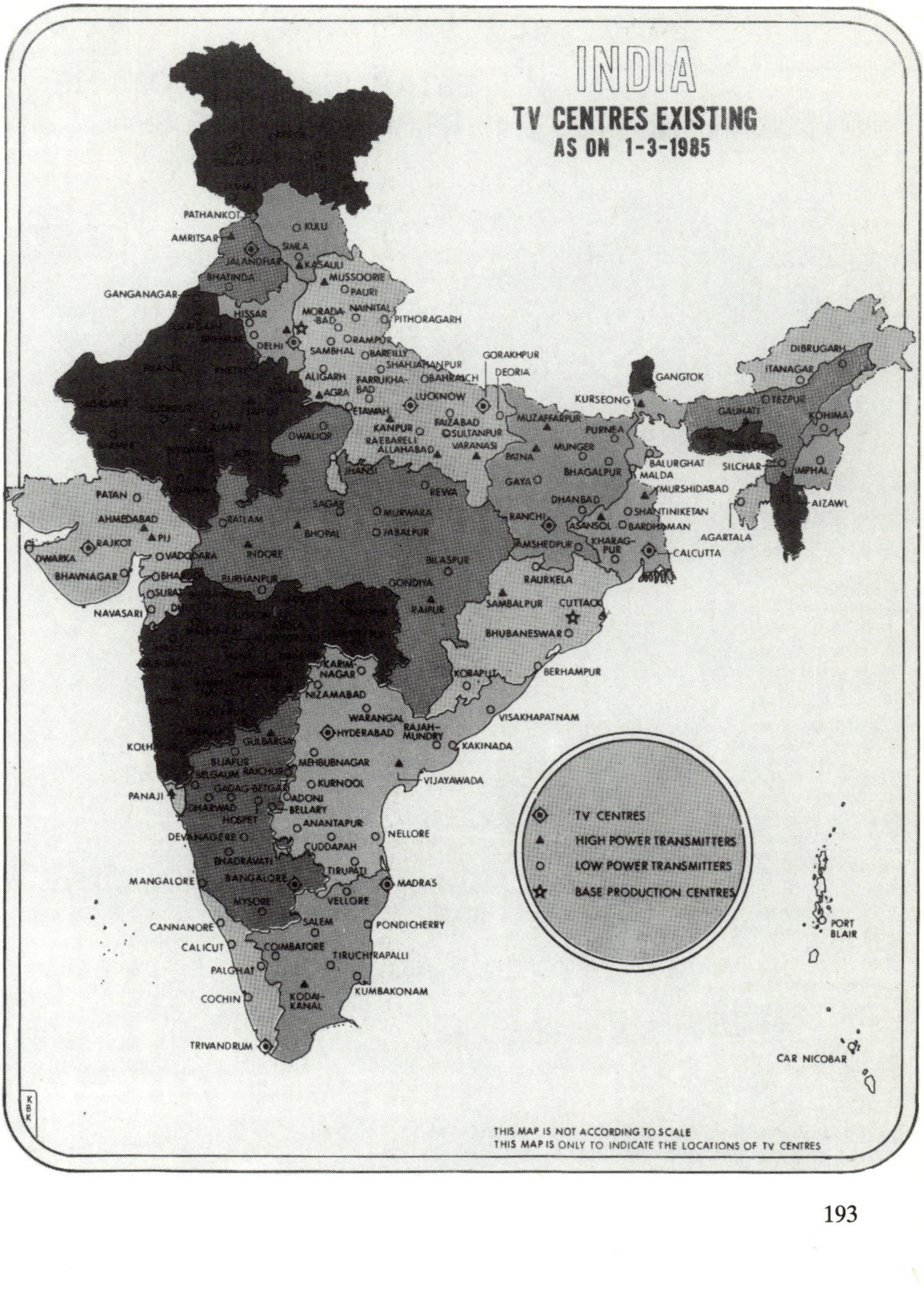
INDIA
TV CENTRES EXISTING
AS ON 1-3-1985
PATHANKOT
AMRITSAR
JALANDHAR
KULU
SIMLA
KASAULI
BHATINDA
MUSSOORIE
PAURI
GANGANAGAR
HISSAR
NAINITAL
MORADA-BAD
PITHORAGARH
DELHI
RAMPUR
SAMBHAL
BAREILLY
SHAHJAHANPUR
GORAKHPUR
DEORIA
ALIGARH
FARRUKHA-BAD
BAHRAICH
AGRA
LUCKNOW
ETAWAH
KANPUR
FAIZABAD
SULTANPUR
RAEBARELI
ALLAHABAD
VARANASI
GWALIOR
JHANSI
REWA
SAGAR
MURWARA
JABALPUR
BHOPAL
PATAN
AHMEDABAD
PIJ
RAJKOT
DWARKA
VADODARA
RATLAM
INDORE
BHAVNAGAR
BURHANPUR
SURAT
NAVASARI
BILASPUR
GONDIYA
RAIPUR
KURSEONG
GANGTOK
MUZAFFARPUR
PURNEA
PATNA
MUNGER
BHAGALPUR
GAYA
BALURGHAT
MALDA
MURSHIDABAD
DHANBAD
RANCHI
ASANSOL
SHANTINIKETAN
BARDHAMAN
JAMSHEDPUR
KHARAG-PUR
CALCUTTA
RAURKELA
SAMBALPUR
CUTTACK
BHUBANESWAR
BERHAMPUR
KORAPUT
DIBRUGARH
ITANAGAR
TEZPUR
GAUHATI
KOHIMA
SILCHAR
IMPHAL
AIZAWL
AGARTALA
KARIM-NAGAR
NIZAMABAD
WARANGAL
HYDERABAD
RAJAH-MUNDRY
KAKINADA
VISAKHAPATNAM
GULBARGA
KOLHAPUR
BIJAPUR
BELGAUM
RAICHUR
MEHBUBNAGAR
VIJAYAWADA
PANAJI
GADAG-BETGARI
KURNOOL
DHARWAD
ADONI
BELLARY
HOSPET
ANANTAPUR
DEVANAGERE
NELLORE
CUDDAPAH
BHADRAVATI
TIRUPATI
MANGALORE
BANGALORE
MADRAS
MYSORE
VELLORE
CANNANORE
SALEM
PONDICHERRY
CALICUT
COIMBATORE
TIRUCHIRAPALLI
PALGHAT
KODAI-KANAL
KUMBAKONAM
COCHIN
TRIVANDRUM
TV CENTRES
HIGH POWER TRANSMITTERS
LOW POWER TRANSMITTERS
BASE PRODUCTION CENTRES
PORT BLAIR
CAR NICOBAR
KBK
THIS MAP IS NOT ACCORDING TO SCALE
THIS MAP IS ONLY TO INDICATE THE LOCATIONS OF TV CENTRES

MAP III

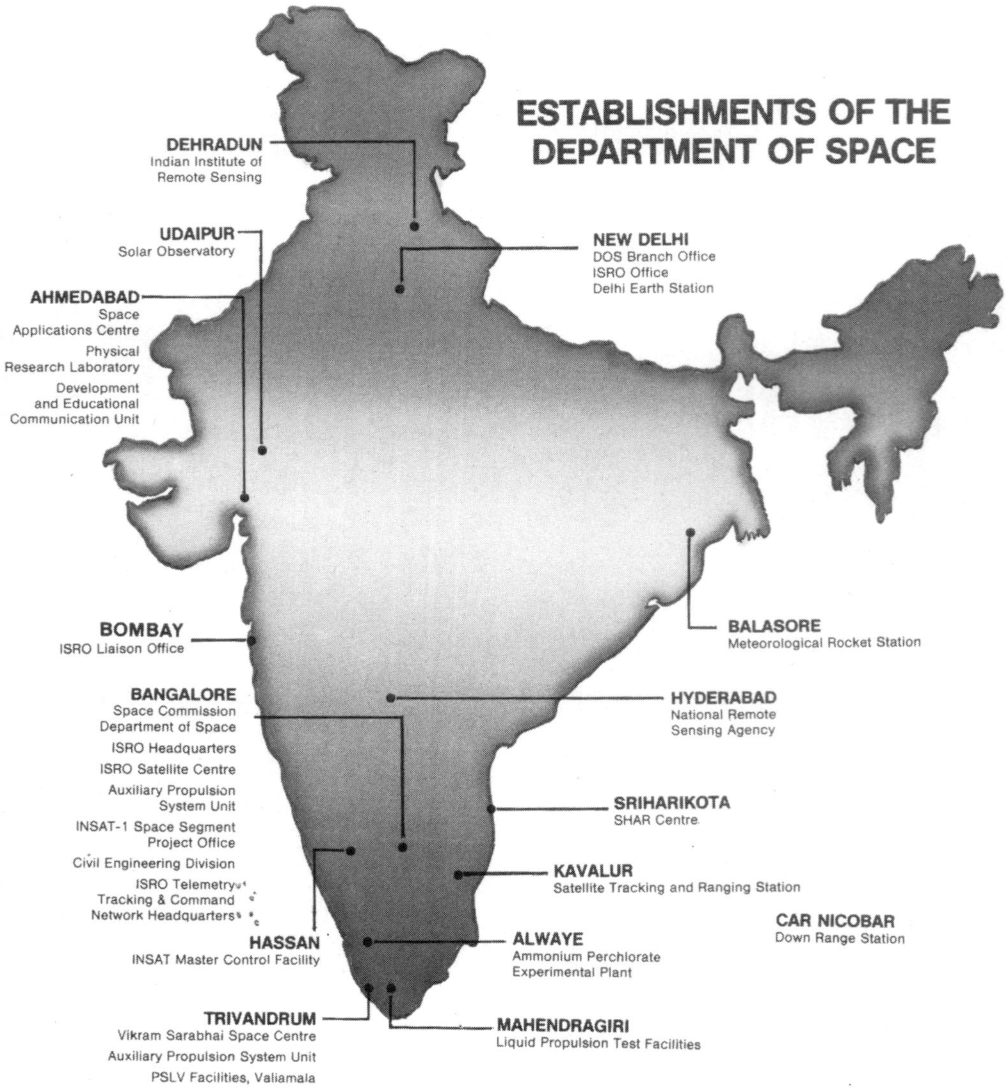

Source: ANNUAL REPORT 1984 p85, DEPARTMENT OF SPACE, GOVERNMENT OF INDIA p. 2

NATIONAL REPORT QUESTIONNAIRE*

Part 1: Telephone services

A. Regulation of transborder telephone services

I. Basic regulations of domestic telecommunications law for transborder telephone services[1]

1. Transformation of international regulations into domestic law and practice
   a) Survey of the relevant international law
      aa) Multilateral agreements
      bb) Bilateral agreements
   b) Scope of questions of transborder telephone services reserved for national regulation
   c) Domestic regulatory power to transform international regulations into domestic law and practice
      aa) Power to issue regulations affecting the domestic sphere[2]
         aaa) Legislature
         bbb) Public administration (administrative agencies)
         ccc) Operating companies (providing telephone services)
      bb) Power to issue regulations affecting foreign states[2]
         aaa) Legislature
         bbb) Administrative agencies
         ccc) Operating companies
   d) Contents of the international regulations as transformed into domestic law (including their application and construction)
2. Domestic law unaffected by international law
   a) Regulatory power[2]
      aa) Legislature
      bb) Administrative agencies

* The Questionnaire was prepared by a Work Group at the Max Planck Institute in Hamburg. Under the direction of Prof. E.-J. Mestmäcker, the Group consisted of Thomas Born, Reinhard Ellger, Beate-Katrin Graben and Detlev Witt.

cc) Operating companies

b) Survey of the contents of the domestic law (including application and construction)

II. Legal relations between domestic carriers (networks) providing transborder telephone services and domestic users of those services

1. Use of telephone services
   a) Public networks (common carriers)[3]
      aa) Who operates public networks?
      bb) Legal requirements for establishment and operation of public networks
         aaa) Contents of the requirements
         bbb) Power to regulate the requirements, to license operating companies, etc.
         ccc) Judicial review or other legal recourse against regulatory decisions
      cc) What services may be offered? What services are actually available?
      dd) Requirements for access to and conditions for use of public networks[4,5]
         aaa) Who has access to the networks?[6]
            (1) Ultimate consumers
            (2) »Resellers« of transmission services (lessees of network capacity)
            (3) Power to regulate access to networks
         bbb) Setting of tariffs
            (1) Tariff principles
            (2) Power to regulate tariffs (or market pricing?)
         ccc) Liability (of operating company for malfunction, etc.)
         ddd) Technical standards (especially standards for terminal equipment and its usage)
            (1) Power to regulate standards (source of regulation: international/national, governmental/private?)
            (2) Contents of technical standards
         eee) Judicial review or other legal recourse against regulatory decisions

b) Private networks
   aa) Who operates private networks?
   bb) Legal requirements for establishment and operation of private networks[6]
      aaa) Contents of the requirements[7]
      bbb) Regulatory power[7]
      ccc) Judicial review or other legal recourse[7]
   cc) What services may be offered? What services are actually available?
   dd) Are private network operators allowed to sublease networks? If so, under which conditions?

c) Networks operated by closed user groups
   aa) Who operates closed-user-group networks? (e.g., SITA, SWIFT)
   bb) Legal requirements for establishment and operation of closed-user-group networks[6]
      aaa) Contents of requirements[7]
      bbb) Regulatory power[7]
      ccc) Judicial review or other legal recourse[7]
   cc) What services may be offered? What services are actually available?
   dd) Requirements for access to and terms of usage of closed-user-group networks[6,7]
      aaa) Who can become a member of the »user group« and thereby gain access to the network?
      bbb) Setting of tariffs
         (1) Tariff principles
         (2) Who sets the tariffs?
      ccc) Liability (for errors, malfunction, etc.)
      ddd) Technical standards
      eee) Judicial review or other legal recourse; government supervision

2. Admission of terminal equipment to the network[8,9]
   a) What terminal equipment is part of the network – according to domestic telecommunications law – and therefore subject to the regulatory powers governing the telephone services?
   b) Who regulates the admission of terminal equipment to the network?
      aa) Administrative agencies

bb) Network operators
c) Criteria for admission (e.g., technical compatability)[5]
d) Judicial review or other legal recourse

III. Legal relations between domestic and international or foreign network operators

1. Access of domestic networks to and terms of usage of foreign networks
   a) Requirements of domestic telecommunications law[6] for access to the international network[10,11]
      aa) Contents of the requirements
         aaa) International law (multilateral/bilateral agreements) and domestic implementation thereof
         bbb) Domestic law unaffected by international law
      bb) Regulatory power
         aaa) International organizations
         bbb) Bilateral coordination
         ccc) Domestic legislature
         ddd) Domestic administrative agencies
         eee) Operating companies
      cc) Judicial review or other legal recourse
   b) Requirements of domestic telecommunications law for the use of the international network (to what extent does domestic law influence these requirements?)[12]
      aa) Contents of the requirements
         aaa) Setting of tariffs, accounting
            (1) International framework (multilateral/bilateral) agreements, including their transformation into domestic law)
            (2) Domestic law unaffected by international law
         bbb) Technical standards
            (1) International framework
            (2) Domestic law
         ccc) Liability (for malfunction, etc.)
      bb) Regulatory powers for setting tariffs and technical standards
         aaa) International organizations
         bbb) Bilateral coordination
         ccc) Domestic legislature

ddd) Domestic administrative agencies
eee) Operating companies
cc) Judicial review or other legal recourse

2. Access of foreign networks to and terms of usage of domestic networks
   a) Are several domestic networks accessible from abroad?
   b) Requirements of domestic telecommunications law[6] for access to domestic network(s)
      aa) Contents of the requirements
         aaa) International regulations (including their transformation into domestic law)
         bbb) Domestic law unaffected by international law
      bb) Regulatory powers
         aaa) International organizations
         bbb) Bilateral coordination
         ccc) Domestic legislature
         ddd) Domestic administrative agencies
         eee) Operating companies
      cc) Judicial review or other legal recourse
   c) Terms of usage of the national networks
      aa) Contents of the terms
         aaa) Tariffs, accounting between networks
            (1) International framework (including transformation into domestic law)
            (2) Domestic law unaffected by international law
         bbb) Technical standards
            (1) International framework (including transformation into domestic law)
            (2) Domestic law unaffected by international law
         ccc) Liability (for errors, malfunction, etc.)
      bb) Power to regulate tariffs and technical standards
         aaa) International organizations
         bbb) Bilateral coordination
         ccc) Domestic legislature
         ddd) Domestic administrative agencies
         eee) Operating companies
      cc) Judicial review or other legal recourse

B. Legal regulation of the terminal and network equipment markets
- I. Demand side (procurement)
  - 1. Impact of the regulation of telephone services on the terminal and network equipment market
    - a) Who procures the equipment?
      - aa) To what extent does the domestic telecommunications law allow the network owners/operators and the users to purchase equipment according to their own choice?
      - bb) Competitive situation of network owners/operators in purchasing network and terminal equipment
    - b) Conditions of the procurement of equipment
      - aa) Power to set the conditions
        - aaa) International framework
        - bbb) Domestic legislature and administrative agencies
        - ccc) Operating companies
      - bb) Contents of the conditions
        - aaa) Technical standards and research/development of equipment
        - bbb) Pricing, contractual terms
        - ccc) Who maintains the equipment; under what conditions?
        - ddd) Criteria for choice among several suppliers
  - 2. Impact of further regulations (besides telecommunications law) on the terminal and network equipment markets
    - a) Impact of the regulation of foreign trade on the domestic procurement of terminal and network equipment
      - aa) General rules for foreign trade in goods
      - bb) Particular rules for foreign trade in terminal and network equipment
    - b) Impact of other regulations (e.g., antitrust law; general regulation of economic activities)
- II. Supply side
  - 1. Effect of demand-side situation on the access to the market of network and terminal equipment for suppliers
  - 2. Impact of economic dependencies and other relations between demand and supply sides on the market for network and terminal equipment

Annotations to Part 1

1. This part calls for a survey of the regulations. Details should be given at parts II and III.
2. It should also be described to what extent the relevant institutions have actually exercised their regulatory powers.
3. The notion »public networks« means common carriers that offer their telephone services to all interested parties. The notion includes operators being owners of the networks as well as companies that offer telephone services by means of leased lines.
4. The »users« of public networks may be:
   - customers, who use telephone services for their own needs
   - lessees, who offer telephone services to third parties by means of leased lines
5. In the following parts, the international regulations and their transformation into domestic law should also be considered even if this may not be particularly mentioned in the outline.
6. General regulations other than telecommunications law should also be considered (e.g., antitrust law)
7. As far as private networks are operated by means of lines leased from common carriers, the conditions for access and usage, as stated at Part II.1.a) dd), should be referred to.
8. The different kinds of telephone networks have to be taken into account (see Part II.1.a)–c) above).
9. In this part, regulations regarding terminal equipment should only be dealt with, insofar as the admission of the equipment to the network is concerned. The impact of these regulations on the market for terminal equipment is to be treated in Part B of the outline.
10. The notion »international network« embraces all networks used for transborder telephone services except domestic networks.
11. »Requirements of access« means the criteria for determining which domestic carrier has access to foreign networks.
12. The conditions for access to and usage of networks used for transborder services can only be described comprehensively if the respective foreign telecommunications law is taken into account. This would go beyond the scope of a purely national report. However, information on bilateral relations should be added if available.

Part 2: Remote data processing (also: Videotex and remote sensing)

A. Legal regulation of transborder data processing

I. General legal rules that may be applicable to transborder data processing

1. Export of data
   a) General laws for the protection of national security and public safety (e.g., protection of secrets related to national security)
   b) Rules for the protection of domestic economic interests (e.g., regulations imposing tariffs on exports of data, disquettes, cassettes, hardware and software)
   c) General laws for the protection of private and individual interests
   d) Privacy protection

2) Import of data
   a) General laws for the protection of national security and public safety
   b) Rules for the protection of domestic economic interests (e.g., regulations imposing tariffs on the import of data, disquettes, cassettes, hard- and software)
   c) General laws for the protection of private and individual interests
   d) Privacy protection

II. Regulations relating to transborder data processing as a service
1. Import of data processing services
   a) Commercial data processing services (data processing services offered to third parties that are not members of closed-user-group networks)
      aa) Principles of international business transactions law of the reporting country for transborder business in services in general (especially import regulations)
      bb) Particular rules for data processing services

aaa) Data processing
bbb) Data storage and retrieval

b) Intra-company communication
   aa) Data processing
   bb) Data storage and retrieval
c) Closed-user-group networks
   aa) Data processing
   bb) Data storage and retrieval

2. Export of data processing services
   a) Commercial data processing services (data processing services offered to third parties that are not members of closed-user-group networks)
      aa) Principles of international business transactions law of the reporting country for transborder business in services in general (especially export regulations)
      bb) Particular rules for data processing services
         aaa) Data processing
         bbb) Data storage and retrieval
   b) Intra-company communication
      aa) Data processing
      bb) Data storage and retrieval
   c) Closed-user-group networks
      aa) Data processing
      bb) Data storage and retrieval

III. Regulations applicable specifically to transborder data processing survey of international law

1. Basic legal principles of domestic telecommunications law for the transborder transmission of data[1]
   a) Transformation of legal requirements set up by international law into domestic law and practice
      aa) Survey of the relevant international law
         aaa) Multilateral agreements (e.g., ITU, regional organizations)
         bbb) Bilateral agreements
      bb) Scope of the issues of telecommunications reserved for domestic regulation
      cc) Domestic regulatory power to transform international requirements into domestic law and practice

aaa) Power to issue regulations affecting the domestic sphere and regulations issued[2]
(1) Legislature
(2) Administrative agencies
(3) Operating companies providing data transmission services
bbb) Power to issue regulations affecting the international or foreign sphere
(1) Legislature
(2) Administrative agencies
(3) Operating companies providing data transmission services
dd) Content of the international rules as transformed into domestic law (including application and construction of the rules)
b) Domestic law unaffected by international law
aa) Regulating Power
aaa) Legislature
bbb) Administrative agencies
ccc) Operating companies
bb) Survey of the contents of the domestic law (including application and construction)

2. Rules of domestic law regulating the relations between domestic operating companies providing international data transmission services and domestic users of those services
a) Use of data transmission services
aa) Public networks (common carriers)[3]
aaa) Who in fact operates public networks?
bbb) Legal requirements for installation and operation of public networks
(1) Content of requirements
(2) Jurisdiction (for making the regulations and granting licenses, etc.)
(3) Judicial review or other legal recourse against regulatory decisions
ccc) What services legally may be offered via the public network?
(1) Transmission services alone
(2) Enhanced services (i.e., transmission *and* data

processing services)

ddd) Requirements for access to and use of public networks[4,5]

(1) Jurisdiction to regulate access and use of networks – who actually regulates?

(2) Who has access to the networks?[6]

(2.1) Users (ultimate consumers) of data processing services

(2.2) Offerors of data processing services (who offer data processing services to other parties.

(2.3) Lessees of networks, who offer either transmission services alone or enhanced services

(2) Setting of tariffs

(1.1) Regulatory jurisdiction (or market pricing)

(2.3) Principles of setting tariffs

(3) Liability for errors in data processing

(4) Technical standards (especially for terminal equipment and its usage)

(4.1) Source of regulation: international or national; governmental or private

(4.2) Contents

(5) Judicial review or other legal recourse

bb) Private networks

aaa) Who operates private networks?

bbb) Legal requirements for installation and operation of private networks[6]

(1) Regulatory power[7]

(2) Judicial review or other legal recourse

(3) Contents of requirements[7]

ccc) Which services are offered through private networks?

(1) Data transmission for the network operator only

(2) Data transmission also for third parties

ddd) Are private network operators allowed to sublet the networks? If so, under which conditions is a sublease allowed?

cc) Networks operated by closed user groups[6]
aaa) Who operates closed-user-group networks (e.g., Swift, Sita)?
bbb) Legal requirements for installation and operation of closed-user-group networks[6]
(1) Contents of requirements[7]
(2) Regulatory power[7]
(3) Judicial review and other legal recourse
ccc) What services are offered?
(1) Data transmission for the network operating company only
(2) Data transmission also for third parties
ddd) Conditions for access to and usage of the networks
(1) Who can become a member of the »user group« and thus gain access to the network?
(2) Setting of tariffs
(2.1) Principles
(2.2) Who determines the tariffs?
(3) Liability for errors in data processing
(4) Technical standards
(5) Judicial review or other legal recourse
(6) Government supervision of private networks

b) Admission of terminal equipment[8,9]
aa) Who regulates the admission of terminal equipment to the network?
aaa) Public authorities
bbb) Operating companies
bb) What terminal equipment is part of the network according to domestic telecommunications law and is therefore subject to the respective regulatory powers?
cc) Criteria for admission (e.g., technical standards for compatibility; non-discriminatory competition for foreign suppliers of terminal equipment)
dd) Judicial review or other legal recourse

3. Rules regulating the relations between domestic and international or foreign network operators
a) Access to and modes of usage of international networks[10,11] by domestic carriers
aa) Requirements of domestic telecommunications law for access to international networks[12]

aaa) Contents of requirements
(1) International preconditions (multilateral or bilateral agreements)
(2) domestic telecommunications law
bbb) Regulatory powers
(1) International organizations
(2) Bilateral agreements
(3) Domestic legislation
(4) Domestic administrative agencies
(5) Operating companies
bb) Requirements of domestic telecommunications law for the use of international networks (to what extent are these conditions influenced by domestic law?)[14]
aaa) Contents of conditions
(1) Tariffs, accounting
(1.1) The international framework (bilateral and multilateral agreements and their transformation into domestic rules)
(1.2) Domestic law unaffected by international law
(2) Technical standards
(2.1) International framework
(2.2) Domestic Law
(3) Liability for errors in data transmission
bbb) Regulatory powers for setting tariffs and technical standards
(1) International institutions
(2) Bilateral agreements
(3) Domestic legislation
(4) Domestic administrative agencies
(5) Operating companies
ccc) Judicial review and other legal recourse
b) Access to and modes of usage of domestic networks by foreign network operators
aa) How many domestic networks are accessible from abroad?
bb) Requirements set by domestic telecommunications law[6] for access to domestic networks
aaa) Contents of requirements
(1) International framework

(2) Domestic law

bbb) Regulatory powers

(1) International organizations

(2) Bilateral agreements

(3) Domestic legislation

(4) Domestic administrative agencies

(5) Operating companies

ccc) Judicial review or other legal recourse

cc) Conditions for the use of domestic networks

aaa) Contents of conditions

(1) Tariffs, accounting between domestic and international networks

(1.1) International framework and transformation into domestic law

(1.2) Domestic law

(2) Technical standards

(2.1) International framework and transformation into domestic law

(2.2) Domestic law

(3) Liability for errors in data transmission

bbb) Regulatory powers over tariffs and technical standards

(1) International institutions

(2) Bilateral agreements

(3) Domestic legislation

(4) Domestic administrative agencies

(5) Operating companies

ccc) Judicial review or other legal recourse

B. Regulation of the markets for network and terminal equipment

I. Demand side

1. Impacts of the regulation of data transmission services on the markets for network and terminal equipment

a) Demand

aa) To what extent does the domestic telecommunications law allow the operating companies or the users to purchase network and terminal equipment according to their own choice?

bb) Competition among the network operators in purchasing network and terminal equipment

b) Conditions of procurement of network and terminal equipment

aa) Regulatory powers to set conditions

aaa) International framework

bbb) Domestic legislature and administrative agencies

ccc) Conditions set by operating companies themselves

bb) Contents of the conditions

aaa) Technical standards and development of equipment

bbb) Pricing, contractual conditions

ccc) Maintenance of equipment; conditions

ddd) Criteria for choice among several suppliers

2. Impact of other regulations (besides the rules for data transmission services) on the market for network and terminal equipment

a) Effects of the rules regulating international business transactions upon the market for network and terminal equipment

aa) General provisions for the trade in goods

bb) Particular rules for network and terminal equipment within the law relating to international business transactions

b) Impact of other regulations, e.g., antitrust law, especially regulations against misuse of demand power; general regulation of economic activities

II. Supply side

1. Effect of the demand-side situation on access to the market for network and terminal equipment

2. Impacts of economic dependencies and other relations between the supply and demand sides on competition in the market for network and terminal equipment

1. This part of the outline calls for a survey of the regulations. Details should be given at parts III 2 and 3.
2. The constitutional framework of the legislative activities as well as the content of the provisions should be explained.
3. »Public networks« means common carriers, which offer their data transmission services to any interested parties. »Operating companies« includes the owners of the networks and also companies that use leased lines to offer data transmission services.
4. »Users« of public networks may be:
   - customers, who use the data transmission services for the remote processing for their own needs
   - lessees, who use leased lines to offer third parties remote data processing capacities.
5. Also the international regulations and their transformation into domestic law are to be considered, even if this may not be particularly mentioned in the outline.
6. Also legal rules other than telecommunications law should be taken into account here (e.g., antitrust law)
7. If the private networks are operated with lines leased from common carriers, the conditions for access and usage of the networks are to be treated, as stated at part III 2a, aa, ddd, dd above.
8. At this point, the different kinds of data transmission methods have to be taken into account (see part III 2a above)
9. Regulations relating to terminal equipment should be dealt with here only insofar as the admission of the equipment to the network is concerned. The impact of these regulations on the market for terminal equipment is to be treated in part B of the outline
10. Account should be taken of whether the regulation of access to international networks distinguishes
    a) between different kinds of data to be transmitted or different kinds of data transmission services
    b) between »pure« data transmission services and enhanced services.
11. If special rules exist for the transit of data on the way to third countries, they should be mentioned separately.
12. The notion of »international networks« encompasses all networks that are used for transborder data transmissions, except domestic networks.
13. »Requirements of access« means the criteria for determining which

domestic carrier has access to foreign networks.

14. The conditions under which networks for transborder data transmissions may be accessed and used can only be covered comprehensively if the respective foreign telecommunications law is taken into account. Although this goes beyond the scope of a national report, information on bilateral relations should be added if available.

Part 3: Audiovisual media programmes

A. Regulation of the flow of media programmes from abroad to the reporting state (RS)
(Admission of programmes to the domestic territory; principles and conditions of access)

I. Legal relations between foreign states and programme and transmitting companies on the one hand and the reporting state on the other

1. The international framework and its transformation into national law
(Extent of international obligations of RS to give access to its territory for foreign programmes)

a) Multilateral agreements and international organizations subscribed to by RS

aa) ITU convention and rules arising from it

aaa) Relation of RS to ITU

bbb) Audiovisual broadcast programmes

(1) Jamming

(2) Prohibition of reception

(3) Technical standards and import regulations for receiver equipment

(4) Different treatment according to origin and/or domicile of foreign programme/transmitting company

ccc) Direct-Broadcast Satellites (DBS)

(1) Jamming

(2) Prohibition of reception

(3) Technical standards and import regulations for receiver equipment

(4) Different treatment according to origin and/or domicile of foreign programme/ transmitter company

(5) Different treatment of intended/unintended overspill

ddd) Cable TV (CATV)

(1) Ability of foreign cable operators to link their

systems with domestic cable networks
(1.1) General conditions of access
(1.2) Setting of tariffs
(1.3) Technical standards
(1.4) Programme standards
(2) Access to networks for foreign programmes
(1.1) General conditions of access
(1.2) Setting of tariffs
(1.3) Technical standards
(1.4) Programme standards

bb) Transformation of ITU rules into national law (for broadcast, DBS and CATV programmes)
aaa) Power to transform ITU rules into national law
bbb) Form and extent of transformation
ccc) Jurisdiction for application of transformed rules to foreign programmes of companies
ddd) Practice of application
eee) Judicial review or other legal recourse against regulatory decisions

cc) Human Rights Conventions and rules arising from them
aaa) Extent of adoption by RS
bbb) Audiovisual broadcast programmes
(1) Jamming
(2) Prohibition of reception
(3) Technical standards and import regulations for receiver equipment
(4) Preferential treatment of states of programme companies
ccc) Direct-Broadcast Satellites
– subdivided as above bbb)
ddd) Cable television
– subdivided as above bbb)

dd) Transformation of Human Rights Convention into national law (for broadcast, DBS and CATV)
aaa) Power for transformation of Human Rights Conventions into international law
bbb) Form and extent of transformation
ccc) Jurisdiction for application of transformed

rules to foreign programmes of companies
ddd) Practice of application
eee) Judical review or other legal recourse against regulatory decisions
ee) Other multilateral agreements subscribed to by RS
aaa) Audiovisual broadcast programmes
bbb) Direct-Broadcast Satellites
ccc) Cable Television (CATV)
ff) Transformation of other multilateral agreements into national law (broadcast, DBS and CATV)
– subdivided as above dd) –
b) Bilateral agreements
aaa) Scope left for bilateral agreements under ITU rules
(1) Audiovisual broadcast programmes
(2) Direct-Broadcast Satellites
(3) Cable television (CATV)
bbb) Noteworthy bilateral agreements to which RS subscribes
ccc) Special rules provided by bilateral agreements to which RS subscribes
(1) Audiovisual broadcast programmes
(1.1) Jamming
(1.2) Technical standards and import regulations for receiver equipment
(1.3) Preferential treatment for certain states/programme companies
(1.4) Bilateral monopolies
(2) Direct-Broadcast Satellites
– subdivided as above (1)
(3) Cable television
– subdivided as above (1)
c) Summary: Scope of action left to reporting state under international law or international law as transformed into national law for regulation of access of audiovisual broadcast programmes to its territory.

2. National law independent of international framework (Regulations generally governing the emission of audiovisual broadcast, satellite and cable programmes)
a) Structure of the domestic media and their regulation

aa) Constitutional bases of the national media organization
  aaa) Newspapers, magazines and other print media
  bbb) Audiovisual broadcast programmes
  ccc) Direct-Broadcast Satellites
  ddd) Cable television
bb) Power to regulate, legal technique or regulation
  – subdivided as above aa)
cc) Essentials of the national media regulation
  – subdivided as above aa)

b) General laws applicable to media programmes (classified according to legal spheres or objects of legal protection, e.g.:
- General laws
- Penal laws
- Law against obscenity
- Law of advertising
- Antitrust law
- Other telecommunications laws)

c) Specific applicability of national law, actually or potentially, to incoming foreign programmes
  aa) Audiovisual broadcast programmes
  bb) Direct-Broadcast Satellites
  cc) Cable television

II. Legal relations between reporting state and receivers (Regulations governing the *reception* of broadcast/cable transmitted programmes and legal recourse of receivers to enforce rights of reception)

1. The international framework and its transformation into national law
  a) Multilateral agreements
    aa) ITU convention and rules arising from it
      aaa) Audiovisual broadcast programmes
        (1) Prohibition of reception
        (2) Technical standards and import/operating regulations for receiver equipment
        (3) Tariffs for reception
      bbb) Direct-Broadcast Satellites
        – subdivided as above aaa)

ccc) Cable television
(1) Principles of access to networks
(2) Technical standards and import/operating regulations for receiver equipment
(3) Tariffs for access
bb) Human rights convention and rules arising from them
aaa) Audiovisual broadcast programmes
(1) Prohibition of reception
(2) Technical standards and import regulations for receiver equipment
(3) Tariffs for reception
bbb) Direct-Broadcast Satellites
– subdivided as above aaa)
ccc) Cable television
– subdivided as above aaa)

b) Bilateral agreements
aa) Frame for bilateral agreements under multilateral rules
aaa) Audiovisual broadcast programmes
bbb) Direct-Broadcast Satellites
ccc) Cable television
bb) Rules provided by bilateral programmes
aaa) Audiovisual broadcast programmes
(1) Technical standards and import regulations for receiver equipment
(2) Tariffs
bbb) Direct-Broadcast Satellites
– subdivided as above aaa)
ccc) Cable television
– subdivided as above aaa)

c) Transformation of international agreements on receiver's rights into national law (for broadcast, DBS and CATV programmes)
aa) Power for transformation of rules into national law
bb) Form and content of transformation
cc) Jurisdiction for application of transformed rules
dd) Practice of application
ee) Judicial review or other legal recourse against regulatory decisions

d) Summary: Scope of action left to reporting state under international law for regulation of relations between state and receivers of broadcast/cable-transmitted programmes from abroad

2. National law independent of international framework (Regulations governing the *reception* of broadcast/cable transmitted programmes for reasons of public interest)
   a) Constitutional framework of audivisual media reception (Civil rights of receivers and their judicial review)
      aa) Audiovisual broadcast programmes
      bb) Direct-Broadcast Satellites
      cc) Cable television
   b) Power to regulate, legal technique of regulation
      – subdivided as above a)
   c) Content of regulations (Audiovisual broadcast, DBS and CATV)
      aa) Prohibition of reception/principles of access to networks
      bb) Technical standards, manufacturing and operating interdictions for receiver equipment
      cc) Reception tariffs

III. Legal relations between media companies and individuals, including personal claims against companies (Audiovisual broadcast, DBS and CATV)

1. International agreements and their transformation into national law
   a) Protection of privacy law; protection of honour; right to have a counter-statement published
   b) Copyright law
   c) Illicit advertising (individual claims)

2. Conflict law of the reporting state
   – subdivided as above 1.

3. National rules providing individual claims against programme companies and thus potential barriers to free transborder flow of media programmes
   – subdivided as above 1.

B. Establishment and activities of foreign programme companies/programme transmitting companies *on the territory of the RS*

I. International framework

1. Establishment and operation of transmitter stations and cable networks
   a) Audiovisual broadcast programmes
   b) Direct-Broadcast Satellites (including participation in national satellite operating companies, operations of national satellite systems)
   c) Cable television (establishment and operation of cable networks)

2. Establishment and activities of programme companies
   a) Multilateral agreements (e.g., EEC-treaty)
      aaa) Audiovisual broadcast programmes
      bbb) Direct-Broadcast Satellites
      ccc) Cable television
   b) Bilateral agreements (e.g., AFN, RFE)
      – subdivided as above a)

II. National framework
– subdivided as above I.

C. Regulation of the flow of media programmes transmitted from reporting state to other countries (legal relations between RS and programme companies transmitting to other countries)

I. International framework and its transformation into national law

1. ITU convention and rules arising from it
   a) Audiovisual broadcast programmes
      (rights of RS to transmit abroad)
   b) Direct-Broadcast Satellites
      (Orbital positions of RS)
   c) Cable television
      Access of domestic programmes to foreign cable systems)

2. Other multilateral agreements
   – subdivided as above 1.

3. Bilateral agreements
   – subdivided as above 1.

II. National law independent of international framework

1. Regulations governing the establishment and operation of transmitting facilities
   a) Constitutional framework
      aa) Audiovisual broadcast programmes
      bb) Direct-Broadcast Satellites
      cc) Cable networks
   b) Power to regulate, legal technique of regulation
      – subdivided as above a)
   c) Content of regulations
      aa) Principles of authorization
         aaa) Audiovisual broadcast programmes
         bbb) Direct-Broadcast Satellites
         ccc) Cable television
      bb) Rules governing the content of programmes
         – subdivided as above aa)
      cc) Other conditions of authorization, including tariffs
         – subdivided as above aa)

2. Regulations governing the production of programmes for abroad
   – subdivided as above 1.

Joachim Scherer

Nationale und europäische Perspektiven der Telekommunikation

Die Beiträge des Sammelbandes untersuchen – aus ökonomischer, politikwissenschaftlicher und juristischer Sicht – Möglichkeiten und Grenzen einer europäischen Telekommunikationspolitik. Die Telekommunikationsstrukturen in den Mitgliedstaaten der Europäischen Gemeinschaft befinden sich in einem tiefgreifenden Umbruch. Dazu tragen mehrere Faktoren bei: Die zunehmende Integration der Telekommunikationsnetze bis hin zu dem bereits geplanten europäischen »dienste–integrierenden digitalen Fernmeldenetz« (ISDN), die Vervielfachung der Telekommunikationsdienste sowohl durch die von der Telematik eröffneten technischen Möglichkeiten als auch im Bereich von Kabel– und Satellitenrundfunk sowie der aufkommende Wettbewerb zwischen unterschiedlichen Anbietern von Telematikdiensten, zwischen öffentlich–rechtlichen und privaten Rundfunkveranstaltern. Daraus ergeben sich auf nationaler, aber auch auf europäischer Ebene neuartige Regelungsprobleme. Die Autoren – Verwaltungspraktiker und Wissenschaftler – präsentieren Stand und Entwicklung der europäischen Telekommunikationspolitik und analysieren politische und rechtliche Optionen für die nationale und die europäische Neuordnung der Telekommunikationsstrukturen.

1987, 157 S., 48,– DM, ISBN 3-7890-1416-8
(UFITA–Schriftenreihe, Band 70)

NOMOS VERLAGSGESELLSCHAFT
Postfach 610 · 7570 Baden-Baden

Marcellus S. Snow,

The International Telecommunications Satellite Organization (INTELSAT)

– Economic and Institutional Challenges Facing an International Organization.

Die International Telecommunications Satellite Organization (INTELSAT) nimmt unter den internationalen Organisationen eine Sonderstellung ein. Sie ist das bedeutendste internationale Telekommunikationsunternehmen. Professor M.S. Snow untersucht die gegenwärtige Struktur und die Rolle von INTELSAT in einem Umfeld, das durch tiefgreifende Wandlungen der Kommunikationstechniken und der Kommunikationspolitiken gekennzeichnet ist. Im Anhang wird ein White Paper der amerikanischen Regierung über "New International Satellite Systems" veröffentlicht, in dem die Grundzüge der amerikanischen Politik der Deregulierung für internationale Satelliten entwickelt werden. Die Untersuchung von Professor Snow und das Weißbuch zeigen das Zusammenwirken von Völkerrecht, nationalem Kommunikationsrecht und nationalen Politiken für einen immer wichtiger werdenden Teil der internationalen Telekommunikation.

1987, 200 S., 69,– DM, Subskr.-Preis 59,– DM (Bd. 2), ISBN 3-7890-1434-6

NOMOS VERLAGSGESELLSCHAFT
Postfach 610 · 7570 Baden-Baden

Ernst-Joachim Mestmäcker (ed.),

Law and Economics of Transborder Telecommunications – Symposium.

Die Beiträge zu diesem Symposium behandeln das Zusammenspiel zwischen nationalen und internationalen Telekommunikationssystemen. An der Konferenz, die vom 2. bis 6.3.1986 in Malente stattfand, haben die an dem Institutsprojekt beteiligten Wissenschaftler, insbesondere die Autoren der Länderberichte, Beamte der zuständigen Behörden und Vertreter der Wirtschaft teilgenommen. Die Länderberichte, die in dieser Reihe gesondert veröffentlicht werden, ermöglichen den Vergleich verschiedener nationaler Erfahrungen, zeigen deren Bedeutung für die grenzüberschreitende Telekommunikation und enthalten Hinweise auf bereits entstandene und potentielle internationale Konflikte. In der Entscheidung über nationale Politiken für den Export und den Import von Informationen müssen die Staaten den Zusammenhang mit dem internationalen Kommunikationssystem in Rechnung stellen. Die Mehrheit der Beiträge behandelt die daraus entstehenden Zusammenhänge nationaler und internationaler Regulierungen, Harmonisierungen und Kooperationen.

1987, 450 S., 139,– DM, Subskr.-Preis 119,– DM (Bd. 1), ISBN 3-7890-1368-4

NOMOS VERLAGSGESELLSCHAFT
Postfach 610 · 7570 Baden-Baden

Nicolas M. Matte/Ram S. Jakhu,
Law of International Telecommunications in Canada.
1987, 131 S., 49,– DM, Subskr.-Preis 42,– DM (Bd. 3)
ISBN 3-7890-1309-9

Stephen R. Barnett/ Michael Botein/Eli M. Noam,
Law of International Telecommunications in the United States
1988, ca. 192 S., ca. 68,– DM, Subskr.-Preis 58,– DM (Bd. 4)
ISBN 3-7890-1308-0

Die folgenden Bände sind in Vorbereitung:

K. D. Gaur,
Law of International Telecommunications in India.
1988, ca. 208 S., (Bd. 5)
ISBN 3-7890-1310-2

A. Wouter Hins/P. Bernt Hugenholtz,
Law of International Telecommunications in the Netherlands.
1988, ca. 240 S., (Bd. 6)
ISBN 3-7890-1311-0

Youichi Ito/Atsushi Iwata,
Law of International Telecommunications in Japan (Bd. 7)

Verene Wiedemann,
The Law of the Electronic Media in Great Britain (Bd. 8)

Jean-Bernard Blaise/Michael Fromont,
Wirtschaftsrecht der internationalen Telekommunikation in Frankreich
(Law of International Telecommunications in France) – in deutscher Sprache (Bd. 9)

Esteban Lopez-Escobar,
Wirtschaftsrecht der internationalen Telekommunikation in Spanien
(Law of International Telecommunications in Spain) – in deutscher Sprache (Bd. 10)

Joachim Scherer,
Nachrichtenübertragung und Datenverarbeitung im Telekommunikationsrecht
– Eine vergleichende Untersuchung telekommunikationsrechtlicher Regelungsmodelle (Data Communication and Data Processing in Telecommunication Law – A Comparative Analysis of Regulatory Models) – in deutscher Sprache (Bd. 11)
1987, 200 S., 64,– DM, Subskr.-Preis 59,– DM

NOMOS VERLAGSGESELLSCHAFT
Postfach 610 · 7570 Baden-Baden

Jürgen Schwarze (Hrsg.)

Rundfunk und Fernsehen im Lichte der Entwicklung des nationalen und internationalen Rechts

Beiträge zu einem medien-rechtlichen Symposium des Instituts für Integrationsforschung der Stiftung Europa-Kolleg Hamburg am 17./18. Oktober 1985

Die Regelung von Rundfunk und Fernsehen im Bundesstaat und grenzüberschreitend in der Europäischen Gemeinschaft gehört zu den grundlegenden Ordnungsproblemen der Gegenwart.
Fachleute aus den Bereichen privater und öffentlich-rechtlicher Medien, der nationalen und internationalen Verwaltungen, der Anwaltschaft und der Wissenschaft erörtern den Erfahrungsstand mit den Neuen Medien und untersuchen Konzepte für die Gestaltung von Rundfunk und Fernsehen in der Zukunft.
Unter den verschiedenen Blickwinkeln des deutschen Staats- und Verwaltungsrechts, des Europarechts, des Urheberrechts,. des Kartellrechts und des Internationalen Privatrechts entsteht so ein umfassendes Bild von Rundfunk und Fernsehen in ihrer nationalen und internationalen Dimension.
Zu einem umfassenden Überblick über den derzeitigen Entwicklungsstand und die Neuordnungsvorschläge für die Zukunft trägt zusätzlich eine Auswahl wesentlicher Dokumente über Rundfunk und Fernsehen im Gemeinsamen Markt bei.

1986, 398 S., 98,– DM, ISBN 3–7890–1230–0
(Schrr. Europ. Recht, Politik u. Wirtschaft, Bd. 123)

NOMOS VERLAGSGESELLSCHAFT
Postfach 610 · 7570 Baden-Baden